CHARISMATIC EXPERIENCES IN HISTORY

CHARISMATIC EXPERIENCES IN HISTORY

Cecil M. Robeck, Jr., Ph.D.
Editor

HENDRICKSON PUBLISHERS
PEABODY, MASSACHUSETTS 01961-3473

Copyright © 1985 by Hendrickson Publishers, Inc.
P.O. Box 3473, Peabody, Massachusetts 01961-3473
All rights reserved
Printed in the United States of America

ISBN 0-913573-13-2

TABLE OF CONTENTS

Dedicated to the
Society for Pentecostal Studies:
An International
Community of Scholars
Working within the
Pentecostal and Charismatic Traditions

PREFACE

This book is a collection of essays which look at certain of the charismata from the perspective of several disciplines. It includes studies in Old Testament, New Testament, Theology, Church History (Patristic and Modern), Psychology, and Anthropology. Some of the contributors are classical Pentecostals, others are charismatics in the popular sense of that term, still others are Protestant evangelicals or Roman Catholics. Each contributor has been allowed to express himself or herself in whatever manner she or he has chosen to do it. As a result the reader may note that there are differences of emphasis, opinion, and interpretation in the ideas expressed herein. The views expressed by the various contributors are those of the particular contributor. They do not necessarily represent the views of any other contributor, or those of the editor. I have allowed this deliberately to demonstrate that even on such a controversial issue as "gifts of the Spirit," we can testify to the essential Christian unity which is the Church, although there are legitimate differences of opinion.

The 1982 annual meeting of the Society for Pentecostal Studies held on the campus of Fuller Theological Seminary provided the catalyst for this endeavor. It also provided some of the papers. At that time some three-hundred scholars from the Pentecostal/charismatic movements gathered to discuss a variety of topics, each related to the larger subject of "Gifts of the Spirit." From this event come the essays by Richard D. Israel, Father Donald L. Gelpi, S.J., J. Rodman Williams, Ralph P. Martin, James D. G. Dunn, and Edith Blumhofer. To these have been added further reflections by H. Newton Malony, Cecil M. Robeck, Jr., and Paul G. Hiebert.

Richard D. Israel, a Ph.D. student in Old Testament at the Claremont Graduate School at Claremont, California, where he also serves as an instructor in Hebrew, leads off with a paper on a passage critical to much of Pentecostal and charismatic theology. He evaluates the various prophetic streams which ultimately fed into Joel's prophecy in Joel 2:28-30, then he demonstrates how this text was used to underscore the significance of the Pentecost event in Acts.

In a related study, Father Donald L. Gelpi, S.J., Professor of Historical/Systematic Theology at the Jesuit School of Theology in Berkeley, California focuses on a similar theme in the synoptic gospels. Father Gelpi translates the term *pneuma* as "breath" and employing the hermeneutical methods of Bernard Lonergan analyzes the ways in which the concept of "breath-baptism" was understood by the various synoptic writers. He concludes by showing how the theological emphases of these writers came to be placed on moral transformation in the image of Jesus and he makes suggestions for practical application to contemporary Christian life.

J. Rodman Williams, founding President of Melodyland School of Theology, now Professor of Theology at the School of Biblical Studies, CBN University in Virginia Beach, Virginia has given us a carefully argued treatment of the "greater" gifts. He argues that the gifts of prophecy *and* tongues should have a basic role among assembled believers because of their uniqueness as manifestations of God's grace.

From a more traditional perspective comes an exegetical study on 1 Corinthians 14:1-25 by Ralph P. Martin, Professor of New Testament and Director of the Graduate Program of the School of Theology at Fuller Theological Seminary in Pasadena, California. This article, first offered as a paper at the November 1982 SPS meeting, has also appeared as a chapter in Professor Martin's latest book, *The Spirit and the Congregation: Studies in 1 Corinthians 12-15* (Eerdmans, 1984), the publishers of which we are indebted to for permission to print it here.

James D. G. Dunn, formerly Lecturer in New Testament at the University of Nottingham, now Professor of Divinity at the University of Durham, England, has contributed another work with both theological and practical overtones. He has identified Ministry and The Ministry, the subject of giftedness and ordination as *a*, perhaps *the*, major challenge represented by Pentecostal and charismatic theology to traditional ecclesiastical understandings. His paper looks at some of the more recent trends in various traditional and ecumenical settings and proposes that some major rethinking on the subject of ministry, including ordination, should be undertaken in light of the charismatic dimension of ministry.

H. Newton Malony, Professor of Psychology and Director of Programs in the integration of Psychology and Theology from the Graduate School of Psychology at Fuller Theological Seminary, has provided from a behavioral scientific perspective a helpful analysis of those who speak in other tongues. This study, published previously in the *Journal of the American Scientific Affiliation*, demonstrates that those who speak in tongues do not appear to be mentally unhealthy, nor do those who speak in tongues frequently differ from those for whom the experience is less frequent. A special "thank you" goes to the *JASA* for permission to reprint this article for a wider audience.

Two historical pieces are included within this book to demonstrate ways in which certain gifts of the Spirit have been understood and exploited in quite different contexts. The first by Cecil M. Robeck, Jr., a Ph.D. candidate in Historical Theology who also serves as the Director of Academic Services and as an Adjunct Instructor in New Testament and Historical Theology at Fuller Theological Seminary, surveys the treatment which the grace-gifts mentioned in 1 Corinthians 12:8-10 receive in various writings of Origen in the first half of the third century. He argues that Origen was aware of these gifts in their literal sense but suggests that many of Origen's writings speak of these same gifts in a sense which relates them more closely to his "spiritual" treatment of Scripture, primarily to provide a hearing for the gospel among contemporary intellectuals.

Edith L. Blumhofer, Assistant Professor of History at Evangel College in Springfield, Missouri has contributed a study of a more contemporary teacher in the person of John Alexander Dowie and his Christian Catholic Apostolic Church. Her analysis of his role in Zion, Illinois, as background to American Pentecostalism, together with his perspective on the gifts of healings and of speaking in tongues, as well as her assessment of the competing role of Charles H. Parham, help us understand the importance of these doctrines for early Pentecostals.

Finally, Paul G. Hiebert, Professor of Anthropology and South Asian Studies from the School of World Mission at Fuller Theological Seminary has asked the all important question about how one knows the hand of God when it is seen. In a world in which many religions claim to possess signs and wonders, the question of discernment of spirits is a critical one. Hiebert has built upon his earlier article "The Flaw of the Excluded Middle," *Missiology* 10 (1982): 35-47, and suggested several categories to enable the Christian to distinguish between what is from God and what is not.

I would like to add a few words of thanks to the Society for Pentecostal Studies for allowing me to use several of their papers for publication in this book. The administration of Fuller Theological Seminary has been gracious to allow me to place the various manuscripts on its word processor. A special word of thanks goes to Jan Gathright who typed the manuscript in parts and in whole and whose patience and constructive suggestions never cease to amaze me. Last but not least, I would be remiss if I did not acknowledge the role which my wife, Patsy and our four sons, Jason, John Mark, Peter, and Nathan have played toward the publication of this work by giving up many an evening so that I could go back to the office to work on it.

Cecil M. Robeck, Jr. July, 1984

1

JOEL 2:28-32 (3:1-5 MT): PRISM FOR PENTECOST

Richard D. Israel

One conviction of all New Testament writers was that the Old Testament, as Word of God, spoke to the needs and events of their generation. A fitting word to describe this function of Scripture is "prismatic." An event described in the New Testament was often illumined by Old Testament references. It must be acknowledged that in some instances the particular hue cast on a New Testament event by the writers of the New Testament is not visible at the level of the Old Testament context. Nonetheless, the interpreters were convinced that the Holy Spirit illumined the hidden color of the Old Testament text in light of which the events of their times were to be viewed. The metaphor of a prism is suggestive, thus, of the function which Scripture texts performed in the theologizing of the New Testament. This phenomenon was not limited to Christian writers, but was present also in the pesharim of the sectarian Qumran Judaism as well as the midrashim of the more mainstream Judaism of that era.

The passage of Joel 2:28-32 (3:1-5 MT) is adapted in this manner by Peter and Luke to explain the Pentecost event. But Joel 2:28-32 is itself a composite of other prophetic traditions which illuminate Joel's own eschatological scenario. In the following pages we want to respond to four questions which are raised on the basis of these observations: First, how does this passage fit into Joel's view of the future? That is, what is the function of this passage in the overall scope of the book of Joel? Second, how did Joel compose this passage to fit together as a unit? In the first question we are looking at the broad context, in the second we will be looking at the passage itself to try and grasp the inner coherence of the text. Third, what traditions has Joel called upon to depict the situation described in the passage? To what did Joel reach back for his ideas? How has he employed them when compared with their use in other Old Testament contexts? Finally, why did this text suggest itself to Peter and Luke as a means of proclaiming the significance of the Pentecost event? What in the text lent itself to adaptation by Peter and Luke? Or, in more traditional conservative terms, how did Pentecost fulfill the prophetic text in Joel?

A brief look at the date and authenticity of the passage will suffice for the concerns of this paper. Authenticity is a secondary issue at best. Irrespective of whether Joel or a later disciple of Joel is ultimately responsible for the compilation and inclusion of this passage in the book, the passage impinges on the message of the book, and an account must be given for its impact. The question as to when the passage originated must take second place to the question of the book's message including this passage. The quest for authenticity presents the danger of rooting authority in a romantic sentimentality about primitive originality. This ignores the more basic datum that canon, or authority was defined by the function of a passage in a community and not an ontological status such as originality or authenticity inherent within a text. Thus, when Georg Fohrer bypasses Joel 2:28-32 in his outline of the book in his revision of Sellin's *Introduction to the Old Testament*, and when, in his commentary on the prophets, he omits this passage in his treatment of Joel and instead offers a treatment of this passage in a separate section entitled "Words of other unknown prophets," he misses the point.[1] This constitutes a splendid example about how the quest for authenticity has led scholarship down a sidetrack for the better part of three generations, from literary criticism to form criticism.

Concerning the date of Joel, arguments have placed the book from Solomonic times to the Hellenistic period. Wolff's arguments in his *Hermeneia* commentary are to be preferred,[2] and as the present writer has already intimated when speaking about Joel "reaching back," the book comes from post-exilic times. Briefly, the reasons for this are: 1) the lack of mention of any kings' reigns. This puts us in the post-exilic period. 2) The mention of the walls in chapter two places us in the post-Ezra-Nehemiah period, and 3) the picture of Jerusalem as a cultic community corresponds best to this period. The mention of the Javanites in chapter three (English versions) probably means that this pericope comes from the late fourth century, but it may well be later than the main corpus of the book. Let us now focus on Joel 2:28-32, first in relation to the entire book (the super-structure) and then on the passage itself (the infra-structure).

THE CONTEXT EXAMINED

First, how is this passage situated in the book as a whole? What role does it play in the book? What is its function in relationship to the way the book is structured?

There is wide agreement that the book contains two sections. Where that division is to be made, however, is disputed. There are two prevailing options: either our text is the beginning of the second section[3] or 2:18 already begins the second section.[4]

The view that 2:28 (3:1) begins the second section is supported by the following arguments, all based on the content of the book:

1) One may discern a temporal shift at this juncture. Joel 1:4-2:27 deal with a current crisis, that of drought and plague and its resolution, whereas, 2:28-3:21 (MT 3:1-4:21) deal with future concerns, temporally removed from the locust plague and drought.

2) Literarily it appears that 2:21-27 reverse the crisis depicted in 1:4ff., and as such serve as a rhetorical conclusion to that earlier section. Chapters three and four go on to deal with other matters.

3) Theologically chapters one and two deal with what has been termed sustenance or blessing. The provision of food for life is elevated to theological concern. The disruption of the natural cycle determined by Yahweh has threatened the historical existence of Israel. This fundamental issue which offers no clue to its particular historical circumstance is what makes the dating of Joel so difficult. In contrast to the concern of chapters one and two with sustenance, chapters three and four deal with once-for-all, epochal, historical events. Cosmos and history are distinguished in the theology of Joel, the former being the presupposition of the latter.

4) In 1959 a French scholar named Bourke published a seminal study on the Day of the Lord in Joel in which he identified two distinct "days of the Lord", one in Joel 1 and 2, and one in Joel 3 and 4.[5] If this view holds it would be a strong indication that the book should be divided at 3:1 (2:27).

The other option for dividing the book is to make the division according to the criterion of form. H. W. Wolff observes that the narrative form at 1:4, "What the cutting locust left the swarming locust has eaten, what the swarming locust has left, the hopping locust has eaten, and what the hopping locust left, the destroying locust has eaten" (RSV), corresponds to the narrative statement at 2:18 "Then the Lord became jealous for his land, and had pity on his people" (RSV). Both of these verses function in the same way, in that they "recount the essential facts concerning not only the terrible current catastrophe, but also the subsequent renewal of Yahweh's compassion."[6] What follows each of these reports, then, is an "expanded liturgical section"[7] corresponding to a lament ceremony after 1:4, and oracles of response after 2:18.

It appears, then, that we have competing structural signals, one based on form and one based on content. The question is, which is determinative for the structure of the book, form or content? Which determines which? The arguments for dividing the book at 3:1 (2:27) are good observations by and large. Bourke's thesis regarding two distinct Days of Yahweh will not stand a close scrutiny. He believes that the first Day came with the locusts. On closer examination, however, one sees that the locusts have come already (cf. 1:4) but the Day of the Lord in chapters 1 and 2 is only near, it is coming (imperfect aspect in 1:15). This means that the arrival of the locusts does not mean the arrival of the Day, but signals its nearness. The locust plague and drought are *harbingers* of the Day of the Lord. The threatened ultimate destruction of the Day of the Lord is averted by a repentant community. Yahweh repents in 2:14. Now, on the basis of a repentant community, the damage of the plagues will be undone (2:21-27), and the Day of the Lord no longer means destruction for Israel, but blessing (3:1-4:21).

The other observations regarding the different content of chapters three and four are good, but they are not determinative. The generative force of the book was not present concerns (chs. 1-2 MT) versus future concerns (chs. 3-4 MT); rather, the determinative issue was the community's response to the plague and drought (1:4-2:17) and Yahweh's response to the repentant community (2:18-4:21).

The three major sections of part two answer three concerns in part one. 2:18-27 promise a reversal of the crisis caused by plague and drought. 2:28-32 promise a reversal of Israel's role in the Day of the Lord and 4:1-21 promise a reversal of the nations' roles in the Day of the Lord. Thus, our passage (2:28-32 [MT 3:1-5]) functions in the book of Joel as a reversal of the significance of the Day of the Lord for Israel, from judgment to promise, from threatened destruction to safety.

I. The Passage Examined: The Text as a Unit

One implication of the preceding examination of the passage's content is that the passage itself functions as a unit within the book of Joel.[8] We need next to understand wherein that unity inheres. Most commentators do not press their exegesis beyond an analysis of the various parts of the text. They analyze but do not synthesize, they take the passage apart but do not put it together again. It is important, though, to treat the passage as a whole for the reason stated above and also because at least one interpreter saw it as a whole, namely Luke. In light of that, if we want to understand Luke's use of it we should try to understand the unity which may be found in its original context in Joel.

Searching for unity here is extremely difficult. A stylistic analysis of the passage yields the following data: 1) There are a number of converted perfect verb forms as well as imperfect forms. Both perfect and imperfect tenses portray future action; but why the variation from one means of expressing future action to the other? 2) There is a change of speaker in the passage. Somewhere the first person Yahweh speech becomes a third person utterance. Opinions vary as to where this takes place. Some see the third person speech beginning in verse four,[9] since there is a third person reference to Yahweh there; others see it beginning in verse five.[10] 3) There is a change of addressee. Verses one and two are addressed to a plural group—*your* sons and *your* daughters, whereas three through five do not specify to whom they are addressed. 4) There are rhetorical devices in the text which are important stylistically. Verse 2b "In those days I will pour out my Spirit" is a refrain of the opening words of the Yahweh speech. This repetition rhetorically envelopes what goes between and sets these verses off from the rest. Verses three and four are chiastically arranged: 3a speaks of signs in heaven and on earth and verses 3b-4a specify the signs, first on earth then in heaven. Verse five reflects a subtle play on the verb *qará* ("to call") by affirming deliverance offered to those who call upon Yahweh in 5a, and those who are called by Yahweh in 5b. 5) There are three different forms of prophetic speech in these verses: verses 1-2 are called by Wolff an "absolute assurance of salvation," verses three and four are "announcement of a sign," and verse five is a "conditional announcement of salvation."[11] 6) The scope of the promised blessing is broadly called "all flesh" in verse one, whereas in verse five deliverance is granted only to those who call upon Yahweh and who are called by Yahweh. 7) There are three temporal phrases, which orient the reader "after this," "in those days," and "before the coming of the day of the Lord."

All seven of these observations must be accounted for in analyzing this passage as a unit. The question becomes, where does one subdivide these verses to understand and interpret the structure of the five verses? As mentioned earlier, most subdivide the text at 1-2, 3-4, and 5. Such a subdivision corresponds to most of the stylistic observations above: the rhetorical devices mentioned bind 1 to 2 and 3 to 4, while 5 stands independently. The formal distinctions follow this subdivision. The change of addresses occurs after verse two, also lending support to this division. The other three stylistic observations, change of aspect, speaker switch from first to third person and the universal "all flesh" of verse one versus the particularity of verse five neither support nor call for this structural option.

The difficulty comes in interpreting the relationship of these three sections in the unit 3:1-5. This is the point where many exegetes leave off. What does it mean that an "announcement of a sign" is placed between an "absolute assurance of salvation" and a "conditional announcement of salvation"?[12] Are they three independent oracles listed in a series or do they have a relationship to one another? Their redactional grouping at this point in the book implies an interrelated unity of the passage. They do have a bearing on one another. The issue focuses on the purpose of the signs in verses three and four and their relationship to the blessing and salvation for Israel in verses 1-2 and 5. Joel 3:1-5 have already been characterized as a reversal of Israel's role in the Day of the Lord as contrasted with Israel's role in chapters 1 and 2. Here the structure of the whole book informs the structure of the particular passage; the dark words of verses 3-4 must be explained in light of the positive role of Israel in the Day of the Lord which this section of the book of Joel treats.

Such an explanation may be found by simply reading verses three and four in conjunction with verse five. The fearful portents on earth and in heaven signal the coming of the Day, but deliverance for the chosen in Jerusalem who choose Yahweh is certified by Yahweh's promise. To the question of Joel 2:11 "Great is the Day of the Lord and exceedingly fearful, who is able to survive it?" Joel 3:35 respond that the called of Yahweh shall be delivered by calling on Yahweh. The terrible signs of verses three and four are now not for going under but for going through, or not for passing away, but for passing through.[13]

If this be the case, then we do not have three sections in this text, but two, 1-2 and 3-5, each dealing with the future blessing and deliverance of the descendants of the Jerusalemites of Joel's day. The key words which signal this structure are the two verbs where Yahweh acts: "I will pour out" and "I will place." The text is composed of two divine acts, pouring out the Spirit and placing signs which portend the coming Day of Yahweh in which the true worshippers of Yahweh will be saved. Verses 3-4 are determined by verse 5, that is, the announcement of a sign (vv. 3-4) is infused with salvific significance by the announcement of conditional salvation (v. 5). While the verb "I will place" signals the beginning of the second section, the dominant idea in verses 3-5 is the promised deliverance of verse 5.

Of the seven stylistic observations mentioned above, we find that the verbs are the most important structural signals, and the most important verbal distinction is that of person—the first person Yahweh verbs being determinative. The form critical distinctions, along with the rhetorical devices and change of tenses, speaker and addressee are all subordinated to the actant of the two first person verbs.

Only the last two stylistic observations are problematic for our structure. One may take some comfort in the thought that they are also problematic for any structure. Those two observations, it will be recalled, are the universal scope of the gift of the Spirit in 1-2 versus the particularism of verse five, and the three temporal indicators: "after this," "in those days," and "before the coming Day of the Lord."

Let us take the issue of universalism versus particularism first. The text unabashedly associates the pouring out of the Spirit upon *all flesh* with the strict delimitation of deliverance to those called by Yahweh in Jerusalem in verse five. The "*all* flesh" of verse one is restricted in verse five to "*all* who call upon the name of Yahweh." *All* occurs in both verses, but it is used inclusively in verse 1 and exclusively in verse 5. One possible resolution of this tension is to recognize the categories to which the promises are addressed. The "all flesh" of verse one is defined further by anthropological and sociological categories: gender, age and position in society. The promise in verse five describes a *theological* category, namely the elect who call upon Yahweh. This understanding necessitates viewing the theological category as most basic. Salvation is offered to the elect and it is based on Yahweh's call, but the elect are called from diverse anthropological and sociological groups. Thus deliverance is theologically and not sociologically determined. Liberation is grounded on a theological base more than a sociological base. The oppressed in this text are not delivered because they are oppressed, but because they are *called* along with their oppressors to the worship and service of Yahweh. This means of course that the "all flesh" of verse one is not really universal, but then that is clearly perceived by most exegetes anyway, since the prophet Joel here is speaking only to Israel, as chapter four makes abundantly clear.

The other stylistic aspect of the text which merit discussion is the temporal indicators. The "after this" of verse 1 locates the time in the future following the promised restoration of agricultural bounty in 2:18-27. This is confirmed by the phrase "in those days" (3:1) referring to the distant future in contrast to the near future of 2:18-27. To this point we have an unspecified future period, but the signs of verses three and four specify that at least that action precedes the Day of the Lord. Thus we have a period spoken of as in the future, yet prior to the Day of the Lord, in which Yahweh will perform his two promised deeds. The question remains open as to the temporal sequence of the two acts. It is not specified whether the outpouring of the Spirit will precede the giving of signs, or vice versa, or whether they are associated in contemporaneous fashion. The order of the text may indicate temporal priority of the outpouring of the Spirit, especially if the conjunction and verb of verse three are interpreted consecutively, but this is not at all necessary. The reason for the order of the text may lie in other areas. We cannot at this point be certain as to the temporal relation of the two acts. It must be left open-ended for now, but it will come to our attention again.

II. The Passage Examined: The Sources of Joel's Thought

Joel 3:1-5 (MT) reflect a fairly developed stage of prophetic views of the future. Joel did not invent the material in this passage; nearly every clause in the passage has its antecedent in older prophetic tradition. Yet Joel was not a tradent who simply passed on the traditions he received, but one who used them to speak to the needs of his hearers. Let us examine briefly the tradition history of the major concepts of which Joel availed himself and see how they were used by Joel to offer his prophetic word of promise to his hearers.

Verses 1-2 invite comparison to two traditions which are very broadly anchored in the Old Testament: the Spirit of God and prophecy. We could spend more space than we have on these two independent of each other, but in order to focus our attention we will discuss these two only as they impinge on one another in the Old Testament tradition.

Spirit-inspired prophecy is a very ancient modality which dominated Israel's early prophetic heritage. First Samuel records two instances when Saul was overcome by the Spirit and prophesied, both of which claim to be the reason for the proverb "Is Saul also among the prophets?" First Samuel 10:10 reads: "When they came to Gibeah, behold a band of prophets met him (Saul); and the spirit of God came mightily upon him, and he prophesied among them" (RSV). Later, when Saul was searching for David to kill him, according to 1 Sam. 19:23-24 "the Spirit of God came upon him (Saul) also and as he went he prophesied . . . and he too stripped off his clothes and he too prophesied before Samuel, and lay naked all that day and all that night" (RSV). One important aspect of these verses is the stem of the verb "to prophesy." It is the *hithpa'el* stem. The particular nuance indicated by the use of the *hithpa'el* seems to be ecstatic phenomena accompanying the Spirit-induced prophecy. Note the musical aspect in 1 Samuel 10 and Saul's bizarre behavior in 1 Samuel 19:24. This ecstatic prophecy seems to be characteristic of prophecy in this early phase.

A curious but well-known passage in Numbers 11 speaks of an incident when Moses and the elders of Israel were gathered at the tent of meeting. Yahweh took some of his Spirit from Moses and placed it upon the elders and they prophesied. Two other registered elders who remained in the camp also received the Spirit and prophesied. When Moses heard of it the young man Joshua urged him to forbid the prophesying in the camp, to which Moses replied: "Would that all the Lord's people were prophets, that the Lord would put his spirit upon them" (Num. 11:29 RSV). Once again the verb is in the *hithpa'el* in this passage. This prophesying of the elders was a one time phenomenon according to Numbers 11:25, though Moses' desire was for all Israel to have the experience. Our passage in Joel thus stands as the promised fulfillment of Moses' wish in Numbers 11.

It is important to note the stem used and the implication therein that Spirit-induced ecstasy was part of the prophetic experience. This early mode of prophecy characterized by the Spirit gave way to a prophecy characterized by the Word during the period of the two kingdoms. Certain texts seem to indicate the desire of prophecy to dissociate itself from the Spirit. Jeremiah 29:26 may have a trace of the derision of prophecy of the word by associating it with the prophesying by Spirit when the phrase "every madman who prophesies" is used. Similarly, Hosea 9:7, "The prophet is a fool, the man of the Spirit is mad," contains a view of Spirit-induced prophecy which would provide motivation for the prophets to dissociate themselves from the Spirit. More important than these texts, though, is the use of the *niph 'al* stem to denote prophetic speech from this period onward. No longer is the prophetic behavior highlighted by the *hithpa 'el* stem; rather, the prophetic speech and actions are described by the *niph 'al* stem.

This holds true until the exilic period when prophecy again became associated with the Spirit, though now the *niph 'al* stem is used. Ezekiel seems to be a key figure in this renaissance of Spirit and prophecy. In fact, Joel 3:1-2 are verbally linked with Ezekiel 39:29 "when I pour out (Heb. *shaphakti*) my Spirit upon the house of Israel." While this text does not speak of prophecy, other passages in Ezekiel relate that prophet's ministry to the Spirit. This provided for Joel at least the concepts to forge his own view of the outpouring of the Spirit, where the prophetic relationship with God is once again characterized by the reception of the Divine Spirit.

The other major tradition complex to which Joel lays hold is that of the Day of the Lord.[14] In rough outline it may be said that the Day of Yahweh concept was a time of judgment of God on those who opposed him and bestowal of blessing on his elect. The relationship of the Israelites to God determined its significance for them. Thus Amos perceived Israel as apostate and the Day of the Lord became darkness and not light. This reflects an apparent reversal of the meaning of the Day for Israel, and in essence, it became the dominant meaning among the pre-exilic "writing" prophets. The battle of Jerusalem was perceived as the Day of the Lord (Lam. 2:22; Ezek. 13:5), but the concept was soon thereafter re-eschatologized with a concomitant change in its significance for Israel. Now the Day was seen more and more as a day of deliverance for Israel and judgment for the nations.

The Day of Yahweh for Joel has both of these aspects. In chapters one and two the Day bodes ill for the Israelites because they practice ritual without sincerity of heart (Joel 2:13). The prophet is not afraid to recall the menace of the Day of Yahweh which Amos preached. Joel stands in the best tradition of the prophets when he offers this critique as an explanation of the locust plague and drought

of chapters one and two. Based upon repentance of the community this significance
of the Day changes for Israel. It no longer poses a threat to the Israelites, for
they will be brought through the perilous times preceding the Day of Yahweh
in safety. Now the Day is the Day of Judgment against the nations, when Israel's
shame will be vindicated in a strict sentence against the nations and a Holy War
will be waged against all the nations (cf. Joel 4).

Many other traditions are present, including two sentences which correspond
exactly to Malachi 3:23 and Obadiah 17. However, we will conclude this section
by reflecting briefly on Joel's hermeneutic in these verses. The message of Joel
in these verses is definitely "Yahweh for us," but it is not unconditionally so.
The Day of Yahweh meant destruction for Yahweh's people until they became
repentant and rent their hearts as well as their garments. Only those who call
upon Yahweh will experience the deliverance in Jerusalem assured by Yahweh.
Joel knows how to preach the Word of Judgment as well as the Word of Grace.
To a community which was experiencing drought and plague he preached the
Deuteronomic doctrine of two ways, the path of cursing and the path of blessing.
He was not overanxious to comfort and assure the people of God's blessing until
he called them to repentance. Based on that repentance, the community could fulfill
its calling and be assured that they were on the path of blessing. To a community
ravaged by agricultural distresses as judgment of God Joel calls for repentance.
To a repentant community which calls upon the name of the Lord, Joel preaches
comfort and offers hope of physical and spiritual blessing for both the immediate
and distant future.

III. PETER AND/OR LUKE'S USE OF JOEL 3:1-5

The Pentecost event and its meaning are a key to the theology of the book of
Acts. Whereas in Luke 4 Jesus proclaims himself as recipient of the Spirit for
his ministry, in Acts 2 the Church becomes the recipient of the Spirit for its
ministry. The passage which we have treated in Joel becomes the central text
for understanding Pentecost.

Acts 2 is a narrative report of the first Pentecost after the resurrection and
ascension of Jesus. Often the passage is treated as two largely separate units,
one dealing with the event of Pentecost 2:1-13, and the other dealing with Peter's
sermon (2:14-36). Such an approach tends to overlook the close correspondence
between the crowd's response to the event in 5-13 and Peter's address in 14-36.
This implies a division between the report of the event in 1-4, and subsequent
events in 5-40. In other words, the crowd's response to the marvels of Pentecost
is not an end in itself, but is used in Acts 2 as an introduction to Peter's sermon.
Rather than grouping 2:1-13 together as a report on the event and the crowd's

response, Luke seems to be more concerned to report briefly the event in 2:1-4 and then to explain the meaning of the event by recording Peter's response to the crowd's reaction. Acts 2 seems to be grouped into two major sections, then a report of the Pentecost event, followed by a "dialogue" between the crowd and Peter in which each party participates twice. The first "round" of dialogue occurs in verses 5-36, the crowd's reaction in 5-13 and Peter's response in 14-36. Acts 2:37-40 have another "round" where the crowd speaks in 37 and Peter responds in 38-40, while 41-47 are a concluding report of the results of Peter's sermon.

Note how Peter's response in 14-36 exactly counterpoints the reaction of the crowd. To the mockery of verse thirteen Peter responds in verse 15, to the question concerning the *meaning* of the event in verse 12, Peter responds in verses 16-36. This chiastically structured "dialogue" reflects Luke's preoccupation with the meaning of the event of Pentecost. His usage of Joel 3:1-5 (2:28-32) reveals his interest.

One must say that the text of the Joel passage does not really accord well with the phenomena described in Acts 2:1-4. The only real point of contact is the reception of the Spirit, though even at this point, the word "filled with the Spirit" does not really tally with the effusion referred to by the Hebrew word for "pouring out." Note also that the accompanying phenomena of wind, tongues of fire, and speaking in tongues are not explained by the quotation of the Joel passage. Conversely, many things in the Joel passage do not accord well with the report of events in Acts 2:1-4. Where does the prophesying of Joel 3:2 fit? What about the signs and wonders in Joel? Where do they occur at all in the Pentecost event? Why did the quotation not stop after Joel 3:2? Why is the line about the remnant in Jerusalem in the Joel passage omitted in Acts, especially since the LXX uses a participial form of *euaggelizein* "to evangelize" to describe those left in Jerusalem? It would seem that the LXX might have served as grist for Luke's evangelistic mill.

In light of this disparity between the events of 2:1-4 and the prophetic explanation offered from Joel 3:1-5, how are we to understand the use of that passage in this circumstance? One thing seems clear from the start, and that is that Peter and/or Luke are not trying to explain the phenomena which accompanied Pentecost. Instead, they are concerned with the meaning of the event of Pentecost on a salvational-historical scale. This can best be seen by an investigation of the Joel passage as it occurs in Acts.

There are several notable differences between the Joel passage as it occurs in Joel and in Acts. Responsibility for most of these is probably best assigned to the Septuagint. At least two significant changes, though, are directly attributable to Peter and/or Luke. The first is the change of the Hebrew '*ah^{e}rey ken* (LXX, *meta tauta*), English "after this," to *en tais eschatais hēmerais* "in the last days." The other change is the omission of Joel 3:5b. "For in Mt. Zion and in Jerusalem will be an escaped remnant, just as Yahweh said and those among the survivors whom Yahweh shall call." (The last words of Joel 3:5 seem to be echoed in Acts 2:39 where the promise extends to everyone whom the Lord calls.)

What is accomplished by these changes? Let us consider them in order of occurrence in the text. First, by inserting "in the last days" before the promise of the Spirit's outpouring the Acts passage understands the Pentecost event as occurring in the eschaton. When the Spirit is poured out, then it is already the last days. Now, since Pentecost, the last days have dawned. This is the "already" aspect of New Testament theology. The second act of the Lord, the giving of signs in heaven has not yet occurred, but will yet occur before the coming of the Day of the Lord. This partakes of the "not yet" aspect of early Christian eschatology. Luke has thus eschatologized the Joel passage by placing its fulfillment in the last days. This may have been implicit in Joel's intent of the "after this" in Joel 3:1, but it is made explicit in the citation of this passage in Acts.

Second, Luke has sequentialized the passage of Joel. First come the last days in which the Spirit is poured out, and then comes the Last Day, which will be preceded by the cosmic signs in heaven and on earth. If this is what Peter and/or Luke are doing here, then the failure of the Joel passage to line up with the phenomena of the Pentecost event is not coincidental, but by design. The concern is not to explain the phenomena accompanying Pentecost but its place in the saving history of God's plan. Conzelmann's *Theology of St. Luke* comes to mind here, since he first identified Luke's theological intention as an attempt to understand Jesus' ministry as the center of time, to be followed by a church age prior to the Parousia.[15]

Let us turn now to the omission of Joel 3:5b in Acts 2. As noted earlier, this is all the more surprising since Peter and/or Luke are relying on the LXX text, which states that the Lord will call evangelists (heralds of good tidings) to Jerusalem. The apparent reason, though, for this omission is not difficult to come by. It is the universal scope of the witness proclaimed in Acts 1:8 which dictates the omission of Joel 3:5b. "But you shall receive power when the Holy Spirit has come upon you, and you shall be my witnesses in Jerusalem and in all Judea and Samaria and to the end of the earth." Luke is careful to strip all vestiges of Jerusalemite particularism from the universal scope of his proclamation. It is interesting to note that the divine call of Joel 3:5b, though absent in this citation, resurfaces at Acts 2:39 "The promise is to . . . every one whom the Lord our God calls to him" (RSV).

In sum, Luke sees the same structure of Joel 3:1-5 that was offered in the preceding analysis, namely two divine acts, the bestowal of the Spirit and giving of signs before the coming of the Day of the Lord. Luke "eschatologizes" the bestowal of the Spirit and sequentializes the two divine acts—first the pouring out of the Spirit and then the signs of the End. The church in Acts exists in between those two divine acts. It may be also significant that exactly those two issues which were difficult for us to determine—namely the relation of the two events in Joel 3:1-5 to one another and the problem of the universal blessing versus limited deliverance—are where Luke is most forthright in his editing of the passage to explain the Pentecost event.

What we have seen in our study, then, is a stream of traditions flowing into Joel where they are prismatically refracted to illuminate the true colors of the Pentecost event. The belief in the continuity and applicability of the divine revelation to the present is the factor which accounts for this picture.

SOME REFLECTIONS FOR MODERN PENTECOSTALS

In *fine*, let us consider what modern Pentecostals may glean from such a study. One lesson may be drawn from the focus on the meaning of the Pentecost event. Only four verses in Acts 2 report the event, while the following thirty-six verses center around the meaning of the event. In Pentecostal churches far more sermons have been preached on Acts 2:1-4 than on Acts 2:5-36. There is far more Pentecostal literature suggesting how to reexperience the historical event of Pentecost than on applying the meanings as expounded in Acts 2:5-36 to Pentecostal faith and practice. Perhaps this was necessary in order to justify the existence of the Pentecostal experience in modern times. Further, the history of Pentecostal missions is a splendid example of applying the meaning of Acts 2:5-40 to modern Pentecostal faith and practice. Yet, I still sense an imbalanced preference for application of the Pentecostal event and lack of regard for working out its ethical and theological meaning for Pentecostal faith. The tendency is to emphasize the phenomena and overlook the implications of their meaning. Acts 2, on the contrary, mentions almost incidentally the phenomena accompanying the event, and spells out in great detail its meaning for salvation history, and its impact on that initial congregation.

Some questions which arise from the meaning of the Pentecost event described in Acts 2 include the following. What kind of lives should be lived in light of the Pentecostal experience of Spirit endowment? How does the eschatological existence in the Age of the Spirit impinge on our conduct? What does it mean to lead a prophetic life as a result of Spirit-Baptism? Certainly the Church is a Church in mission empowered by the Spirit, and it operates under the certainty of the coming of the Day of the Lord. But what does it mean "to call upon the name of the Lord"? What kind of community existence does that imply? What these question attempt to do is ask whether or not a Pentecostal ethic ought not to be grounded in the Pentecostal experience. If so, then our task is to build from Pentecostal experience to Pentecostal ethic. Perhaps it is time to reunite *mythos* and *ethos* for Pentecostalism and extend the significance of the Pentecostal experience from faith to practice.

NOTES

[1]G. Fohrer, *Introduction to the Old Testament* ET (Nashville: Abingdon, 1968), pp. 428-9 and G. Fohrer, *Die Propheten des Alten Testaments: Band 6 Die Propheten seit dem 4 Jahrhundert* (Gütersloh: Gütersloher Verlagshaus Gerd Mohn, 1976), pp. 91, 102-103.

[2]H. W. Wolff, *Joel and Amos* (Hermeneia; Philadelphia: Fortress, 1977), pp. 4-6.

[3]A. Weiser, *Das Buch der Zwölf kleinen Propheten I: Die Prophetin Hosea, Joel, Amos, Obadja, Jona, Micha (ADT 24*; Göttingen: Vandenhoeck & Ruprecht, 1974), p. 119.

[4]H. W. Wolff, *Joel and Amos*, p. 7.

[5]J. Bourke, "Le Jour de Yahvé dans Joël," *Revue Biblique* 66 (1959): pp. 5-31 and 191-212.

[6]H. W. Wolff, *Joel and Amos*, p. 9.

[7]H. W. Wolff, *Joel and Amos*, p. 9.

[8]From here on will refer only to MT versification.

[9]H. P. Müller, "Prophetie und Apokalyptik bei Joel," *Theologia Viatorium* 10 (1965/66) (Berlin: Walter de Gruyter, 1966), p. 242.

[10]W. Rudolph, *Joel-Amos-Obadja-Jona* (KAT XIII2; Gütersloh: Gütersloher Verlagshaus Gerd Mohn, 1971), p. 71.

[11]H. W. Wolff, *Joel and Amos*, p. 59.

[12]H. W. Wolff, *Joel and Amos*, p. 59.

[13]A. Weiser, *Das Buch der Zwölf kleinen Propheten* I, 121; ". . . nicht zum Untergang, sondern zum Durchgang. . . ."

[14]The issue cannot here be dealt with as to whether this concept originated in a cultic festival or in a war-event context. Instead we focus on its tradition history and usage in Joel.

[15]H. Conzelmann, *The Theology of St. Luke* ET (New York: Harper & Brothers, 1960), especially Part Five, pp. 207-234.

2

BREATH-BAPTISM IN THE SYNOPTICS

Donald L. Gelpi, S. J.

I

The phrase "to baptize in the Holy Spirit" (or perhaps more accurately "in the Holy Breath") occurs only rarely in the New Testament.[1] Ordinarily New Testament authors preferred other terms to describe graced transformation in God. But the synoptics do place on the lips of John the Baptist a prophecy that a "mightier one" would follow him who would "baptize in a Holy Breath" (Mt 3:11; Mk 1:8; Lk 3:16).

In the paragraphs which follow we will present a dialectical analysis of the ways in which the three synoptic evangelists interpreted the Baptist's prophecy. And from that analysis we will suggest a normative insight into the experience of Breath-baptism.

John's own baptism resembled other ritual washings of purification common among the Jews of his time. It bore superficial likeness to the proselyte baptism of converts to Judaism and to the ritual libations practiced at Qumran. But whatever the antecedents of Johannine baptism in Jewish piety, the rite designated those who submitted to it as John's disciples. The baptized confessed their belief in his proclamation of an imminent divine judgment. Johannine baptism sought therefore to gather together a group of followers whose repentant hope readied them for the saving action God would soon accomplish.

Prior to Jesus' own ministry He certainly moved in the same religious circles as the Baptist. At some point Jesus submitted to John's baptism. We may infer from that act that at the time of His baptism Jesus regarded John as a man sent from God and that He gave assent to the main lines of the Baptist's preaching. We also have solid reason to believe that, either on the occasion itself of His baptism by John or shortly thereafter, Jesus received a divine illumination concerning the scope and purpose of His own religious mission.[2]

However, the two men differed in ministerial style and in doctrine, and that further suggests that Jesus, despite His baptism by John, felt no constraint to assent to every facet of the Baptist's teaching. Jesus did not adopt the Baptist's ascetical practices, nor did He require such behavior of His disciples. He muted the harshness of the Baptist's apocalyptic vision and preached a message of divine forgiveness. He taught that the end-time which John had prophesied was already being accomplished in his Breath-filled proclamation of the kingdom. So far did Jesus differ from the harsher judgmental figure of "mightier one" that John expected, that the imprisoned Baptist began to wonder if Jesus was indeed the "one who is to come" (Mt 11:4-5; Lk 7:18-23).[3]

Jesus for His part seems never to have withdrawn His endorsement of the prophetic character of John's ministry (Mt 11:2-6; Lk 7:18-23; Mk 11:27-33). The Fourth Gospel offers evidence that early in His ministry Jesus administered a baptism similar to John's, although He later abandoned it (Jn 3:22-4:2).[4] If so, then the synoptics further suggest that Jesus replaced the ritual bath with a more demanding proof of committed discipleship—the renunciation of one's personal possessions and their distribution to the poor (Mt 19:16-22; Mk 10:17-22; Lk 18:18-23). But John's Gospel tells us that the disciples baptized even when Jesus himself did not (Jn 4:2). And in the post-resurrectional Church, baptism in Jesus' name would become the ritual sign of Christian discipleship (Ac 2:38).[5]

Since the first Christians needed to explain a rite that imitated the one administered by the Baptist, they had to make two things clear to their converts. They needed to vindicate the superiority of Christian baptism to John's, but they also had to explain why Jesus himself had submitted to a ritual which Christians regarded as inferior to the one that they themselves administered in Jesus' name. The superiority of Christian to Johannine baptism would no doubt have been disputed by the Baptist's followers. And in the defense of the superiority of Christian baptism, the synoptic evangelists found in the Baptist's prophecy of a "mightier one" who would "baptize in a Holy Breath" a powerful polemic argument for the Christian position. The Baptist, they equivalently argued, had himself testified in advance to the superiority of Christian baptism.

John himself, of course, would have uttered his prophecy in oblivion of Christian ritual. His phrase, "to baptize in a Holy Breath," described metaphorically God's sanctifying activity in the age which was about to dawn. The "mightier one" would send the divine Breath to cleanse the repentant of their sinfulness. Moreover, that the Baptist later questioned whether Jesus did indeed fulfill his prophecy suggests that even John remained somewhat vague as to how the prophecy would eventually find fulfillment. Therefore, in citing the Baptist's prophecy as proof of the superiority of Christian Baptism to Johannine, the synoptic evangelists endowed his phrase "to baptize with a Holy Breath" with connotations that far transcended the Baptist's original intent. In the synoptics the Baptist's phrase derives its full meaning retroactively from the Christian experience of Jesus, of His death and resurrection, and of the historical mission of the Holy Breath to the Church. What connotations, then, did the reinterpreted phrase have for each of the synoptic writers?

II

In *Mark's* Gospel the deeper theological meaning of the Baptist's prophecy is intimated in the early events recorded in the Gospel, namely, in Jesus' own baptism and temptations:

> In those days Jesus came from Nazareth of Galilee and was baptized by John in the Jordan. And when He came up out of the water, immediately He saw the heavens open and the Breath descending upon Him like a dove and a voice came from heaven: you are my beloved son; with you I am well pleased. (Mk 1:9-11)

Having cited the Baptist's prophecy, Mark immediately portrays Jesus as divinely designated to fulfill the Baptist's words. The Divine Breath descends upon Him from a rent in the heavens in order to inaugurate His manifestation as the Breath-baptizer foretold by John. We can recognize the rent in the heavens as an apocalyptic image for the beginning of the end-time (Is. 64:1-4). The Divine Breath descends on Jesus to inaugurate the salvation foretold by John and hinted at by Old Testament prophets.

The Holy Breath comes to Jesus under the sign of the dove. The Hebrews kept doves as pets. And the rabbis were fond of depicting Israel as Yahweh's dove, His special pet, the object of His particular delight. That Mark intended the dove to recall such rabbinic teaching becomes clear in the word spoken by the voice from heaven. It designated Jesus as the specially beloved of God and therefore implicitly as the beginning of a new Israel. That Jesus begins a new Israel is further disclosed in His sojourn for "forty days" in the desert. Like the first Israel who wandered in the desert forty years, Jesus, too, must undergo a time of testing in the wilderness (Mk 1:12-13).

The dove hovering over the waters recalls another Old Testament story. A dove's bringing Noah an olive branch told him the flood waters were subsiding (Gn

8:6-12). The unleashing of the waters of chaos has been Yahweh's instrument for cleansing sin from the face of the earth. As the subsiding waters foreshadowed His sealing a new covenant with Noah (Gn 9:8-11), likewise, the dove hovering over Jesus' baptismal waters foreshadows the new and everlasting covenant which God would seal in Jesus' mission, death, and resurrection (Mk 14:22-26).

Through the enlightenment of the Breath, Jesus hears himself proclaimed messianic Son of God by the voice from heaven. Thus the Breath comes to Him as a divine principle of illumination and as the inspiration of His fidelity to His messianic mission. The Breath's descent also recalls the eleventh chapter of Isaiah. There the prophet foretells the coming of the great messianic king who would be a compendium of the great charismatic leaders of Israel (Is 11:1-9). The image probably recalls as well the sixty-first chapter of Isaiah, which prophesied the coming of a messianic leader anointed by God's Breath to proclaim a season of Jubilee to Israel (Is 61:1-4). Luke's Gospel, as we shall see, explicates this last allusion (Lk 4:18-19).

The voice from heaven explains to Jesus the meaning of His baptismal anointing by the Breath by combining two texts from the Old Testament. Jesus is sent to be messiah like the Davidic king addressed in Psalm 2: "You are my son, this day I have begotten you" (Ps 2:7). But unlike that bone-crushing monarch, Jesus undertakes his messianic mission by following in the footsteps of the suffering servant of Deutero-Isaiah: "Here is my servant whom I uphold; my chosen one in whom I am well pleased" (Is 42:1).

Clearly then, for Mark, Jesus fulfills the Baptist's prophecy because the Breath of God and the power to inaugurate the last age of salvation dwells in Him. In consequence of His anointing as Breath baptizer, Jesus stands revealed as the messiah, as Son of God, and as the beginning of a new Israel. The Breath's descent upon Him begins the final recreation of the world. That descent foreshadows the new covenant to be sealed in His blood. It foreshadows the rite of Christian baptism as well, for by that ritual the disciples of Jesus will be incorporated into the new Israel which Jesus in His own person begins. Consequently, the Breath which dwells in the baptized comes to them not merely as the Breath of Yahweh but also as the Breath of His Son. But the Son, the messiah, also confronts the baptized Christian as the suffering servant foretold by Deutero-Isaiah. Hence, Jesus' disciples should anticipate the Breath-baptism will conform them to a suffering messiah.

The promise of conflict and suffering as the price of membership in the new Israel is reinforced in Mark's narrative by Jesus' desert temptations. Jesus' baptismal anointing by the Breath propels Him into immediate conflict with the powers of darkness (Mk 1:12-13). In Mark's Gospel that conflict will persist throughout Jesus' public ministry, and it will culminate in his death as suffering servant.

As we have seen, the images which shape Mark's temptation narrative portray Jesus as the beginning of new Israel. They also depict him as a new Adam. In the biblical story of human origins preserved in the second chapter of Genesis, Yahweh transforms a wilderness into a fruitful garden, creates Adam to be its gardener, and then leads the beasts to him for naming in order to see if Adam can find among them a suitable bride. The failure of this experiment leads to the creation of Eve (Gn 2:18-25). In Mark's temptation narrative Jesus, like Adam, stands in the wilderness surrounded by beasts. Moreover, like Adam Jesus must confront Satan the ancient tempter (Mk 1:12).

In Genesis the serpent appears, not as Satan, but as a vague earth symbol of those created forces outside Adam and Eve that lead them into sin. But long before Mark wrote his Gospel, the book of Wisdom had amalgamated the image of the serpent and that of the devil (Ws. 2:24). And Mark in his reference to Satan may have intended the allusion.

The beasts of the desert which surround Jesus also enjoy a sinister character. The Jews worshipped a living God who creates all living things. Therefore they regarded the lifeless desert as a threatening place, abandoned and cursed by God. They feared it as the haunt of deadly demonic powers, symbolized by the beasts that prowl in desert places (Lv 16:12; Is 13:21, 14:23, 30:6, 34:11-16; Zep 2:13ff.) Mark does not say that Jesus did battle with the desert beasts, but we find a hint of conflict in the ministering angels sent from heaven to assist the messiah as he confronts Satan and the powers of darkness (Mk 1:13).

The desert beasts may well have had a third connotation for Mark. He wrote for Christians who knew persecution under Nero. He may, therefore, have intended his readers to see in the messiah surrounded by wild animals a foreshadowing of the fate that could await any of his Breath-baptized followers: death in the Roman arena.

We find only three other references to the Divine Breath in Mark's Gospel. In the twelfth chapter of Mark, Jesus expresses His belief that David was moved to write the Psalms by the Holy Breath (Mk 12:36). The text adds little to Markan pneumatology, although it supports Christian belief that the Breath in Jesus had been active in the world prior to His coming and had inspired the sacred books of the Hebrew people.

The other two explicit references to the Breath enjoy greater importance. Significantly enough they occur in passages that refer to the struggle against Satan and the enemies of Christ. Both texts, therefore, harken back to Jesus' confrontation with the adversary in the desert after His own baptism. And both yield further insights into Mark's theology of Breath-baptism. In the first text, Jesus' adversaries charge that His power to cast out demons proves that he is possessed by Beelzebub, the prince of devils. Jesus refutes the slander with a double argument. He first uses a *reductio ad absurdam*. He observes ironically that if Satan is indeed working against himself, his kingdom is about to crumble. In other words, even when His adversaries seek to slander Him, they are forced to concede that He has broken the power of Satan over humankind. Jesus then points out the true meaning of His exorcisms: His power to bind the demons reveals that He is in fact mightier than Satan and his minions, implicitly the "mightier one" whom John had foretold (Mk 3:9b-27). Jesus then concludes: "Truly I say to you, all sins will be forgiven the sons of men, and whatever blasphemies they utter; but whoever blasphemes against the Holy Breath never has forgiveness but is guilty of an eternal sin" (Mk 3:28-29).[6]

For Mark one blasphemes the Breath of God by attributing to the Evil One exorcisms done by the power of the Divine Breath. No one truly open to pneumatic inspiration could ever confound divine deliverance with the activity of demons. Moreover, the heart closed to illumination by the Breath of God cuts itself off from the only source of conscious access to God available to human beings. In this life the Breath-blasphemer lives in blindness to the meaning of God's saving action in Jesus and courts damnation in the next. By the same token openness to the Breath's inspiration frees the human heart to recognize the saving presence of God. By implication, then, one may anticipate that Breath-baptism will inspire such discerning openness in Jesus' disciples.

We find one other explicit reference to the Divine Breath in Mark. As Jesus in the course of His Jerusalem ministry moves inexorably to betrayal and death He utters a brief eschatological discourse. In it He warns His disciples that they, too, will one day be drawn into the same violent conflict as He:

> But take heed to yourselves; for they will deliver you up to councils; and you will be beaten in synagogues; and you will stand before governors and kings for my sake, to bear testimony before them. And the gospel must first be preached to all nations. And when they bring you to trial and deliver you up, do not be anxious beforehand what you are to say; but say whatever is given in that hour, for it is not you who speaks but the Holy Breath. (Mk 13:9-12)

These words implicitly recall the prophecy of the Baptist that Jesus would one day baptize His disciples with a Holy Breath. And they further dispel the Baptist's vagueness by clarifying the practical consequences of Breath-baptism in Jesus' name. The Breath-baptized will find themselves drawn into Jesus' own passion;

but they will find strength and inspiration to confound their adversaries through the Breath Jesus will impart.

But Mark's theology of discipleship looks to more than martyrdom. The evangelist also concerns himself with Christian living. Mark's Jesus demands a purity of intention (Mk 7:14-23) irreconcilable with religious hypocrisy, formalism, and legalism (Mk 2:23-3:6, 7:1-13, 12:38-40). He summons His followers to a faith in himself and in God which is touched with moral ultimacy: they must in imitation of their Master be willing, if necessary, to die for Jesus' sake and for the good news He proclaims (Mk 4:40-41, 5:34, 8:34-9:1, 10:38, 11:20-24, 13:3-13, 14:36). Mark's Jesus summons His disciples to a practical faith that binds them to God in petitionary prayer. It demands trust in the Father's providential care as well as obedience to His will and to the moral demands of His covenant (Mk 3:34-35, 10:19-20). Most of all, the Father wills that we love Him above all else and our neighbor as ourselves (Mk 12:29-30).

Jesus reveals the Father's will. The practical faith He demands of His followers goes beyond the moral exegencies of the Torah. Those who would follow Him must be willing to sell their possessions and distribute them as alms to the needy (Mk 10:21-22). They must recognize that hoarded wealth constitutes one of the greatest obstacles to obedient submission to the reign of God (Mk 10:23-27). And they must stand prophetically opposed to rich, pious hypocrites who pray long prayers while oppressing the poor and defenseless (Mk 12:38-40). Instead, the disciples of Jesus must practice an open hospitality toward the dispossessed and the needy that imitates the Lord's own table fellowship with sinners (Mk 2:15-17, 9:37, 10:15-16).

But sharing material possessions in faith through hospitality or almsgiving must itself spring from an intention that is pure. Hence, it must express belief in the divine forgiveness of sins proclaimed by Jesus (Mk 2:5-12, 15-17), and it must incarnate mutual love and forgiveness (Mk 9:41). Indeed, mutual forgiveness must be cherished as the test of the authenticity of prayer (Mk 11:25).

Finally, those who submit in obedient faith to the reign of God must serve one another in the image of Jesus, the suffering servant of God. His disciples must renounce the pride and power of the princes of this world and serve one another, instead, with the simplicity of children. Among the followers of Jesus the least must be treated as the greatest (Mk 9:34-35, 10:34, 41-45). They must scrupulously avoid giving scandal to one another (Mk 9:42-50), and they must pattern their lives on Jesus, who goes to His death forgiving in advance the betrayal of His followers (Mk 8:3-9:1, 14:36). We shall discover the same sets of religious values on Jesus' lips in Matthew and in Luke. Mark links them only implicitly with the action of the Divine Breath who inspires Jesus' entire ministry. But

Matthew and Luke attribute Jesus' moral doctrine more explicitly to the action of the Holy Breath within Him.

We are now in a position to draw a certain number of conclusions about Mark's understanding of Breath-baptism. For Mark, Breath-baptism cannot be equated with the reception of any single charismatic gift. The Breath conforms the baptized to Jesus' image, for He begins the new Israel. The Breath teaches them to bear witness to Him, to testify against the same powers of evil as crucified the Son of God, and if necessary to walk the path of martyrdom. Breath-baptism frees the true disciple to recognize Jesus as the anointed Son of God. It introduces Jesus' disciples into the last age of salvation; it transforms them into a new creation. It seals the new covenant in their hearts. And in doing all these things it reveals the purpose of ritual baptism.

III

Matthew wrote his Gospel for a community in crisis. Its prophetic leadership stood fragmented (Mt 7:15, 24:1). Strife among its members had caused charity to "grow cold" (Mt 24:12). The community had even known mutual betrayal (Mt 10:21). Some members exulted in their charismatic powers in disordered ways that caused them to forget the Lord (Mt 7:21-23).

Matthew responded to this sad state of affairs by recalling his community to fundamentals. They must refocus upon the Lord Jesus. They must relearn obedience to His teachings. Accordingly, Jesus enters the pages of Matthew's Gospel as the Divine Lawgiver. His sayings are grouped in five extended discourses that recall the five books of the Hebrew Torah. In Matthew these discourses explicitate the terms of the new covenant that govern Christian conduct. As we shall see, Matthew's pastoral concerns also color his understanding of Breath-baptism.

Matthew expanded Mark's cryptic account of the ministry of John the Baptist by preserving a sampling of the Baptist's teachings. But he endorsed the substance of Mark's interpretation of the meaning of the Baptist's prediction of a Breath-baptizer mightier than John himself. Harkening possibly to a more primitive tradition concerning the Baptist's words, Matthew modified slightly Mark's version of John's prediction. Mark's Baptist had foretold that the mightier one would baptize "with a Holy Breath." Matthew's Baptist says that He will baptize with "a Holy Breath and with fire" (Mt 3:11).

The addition of the phrase "with fire" contrasts the way the Holy Breath comes to Jesus in His baptism with the way the Breath comes to His disciples. The Breath came to Jesus under the sign of the dove to reveal that He is the beloved son of God, the beginning of a new creation and of a new Israel. Fire, in contrast, symbolizes divine holiness. It purifies those who believe in God; it devastates and devours those who oppose Him. Thus the Breath of Jesus comes to His disciples in purification and in judgment.

Matthew modifies Mark's account of Jesus' baptism in other respects as well. He does not describe the event itself, although he recognizes that it did occur. He prefaces his baptismal narrative with a brief conversation between Jesus and John that underscores the theological implications of the Baptist's prophecy (Mt. 3:13-15). The Baptist protests the impropriety of Jesus' submission to his baptism. Jesus should be baptizing John, not he Jesus. Given the Baptist's later hesitations about Jesus' ministry in Matthew's Gospel (Mt 11:2-3), we may legitimately doubt that this conversation ever occurred. However, Matthew records it primarily for theological reasons in order to vindicate the superiority of Christian to Johannine baptism.

Jesus reassures the Baptist that His baptism by John will "fulfill all righteousness" (Mt 3:15). Minimally, Jesus asserts that in submitting to John's baptism He does what any devout Jew would do. But the word "fulfill" also links Jesus' reply to Matthew's theology of fulfillment. Matthew's Jesus comes not to abolish but to fulfill the Law and the Prophets, including John's prophetic ministry (Mt 5:17). Accordingly, Jesus reminds John that the act they are about to perform enjoys propriety only "for the time being." It occurs as a passing moment in a much larger providential scheme and can be permitted on those terms. The act will fulfill all righteousness, for it will inaugurate Jesus' own revelation as the messiah who baptizes with a sanctifying Breath those who believe in His name.

Matthew also modifies the words spoken to Jesus by the voice from heaven. In Mark the voice addresses Jesus personally: "You are my beloved Son." In Matthew it speaks to the reader and through the reader to all humankind: "This is my beloved Son." The change in wording may reflect Matthew's abiding theological concern to focus the attention of his readers on the person of Jesus (Mt 3:17). But Matthew preserves the basic content of the voice's proclamation as it is recorded in Mark.

By contrast, in his account of Jesus' temptations Matthew departs dramatically from Mark's text. He expands Mark's cryptic reference to Satan into an extended dialogue between Jesus and his diabolical adversary. As we shall see, the dialogue provides an important key to Matthew's understanding of the consequences of Breath-baptism.

Jesus' temptations have often been characterized as messianic. Indeed, Satan in Matthew's narrative addresses Him with the messianic title conferred on Him by the voice from heaven: Satan calls Jesus "son of God" (Mt 4:3, 6). But we cannot assume that the messianic character of Jesus' temptations makes them irrelevant to the religious experience of His disciples. For Matthew's messiah, like Mark's, descends into the desert as the beginning of a new Israel (Mt 4:1-2). He therefore models for the members of the new Israel those attitudes and values they are expected to imitate. For they stand susceptible to the same temptations as Jesus himself: they can be tempted to substitute self-reliance for trust in God. They can test God by trying to set the conditions for their relationship with Him. And they can seek to establish the kingdom on power politics rather than on authentic worship of the Father (Mt 4:1-11, 14:32, 16:23, 20:20-28).

In addition, Matthew's account of Jesus' temptations preface His entire public ministry. The crucified messiah will be taunted on the cross in terms that recall His temptations in the desert (Mt 27:29). As a consequence, the full meaning of Jesus' temptations becomes apparent only as Matthew's narrative unfolds.

The Breath who leads Jesus into the desert presides over His temptations (Mt 4:1). He therefore confronts Satan in the power of the Divine Breath who descended on Him at the Jordan. Moreover, under the Breath's inspiration Jesus three times vanquishes the tempter with a citation of the Torah. That fact enjoys theological importance, for as we have seen, Matthew's Jesus comes to fulfill the Law. His citations of Deuteronomy in the desert find an echo and a fulfillment in His own teachings. As Günther Bornkamm and others have shown, Matthew's Jesus fulfills the Law not only by incorporating into His teaching the substance of Torah piety but also by demanding more of His disciples than ever the Law did.[7] Each citation of Deuteronomy unmasks the deeper intent of each of Satan's temptations. Satan first tempts Jesus to use His messianic power to transform stones into bread. The temptation attacks the meaning of the fast that Jesus has undertaken under the inspiration of the Breath. Jesus has descended into the desert to repeat the experience of the first Israel, when God's people were forced to look for God each day to give them the manna they needed to survive. By fasting Jesus professes His determination to look to God rather than to bread as the ultimate source of His life. Jesus recognizes the tempter's guile and affirms His determination to live not by bread alone but by every word that comes from God's mouth (Mt 4:4; Dt. 8:3).

The second temptation builds on Jesus' reply to the first. Satan tempts the messiah to test God, to set the conditions for trusting in the Father. In rejecting the second temptation Jesus professes His determination to set the conditions under which He will conduct His messianic mission (Mt 4:6; Dt 8:3; Ps 91:11-12). He will demand a similar trust of His disciples.

Having been twice thwarted, Satan is forced to tip his hand. He no longer addresses Jesus as the Son of God. Instead, he offers the messiah the kingdoms of this world if only Jesus will adore Satan as God. In rejecting this third temptation, Jesus rejects a secular messianism based on political power as equivalent to idolatry. He also professes His determination to found the kingdom on authentic divine worship (Mt 4:8-11; Dt 6:13).

As Matthew's narrative unfolds, Jesus explains to His disciples both the practical consequences of unconditional trust in God and the conditions for authentic worship, which He as the messianic beginning of a new Israel had enunciated in the desert. He demands that his followers live, not by bread alone, but by faith and trust in the Father's providential care:

> No one can serve two masters; for either he will hate the one and love the other or he will be devoted to the one and despise the other. You cannot serve God and mammon. Therefore I tell you, do not be anxious about your life, what you shall eat or what you shall drink, or about your body, what you shall put on. Is not life more than food, and the body more than clothing? Look at the birds of the air: they neither sow nor reap nor gather into barns, and yet your heavenly Father feeds them. Are you not of more value than they? And which of you by being anxious can add one cubit to a span of life? And why are you anxious about clothing? Consider the lilies of the field, how they grow; they neither toil nor spin; yet I tell you, even Solomon in all his glory was not arrayed like one of these. But if God so clothed the grass of the fields, which today is alive and tomorrow is thrown into the oven, will He not much more clothe you, O man of little faith? Therefore do not be anxious, saying "what shall we eat?" or "what shall we drink?" or "what shall we wear?" for the Gentiles seek all these things; and your heavenly Father knows that you need them all. But seek first His kingdom and his righteousness, and all these things will be yours as well. (Mt 6:24-34)

Matthew's Jesus also makes the willingness to share one's "bread," one's possessions, with others the most practical expression of faith in the Father. The Father blesses those who do what pleases Him with the gift of the kingdom. He is pleased with the practical sharing of one's goods and oneself with the needy.

> Come, O Blessed of my Father, inherit the kingdom prepared for you from the foundation of the world; for I was hungry and you gave me food, I was thirsty and you gave me drink, I was a stranger and you took me in, I was naked and you clothed me, I was sick and you visited me, I was in prison and you came to me. (Mt 25:31-36)

The true disciple shares personal possessions with the same prodigal love as the Father:

> You have heard it said, "You shall love your neighbor and hate your enemy."

> But I say to you love your enemies and pray for those who persecute you,
> so that you may be sons of your Father who is in heaven, for He makes His
> sun rise on the evil and on the good and sends rain on the just and the unjust
> . . . . you therefore must be perfect as your heavenly Father is perfect. (Mt
> 5:43-48)

Matthew's Jesus also demands unconditional faith in God. Unconditional trust in the Father's providence demands that one set no conditions in principle on the scope of the sharing which expresses that trust. Sharing in the name and image of the Father must reach out to anyone, especially to the dispossessed and the outcast. It must include even one's bitterest foes (Mt 5:43-45, 9:10-13). For it seeks to effect mutual forgiveness and reconciliation in God. "Forgive us our debts as we have forgiven our debtors" (Mt 6:12). Finally, Matthew's Jesus demands that his followers worship only the one true God. But the sincerity of their worship will be measured by their willingness to forgive one another as the Father has forgiven them. Furthermore, in their dealings with one another they must avoid the haughty conduct of the princes of this world and serve one another with the simplicity of children (Mt 2:20-28).

Mark's Jesus, as we have seen, makes similar demands of His followers. But Matthew goes beyond Mark in linking Jesus' proclamation of new covenant morality to the action of the Holy Breath within Him. For in Matthew's Gospel Jesus in His desert temptations proclaims in the power of the Holy Breath the basic tenets of new covenant morality. He does so by enunciating those facets of the old covenant that His own moral doctrine fulfills: unconditional trust in God and authentic worship of the Father in the service of atonement. When these precepts are interpreted in the light of Jesus' own teaching, they commit the members of the new Israel to a life of faith-sharing in which practical concern for the physical needs of others brings into existence a certain kind of community: one concerned to break down the social barriers that isolate people from one another. The new Israel must welcome into its midst the poor, the sinner, the outcast; for its love must imitate the prodigal love of the Father who sends good gifts to saint and sinner alike. Faith-sharing must also express the mutual forgiveness which tests the authenticity of new covenant worship.

Moreover, in other respects Matthew endorses Mark's interpretation of the consequences of Breath-baptism. Like Mark, he reminds his readers of Jesus' warning against the "unforgivable sin." He situates the warning in the same context as Mark: Jesus' adversaries have accused Him of casting out demons by the power of Beelzebul. Although Matthew introduces slight variations in Jesus' reply to His adversaries, its overall sense remains the same as in Mark. Any individual whose heart has so hardened as to lead one to confuse the action of the Holy Breath with demonic activity has cut off the only available source of conscious access to God in faith. Such a person remains blind to the action of God in this life and courts damnation in the next. There are, however, further hints in Matthew's Gospel that blasphemy against the Breath also bears fruit in the inability to believe in the risen Christ (Mt 12:25-37).[8] Presumably, the Breath-baptized will labor under no such religious obtuseness. Matthew qualifies Mark's account of this incident in theologically suggestive ways. He prefaces the story of Jesus' false accusation by His enemies with a reminder of the large numbers of people whom the Savior cured (Mt 12:16). Like Mark he describes Jesus as forbidding the publication of the cures. In Mark's Gospel, such prohibitions are linked theologically to Jesus' "messianic secret," that is, to His gradual disclosure as Son of God and Son of Man. Matthew takes note of this Markan theme but explains it in his own terms as the fulfillment of the first of the servant songs of Deutero-Isaiah. There the servant is described as modest: he "neither contends nor cries out." But in the same song the servant is also depicted as a special vessel of the Divine Breath. "I will pour out my Breath upon him and he will speak judgment to the nations" (Is 42:1-4). The prophecy, therefore, stands in stark contrast to the blasphemous accusations made by Jesus' adversaries that his exorcisms and cures were demonic in origin. And it points to his reply as a divine judgment uttered in the power of the Holy Breath (Mt 12:15-28).

Mark's Jesus, it will be recalled, dismissed the charge of His slanderers by reducing it to an absurdity: if Jesus casts out demons by the devil's power, then Satan's kingdom is internally divided. Matthew also explicitly links His exorcisms to the advent of God's reign. Through the miracles of the Breath-filled messiah, the kingdom of God has already begun to replace the kingdom of Satan. Moreover, by portraying Jesus' exorcisms as the triumph of God's kingdom over that of Satan, Matthew links them thematically to Jesus' third temptation in the desert.

But while Matthew presents Jesus as a charismatic wonderworker, he cautions Christians against egocentric preoccupation with one's own charismatic powers. Matthew's Jesus warns:

> Not everyone who says to me, "Lord, Lord," shall enter the kingdom of heaven, but he who does the will of my Father in heaven. On that day many will say to me "Lord, Lord, did we not prophesy in your name, and cast out demons in your name, and do many mighty works in your name?" And then I will declare to them, "I never knew you; depart from me you evildoers." (Mt 7:21-23)

The intent of this saying approximates the thirteenth chapter of First Corinthians. There Paul warns that charismatic activity uninformed by faith, by hope, and especially by love cannot save. Here Matthew insists that authentic charismatic activity must incarnate the precepts of new covenant religion.

Like Mark, Matthew anticipates that Breath-baptism will draw Jesus' disciples into His passion. In the face of persecution they must stand fast, for the Holy Breath that the Father will send will give them words to confound their adversaries (Mt 10:17-20).

Matthew nowhere depicts the Breath's arrival in the Christian community. But his Gospel closes with a command of the risen Christ:

> Full authority has been given to Me in heaven and on earth. Go, therefore, and make disciples of all nations baptizing them in the name of the Father and of the Son and of the Holy Breath, teaching them to obey whatever I commanded you. And, behold, I am with you all days, until the end of the age. (Mt 28:18-20)

And presumably the baptism of the nations in the triune name reveals Jesus as the Breath-baptizer foretold by John the Baptist.

How then does Matthew understand the significance of Breath-baptism? And how does his position compare with that of Mark? We find broad areas of agreement between the two evangelists. Both agree that Breath-baptism reveals the meaning and purpose of the rite of Christian baptism and establishes the superiority of the Christian ritual to that administered by John the Baptist. Both look upon Breath-baptism as an eschatological event inaugurated by Jesus' own Breath-inspired mission. Both understand Breath-baptism as incorporation into the new Israel. Each looks upon it as a re-creation in grace. Both believe that Breath-baptism commissions one to bear witness to Jesus even under persecution. Each contends that the Breath-baptized will be tested by Satan as Jesus was and that they will be drawn into Jesus' passion.

Matthew, though, advances beyond Mark by insisting more explicitly on the moral consequences of Breath-baptism. As the Breath-inspired beginning of a new Israel, Matthew's messiah proclaims in the desert those facets of old covenant morality which His own doctrine fulfills. Moreover, for Matthew, moral transformation in the name and image of Jesus provides a more basic test of responsiveness to the Holy Breath than the reception of any charismatic gift.

IV

In his account of Jesus' baptism by John, *Luke*, drawing perhaps on the same primitive traditions about the Baptist as Matthew, includes the words "and with fire" to the Baptist's prophecy that another would come who would "baptize you with a Holy Breath" (Lk 3:16). For Luke, as for Matthew, the divine Breath relates differently to Jesus on the one hand and to the Christian community on the other. The Breath comes to Jesus to reveal Him as messiah, beloved of God, and the beginning of the new Israel. The Breath comes to the community in purification and in judgment.

With Matthew, Luke elects not to describe the actual event of Jesus' baptism. But in contrast to Matthew he omits the Baptist's deferential protest to Jesus before the baptism as well as Jesus' assurance that their action will "fulfill all righteousness." And with Mark, Luke portrays the voice from heaven as speaking to Jesus alone (Lk 3:22).

Of the three synoptic evangelists Luke alone states that the Breath descended upon the messiah "in bodily form (sōmatikō eidei)" (Lk 3:22). The phrase attenuates somewhat the apocalyptic tone of the narrative and transforms Jesus' vision into a semi-miraculous public event.[9] It may in all likelihood reflect Luke's concern to date the start of the last age of salvation from Jesus' conception rather than from His baptism (Lk 1:33).

Luke, in contrast to both Matthew and Mark, states that Jesus' messianic commissioning in the power of the Breath occurred only after John had finished baptizing and while Jesus was at prayer (Lk 3:21). Matthew and Mark both situate the vision immediately after Jesus emerges from the water (Mt 3:16; Mk 1:10). Very likely Luke separates Jesus' vision and the descent of the Breath from the event of the baptism itself lest his readers misinterpret John's baptism as the cause of Jesus' messianic anointing. But he may have also desired to parallel the descent of the Breath upon Jesus at the Jordan with the Breath's descent on the apostles at Pentecost. In Acts the Holy Breath seems to arrive while the disciples are gathered in prayer (Ac 1:14).

But despite these minor variations, Luke, like Matthew, endorses the main lines of Mark's theological understanding of the meaning of Jesus' baptism. It inaugurates Jesus' public revelation in the power of the Divine Breath as messiah, Son of God, suffering servant, Breath-baptizer, the new Adam, and the beginning of a new creation.

In describing the messiah's temptations in the desert, Luke (like Matthew) portrays Jesus as the new Moses vanquishing the devil through the proclamation of a new covenant morality. Like Matthew he also affirms that proclamation was inspired by the Holy Breath (Lk. 4:1-13).

In describing the confrontation between Jesus and the Adversary, Luke insists more vigorously than Matthew that the devil exercises dominion over the kingdoms of this world (Lk 4:6-7). But he diverges from Matthew primarily in the way he orders the temptations. In Luke, Jesus' final temptation takes place on the pinnacle of the temple in Jerusalem (Lk 4:9-11).

The revised order of the temptations foreshadows the movement of Luke's Gospel as a whole, a movement from Galilee to Jerusalem, to the hill of Calvary, and finally to the mount of the ascension. By locating Jesus' final temptation in the Holy City, Luke also looks forward to Jesus' passion. At the close of the desert temptations the vanquished tempter departs from the victorious messiah to return at "an opportune time," at the moment of Jesus' betrayal in the Holy City (Lk 4:13). In this respect Luke's handling of Jesus' temptations contrasts sharply with Mark's. In Mark the desert temptations inaugurate an ongoing struggle between Jesus and the power of the Evil One. But Luke's Jesus emerges from the desert serenely victorious. This, too, foreshadows Jesus' death. In Luke's account of the passion, the messiah will die with a similar serenity, confident that His victory is already achieved (Lk. 23:46).[11] We may, however, discern in Luke's text a third reason why he puts Jesus' temptation to test God last. As we have seen in reflecting on Matthew's Gospel, one tests God by placing conditions on one's willingness to trust in His providential care through sharing one's possessions with the dispossessed. For Luke such a reluctance constitutes the supreme temptation of any follower of Jesus (Ac 5:1-11). For not only does Luke endorse the main lines of Matthew's understanding of New Testament morality; in what concerns the renunciation and sharing of material goods, Luke's Jesus makes even more radical demands than Matthew's.

In Matthew's temptation narrative, for example, Jesus replies to the tempter with the words "Man shall not live by bread alone, but by every word that proceeds from the mouth of God" (Mt 4:4). Luke's Jesus replies: "Man shall not live by bread alone" (Lk 4:4). The omission of the second part of the saying hints at a greater austerity in the use of worldly goods. Similarly, in Matthew the first beatitude reads: "Blessed are the poor in spirit" (Mt 5:3). Luke writes "Blessed are you poor" (Lk 6:20). Here both the omission of the phrase "in spirit" and the change of person hints at the need for personal austerity and great compassion toward the poor and the dispossessed.

Throughout his Gospel Luke proclaims God's merciful love for the poor and the outcast. He states twice that Jesus was especially concerned to preach to the poor (Lk 4:18, 7:22), and in both cases he associates this concern of the messiah with His anointing by the Divine Breath. Of all the evangelists, Luke alone records both the parable of Lazarus and the rich man (Lk 16:19-31) and the parable of the rich fool, who hoards his possessions into one place only to die and have them scattered among his relatives (Lk 12:13-21). And, as we shall soon see, Luke preserves a number of other teachings of Jesus concerning the use of worldly goods omitted by the other evangelists.

Luke does agree substantially with the other synoptic writers concerning the moral demands of Christian living. He regards the renunciation of personal possessions in order to distribute them to the needy and the destitute as the most immediate practical expression of faith in the Father's providence. Such sharing introduces the disciple of Jesus into the kingdom of God, and it will be especially rewarded in the life to come. "And I tell you, make yourselves friends from the mammon of iniquity, so that when it fails they may receive you into the tents of eternity (Lk 16:9, 12:22-32, 16:10-13, 12:33-34, 18:28-30). Luke's Jesus excoriates the Pharisees' love of wealth as "a loathsome thing (*bdelygma*)" in God's eyes (Lk 16:14-15, 12-39). He warns against trusting in wealth as the source of one's life (Lk 12:15, 16:10-12). For not only does attachment to wealth enslave one in ways that prevent one's entry into the kingdom, it also renders the service of God impossible (Lk 16:13, 18:18-27). And gross avarice will plunge one, like Dives, into the fires of Gehenna (Lk 16:19-31). Luke further hints that the cynical love of wealth so contradicts obedient trust in God that it prevents belief in the resurrection (Lk 16:31).

By the same token, the willingness to live poorly with a servant messiah manifests true discipleship. "Whoever of you does not renounce all that he has cannot be my disciple" (Lk 14:33, 10:57-58). Moreover, one must share one's intimate personal possessions with others. Hospitality, then, especially for the poor, finds its special reward in the resurrection of the just (Lk 14:12-13, 21).

In his account of Jesus' desert temptations, Luke, like Matthew, portrays the new Moses as demanding not only faith in God, but unconditioned faith. Since like Matthew, Luke also regards the sharing of worldly possessions as a test of faith, it comes as no surprise to discover Luke's Jesus insisting on the unconditional character of Christian faith-sharing. The disciples of Jesus must share even their intimate personal possessions.

> When you give a dinner or banquet, do not invite your friends or your brothers or your kinsmen or rich neighbors, lest they also invite you in return and you be repaid. But when you give a feast, invite the poor, the maimed, the lame, the blind, and you will be blessed, because they cannot repay you. You will be repaid at the resurrection. (Lk 14:12-14; cf. 10:29-37)

Indeed, for Luke as for Matthew, we live as the children of God when we share our possessions with a universality and freedom that imitates God's own love. For God is "kind to the ungrateful and the selfish. Be merciful, even as your Father is merciful" (Lk 6:32-36).

Finally, in both Luke and Matthew, Jesus establishes God's kingdom not on power politics but on a worship whose authenticity is measured by personal repentance and by mutual forgiveness (Lk 5:32, 6:36-37, 11:3, 17:4).

Luke also insists more explicitly than either Matthew or Mark that Jesus conducted His entire public ministry under the inspiration and guidance of the Divine Breath. All three synoptic evangelists follow their account of Jesus' desert temptations with a brief description of His early ministry. Both Matthew and Mark state that Jesus did not begin His own ministry until after John's arrest by Herod; and both summarize Jesus' initial message as one of repentance and of faith in the imminent arrival of God's reign (Mt 4:12-17; Mk 1:14-15).

Luke, unlike Matthew and Mark, concludes his account of Jesus' early ministry with the story of messiah's rejection by His own friends and neighbors at Nazareth. The conflict begins when Jesus claims to be the fulfillment of a messianic prophecy in the book of Isaiah.

> The Breath of the Lord is upon me because he has anointed me to preach good news to the poor. He has sent me to proclaim release to the captives and recovering of sight to the blind, to set at liberty those who are oppressed, to proclaim the acceptable year of the Lord. (Lk 4:16-19; Is 61: 1-2)[12]

For Luke, then, the Holy Breath of God that presided over Jesus' ministry impelled Him to proclaim a season of Jubilee in which misery and oppression would end, and the poor and suffering would be gathered into God's kingdom.[13] But as Luke's narrative proceeds, the widespread wonderment and joy which greeted the initial gracious teaching of the Breath-filled Messiah contrasts sharply with His violent repudiation by His own townsfolk. Their vicious stubbornness and their attempted murder of the messiah foreshadow both Jesus' repudiation by Israel and the suffering that awaits the Breath-baptized followers of a servant messiah (Lk 12:4-12).

Later in the Gospel Luke asserts that the Breath inspires Jesus' personal self-understanding as Son. When the seventy(-two) disciples return from their mission of proclamation, they report joyfully to Jesus that "even the devils submit to us when we use your name." Jesus assures them that their success is indeed a sign that Satan has been cast out from the heavenly court. But in terms reminiscent of Matthew He cautions them against self-infatuated preoccupation with their own charismatic prowess (Lk 10:17-20). Then Luke notes:

> In that same hour, He rejoiced in the Holy Breath and said, "I thank you Father, Lord of heaven and earth, that you have hidden these things from the wise and understanding and revealed them to babes; yes, Father, for such was your gracious will. All things have been delivered to Me by My Father, and no one knows who the Son is except the Father, or who the Father is except the Son and anyone to whom the Son chooses to reveal Him." (Lk 10:21-22)

Jesus' hymn of praise recalls a common theme in wisdom literature: true wisdom descends from on high as God's free gift. It enlightens neither the self-satisfied intellectual nor the self-reliant student of the Torah; rather, it reveals itself to the humble of heart who seek it as a grace given from above. Jesus, however, offers here a new interpretation of the enlightenment which descends from heaven. He does so in light of His own conscious sense of mission. True wisdom, true enlightenment, bears fruit in the freedom of heart to recognize the arrival of the messianic era in the person of Jesus and in His proclamation of the Father. That proclamation emerges from Jesus' awareness that He stands in a unique and special relationship to the Father. Moreover, Luke's Jesus himself proclaims this double truth under the inspiration of the Divine Breath sent Him by the Father. It comes as no surprise, then, that the Holy Breath who inspires Jesus' messianic awareness of being the Son of God in a unique and privileged sense will lead the Breath-baptized to confess the same truth fearlessly (Lk 12:4-12).[14]

But paradoxically, despite the abundant references in Luke to the Breath's inspiration of Jesus' mission, the evangelist's rendering of the controversy over Beelzebul makes no mention of the Holy Breath whatever. As we have seen, Matthew's Jesus replies to the charge that He performs His exorcisms by the power of Beelzebul with the words "But if it is by the Breath of God that I cast out demons, then the kingdom of God has come upon you." Luke replaces the phrase "Breath of God" with "finger of God." And in contrast to Matthew and Mark he postpones Jesus' warning against blaspheming the Divine Breath to another context (Lk 12:10). Luke's rendering of Jesus' answer is charged with theological irony. In the book of Exodus, Pharoah's magicians had recognized that Moses and Aaron performed miracles by the "finger of God" (Ex 8:15-19). These pagans were possessed of more discernment than Jesus' own Jewish contemporaries! Both versions of Jesus' reply enjoy historical plausibility.[15]

Two other references to the Holy Breath occur in Luke's account of Jesus' public ministry. Matthew's Jesus exhorts His disciples to persevering prayer with the assurance: "If you, then, who are evil, know how to give good gifts to your children, how much more will your Father who is in heaven give good things to those who ask Him?" (Mt 7:11). Luke modifies Jesus' words by substituting "the Holy Breath" for the phrase "good things." Luke's Jesus therefore asks: "how much more will the heavenly Father give a Holy Breath to those who ask Him?" (Lk 11:13). Luke's substitution obviously reflects the importance of the role which the Divine Breath plays in bringing salvation. But the substitution may also express a deeper intent. The words of Luke's Jesus foreshadow the day of Pentecost, when the Holy Breath will descend on the praying disciples in order to draw them into Jesus' own baptismal experience (Ac 1:1-14, 2:1-13). The evangelist may have also intended to suggest a parallel between Jesus' relation to the Divine Breath and the disciples. As we have seen, Luke's Jesus comes to a conscious sense of divine sonship through the anointing and illumination of the Holy Breath sent Him by the Father. When we beg from the Father the gift of the same Breath, we ask the Father that He teach us through the Breath's enlightenment to live as children of God in Jesus' image. How can He possibly refuse such a petition?

Luke eventually records Jesus' prohibition of blasphemy against the Divine Breath, but he inserts the saying in a different context. Jesus, having warned His disciples against the hypocrisy of the Pharisees, begins to instruct them concerning their proper relation to each member of the divine triad during times of persecution. For the Father they must have a reverential fear and a trust strong enough to carry them through martyrdom. Their relationship to the Son of Man must be one of fearless confession. As regards to the Divine Breath they must avoid the unforgivable sin of blasphemy. They must also trust the Holy Breath to teach them what to say to confound their adversaries. Therefore, Luke, in contrast to Matthew and to Mark, here associates the "unforgivable sin" with the apostasy of the Breath-baptized Christian (Lk 12:4-12).[17]

We may conclude that Luke's Gospel offers us a fairly elaborate interpretation of the purpose and scope of Breath-baptism. His subsequent description in Acts of the Breath's arrival on Pentecost and of the Breath's action in the Christian community must be read in the light of the theology of Breath-baptism elaborated in his Gospel. Like Matthew and Mark, Luke believes that Breath-baptism reveals the significance, scope, and purpose of the Christian rite of baptism. It proves the superiority of the Christian ritual to that administered by John the Baptist. It introduces the Breath-baptized into the last age of salvation inaugurated at Jesus' conception and publicly manifested in His baptism, ministry, death, resurrection, and ascension. Breath-baptism draws Jesus' disciples into the Lord's own experience of living as a child of God. By comparison, Luke endorses and yet radicalizes Matthew's interpretation of the moral demands of new covenant living which Jesus inculcated. Luke insists even more than Matthew that practical concern for the poor, the oppressed, and the downtrodden is the expression of Christian faith in the Father's providential care. Like Mark and Matthew, he points to mutual forgiveness as the test of authentic worship of the Father. And Luke, like Matthew, portrays Jesus in the desert proclaiming the basic principles of new covenant morality under the inspiration of the Holy Breath. As the Breath-filled beginning of a new Israel, Luke's Jesus (like Matthew's) established fidelity to new covenant morality as the most fundamental proof of Breath-baptism. However, Luke asserts even more explicitly than Matthew or Mark that Jesus' entire mission proceeded under the inspiration of the Holy Breath. But Luke agrees with the other synoptic writers that Breath-baptism not only conforms the disciples to Jesus and to the religious vision He proclaimed and incarnated, but it also draws them into an experience of Jesus' passion. Like Him they must confront the principalities and powers of this world. They must avoid the blasphemy of apostasy and trust the Holy Breath to teach them what to say under persecution.

V

Luke planned a two volume work on the origins of the Christian community. Accordingly his Gospel concludes with a cryptic foreshadowing of Pentecost. Before the risen Christ is taken up into heaven, He promises: "And behold, I send the promise of my Father upon you; but stay in the city until you are clothed with power from on high" (Lk 24:49). The phrase "the promise of my Father" seems to refer to the Baptist's prophecy of the coming of the Breath-baptizer, a prophecy which Jesus now intends to fulfill (Ac 1:5). His free gift of the Pentecostal Breath will clothe His disciples with "power from on high." That is to say, in their witness to Jesus they will speak with divine and messianic authority through the action of the Breath of Christ dwelling within them.[17]

The same promise is repeated at the beginning of Acts, and its meaning is further clarified: "But you shall receive power when the Holy Breath has come upon you, and you shall be my witnesses in Jerusalem and in all Judea and Samaria and to the end of the earth" (Ac 1:8). Here the purpose of Breath-baptism becomes more explicit: it will effect the universal proclamation of Christ. Furthermore, as the good news spreads, the universal scope of the salvation Jesus brings will become increasingly manifest. The gospel will spread first to the Jews, then to the Samaritans, and finally to the Gentiles.[18]

Luke surrounds his account of Pentecost with rich symbolic imagery. The Holy Breath arrives under the double sign of wind and of fire. The same signs had accompanied the ascension of Elijah into heaven; and the vision had revealed to the prophet's disciple Elisha that he would receive a double portion of his master's prophetic *Rûah* (2 Kg 2:9-15).[19] But now the *Rûah* of Elijah has become the Breath of Jesus Christ, and instead of descending on a single individual the Breath comes to fulfill Joel's prophecy that one day the Divine Breath would be poured out on "all flesh," men and women alike (Ac 2:14-22).[20]

The Pentecostal fire recalls the prophecy of the Baptist that the Breath would be poured out in purification and in judgment. But the Breath comes concretely under the sign of "tongues like fire" (Ac 2:3).[21] The image of tongues envisages the disciples' judgmental proclamation of Jesus in power even to the ends of the earth. But the arrival of the Divine Breath effects most immediately the eruption of glossolalic speech among those gathered in the upper room. "And they were all filled with the Holy Breath and began to speak in other tongues as the Breath gave them utterance" (Ac 2:4). Luke interprets the appearance of glossolalia among the disciples symbolically. It symbolizes the gathering of the new Israel from the four corners of the earth. For through the Pentecostal miracle of tongues Jewish pilgrims assembled in Jerusalem from a variety of lands all hear the apostles proclaim the risen Christ in their own native tongue (Ac 2:5-13).

In linking Joel's prophecy of a universal outpouring of the Breath (Jl 2:28-32) to the phenomenon of glossolalia, Luke may also have intended to portray the arrival of the Breath as the reversal of Babel. At Babel, Yahweh had confounded tongues as a sign of the universal sinfulness of humankind (Gn 11:1-9). Now He does it anew through the Breath of Christ as a portent of universal salvation.[22]

Finally, because the arrival of the Pentecostal Breath effects the Breath-baptism promised in God's name by the Baptist, the meaning of Pentecost stands inseparably linked to the meaning of Jesus' own baptism. The Breath comes in purification and in judgment in order to conform not only the disciples' witness but their very persons and lives to the image of Jesus, the servant of God. Peter makes the point clearly. He confronts his audience boldly with their sin in crucifying God's anointed, and he then explains that the risen Christ has now poured out on His followers the same Divine Breath given Him by the Father. The apostles are then asked, "Brethren, what shall we do?" Peter's reply is direct:

Repent, and be baptized every one of you in the name of Jesus Christ; and you shall receive the gift of the Holy Breath. For the promise is to you and to your children and to all that are far off, every one whom the Lord our God calls to Him. (Ac 2:37-39)

Repentance, faith in Jesus, and ritual baptism in His image—these are the conditions for sharing in His baptismal Breath.
Luke planned a two volume work on the origins of the Christian community. by proclaiming the three basic tenets of new covenant morality. Now the Pentecostal Breath immediately conforms the lives of the disciples to the morality that had been proclaimed by the new Moses in the power of the same Breath:

So those who received his word were baptized, and there were added that day about three thousand souls. And they devoted themselves to the apostles' teaching and fellowship, to the breaking of bread and the prayers. . . . And all who believed were together and had all things in common; and they sold their possessions and goods and distributed them to all. And attending the temple together and breaking bread in their homes, they partook of food with glad and generous hearts, praising God and having favor with all the people. (Ac 2:41-47)

In other words, even though in Luke's Pentecost narrative glossolalia symbolizes the creation of a new Israel by a reversal of Babel that will draw every nation into the ambit of God's saving activity, Luke, as Matthew, equates the first practical effect of Breath-baptism with fidelity to the new covenant morality which Jesus proclaimed and incarnated.

Luke's subsequent description in Acts of the lifestyle of the Jerusalem community reinforces this important point. The evangelist contrasts the faith-sharing practiced by the first Christians with the sin of Ananias and Sapphira. The unfortunate couple is struck dead for lying to the Holy Breath and to God. They pretend to have shared all of their possession with the other members of the community, when in fact they have secretly kept back something for themselves.

Peter condemns their sin as "testing God." The phrase recalls Luke's account of Jesus' third temptation in the desert. So, too, does Peter's question to Ananias: "Ananias, why did Satan fill your heart to lie to the Holy Breath and keep back part of the proceeds of the land?" Like Jesus in the desert, the couple is being sifted by the tempter. But unlike Jesus they have succumbed to His third and greatest temptation.

But how precisely did Ananias and Sapphira test God? Their lie itself might conceivably have done so. But as we have seen, for Luke as for Matthew, one tests God by setting conditions on one's willingness to trust Him. And trust in the Father's providential care bears practical fruit in personal willingness to share one's possessions, the physical supports of one's life, with others. Unconditional trust demands unstinting renunciation of one's goods to share them with others without reserve or restriction. By setting conditions on their willingness to share, Ananias and Sapphira stand convicted of setting conditions on their willingness to trust God. That is to say, they have "tested Him" (Ac 4:32-5:11).[23]

Each synoptic Gospel traces the authority of Jesus' teaching and His healings and exorcisms to the action of the Divine Breath within Him. In Acts, the arrival of the Pentecostal Breath is followed by a diffusion of charismatic gifts throughout the community of disciples: tongues and prophecy, cures and exorcisms, preaching, and works of mercy (Ac 2:1, 3:6, 16, 4:7, 10, 12, 30, 10:46, 13:17, 16:18, 19:6). The apostolic witness to the risen Christ is specially confirmed by signs and wonders (Ac 2:43, 5:12-16, 14:13, 15:12). But that same witness plunges the apostles into conflict with the powers who crucified Jesus. As Jesus had promised in Luke's Gospel, therefore, Breath-baptism draws them inexorably to share in Jesus' passion. The Sanhedrin harasses, arrests, and flogs the Twelve. And Peter escapes Herod only through angelic intervention (Ac 4:1-31, 5:21-42, 12:1-19).

The conversion of Paul, the Apostle to the Gentiles, promises the former persecutor a similar fate. Ananias, before baptizing Saul is assured that he is "a chosen instrument of Mine to carry My name before the Gentiles and the kings and sons of Israel; for I will show him how much he must suffer for the sake of My name." And Ananias obediently summons the temporarily blinded Saul to baptism with the assurance that he will be "filled with the Holy Breath" (Ac 9:15-16). The Breath imparted to Paul in baptism presides over his ministry. The Breath sets apart Paul and Barnabas for the missionary evangelization of Asia Minor (Ac 3:12). Their practice of baptizing uncircumcised Gentiles is confirmed by the Breath's action at the council of Jerusalem (Ac 15:5-29). On Paul's second missionary journey, the Breath prevents him from going to Bithynia (Ac 16:7). At Troas, Paul is called by a vision to Macedonia (Ac 16:9) and the Breath descends in Pentecostal plentitude on the disciples of the Baptist whom Paul baptized at Ephesus (Ac 19:1-7). Likewise, Paul's entire ministry is confirmed with abundant charismatic signs of healing and deliverance (Ac 19:11-12).

But the Breath-filled apostle must suffer in Jesus' name and image. He is repeatedly harassed and imprisoned by the enemies of the gospel. In Philippi he is flogged (Ac 16:22), and as he turns back from his second journey to Jerusalem he is prophetically warned by the Holy Breath in town after town that imprisonment and persecution await him in the Holy City (Ac 20:22-23, 21:11-14). But he is content to suffer anything for the sake of the apostolate. His tranquil return to Jerusalem recalls Jesus' own courageous journey from Galilee to Jerusalem and to death.

In making his final farewell at Ephesus, Paul commends the community to its elders. The Divine Breath has constituted them overseers of God's flock and will abide with them after the apostle is gone (Ac 20:28). The guard is being changed. The end of the apostolic era approaches. The age of the presbyter-bishop dawns. But the Holy Breath abides.

We must, therefore, conclude that Luke in Acts echoes the theology of Breath-baptism which he elaborated in his Gospel. In Acts the promise that Jesus will baptize with a Holy Breath finds fulfillment not simply on Pentecost Day but in the ongoing Pentecost of the Church effected by the Breath-filled proclamation of Jesus to the ends of the earth. The miracle of tongues on Pentecost together with the appearance of tongues like fire foreshadow that proclamation. In Acts as in the Gospel, Breath-baptism reveals the scope and purpose of ritual baptism in the name of Jesus: namely, the gathering of a new Israel covenanted to God in the power of the Divine Breath and composed of Jews and Gentiles alike. Although the Holy Breath confers a variety of charisms on the Christian community, in Acts as in Luke's Gospel, the first and most fundamental proof of Breath-baptism remains the disciples' willingness to live the new covenant morality Jesus proclaimed by sharing their bread with those in need as an expression of trust in the Father's providential care. Those who refuse to do so test God as did Ananias and Sapphira. In Acts as in Luke's Gospel, Breath-baptism draws one into Jesus' passion and suffering; for in empowering Jesus' disciples to bear witness to Him, it sets them in opposition to the powers of evil that sought to destroy Him. Finally, as Luke's Gospel had foretold, the Breath comes to the Christian community in purification and in judgment. The Breath pronounces judgment by acting through the apostles to summon unbelievers to repentance and to faith, to rebuke the hypocrisy of sinful Christians, and to guide the Christian community by making sound decisions about its internal belief and discipline.

VI

We are now in a position to draw some general conclusions concerning the meaning the synoptics give the term "baptism in a Holy Breath." It occurs rarely in the New Testament, but it does appear on the lips of John the Baptist. The synoptic authors agree substantially on the way Christians should interpret the Baptist's prophecy, even though their interpretations go beyond the Baptist's own intent and complement and enrich one another theologically. In none of the synoptics can Breath-baptism be equated exclusively with the reception of a specific charism or gift including the charism of tongues. The term envisages a more complex experience of graced witness and transformation in faith. Breath-baptism conforms Jesus' disciples to His teaching and example. That moral transformation cannot be restricted to a single moment. It cannot be dated by hour and minute. It encompasses a lifetime. It begins with baptismal faith in the risen Christ and renders the baptized open to the gift-giving Breath. But mutual service in response to the Breath's charisms ought always to express a more fundamental fidelity to new covenant morality.

The Breath-baptized live in obedience to Jesus' moral vision. Their faith leads them to trust in God's providential care. And that trust frees them to share their possessions, the physical supports of their life with others. That sharing seeks to imitate the unconditional character of the Father's love. It therefore reaches out to others irrespective of their merits, goodness, or social status. Christian sharing shows special concern for the poor and the dispossessed, and it should express a mutual forgiveness that authenticates Christian worship. Such practical attitudes constitute the most basic graces of Breath-baptism.

Prophetic confrontation with the forces of antichrist constitutes a second important practical test of Breath-baptism. Breath-baptism seeks to transform Christians into a prophetic community that confronts sinners and summons them to repentance and faith in Jesus. The forces of antichrist incarnate values and attitudes which Jesus condemned. They are symbolized by the figure of Satan. The antichrist manifests hypocrisy, unbelief, greed, oppression, violence, hatred, and the violently enforced rule of law. And the forces of Satan divide human society into warring classes and factions. The Breath-baptized oppose these satanic powers in the name and image of Jesus by trusting in the illumination of His Holy Breath for courage and for wisdom to speak and act as Jesus did.

But if Breath-baptism enlightens one to acknowledge God's saving action in Jesus and to proclaim Him fearlessly, by that very fact it also preserves one from Breath-blasphemy, whether one interpret that sin in the manner of Luke or in the manner of Matthew and Mark. Luke equates Breath-blasphemy with the apostasy of the persecuted Christian; Mark and Matthew with attributing the Breath's saving action to demons. In both interpretations Breath-blasphemy closes one to the saving illumination from the Breath of Jesus. In avoiding Breath-blasphemy the Breath-baptized manifest a capacity to distinguish the Breath's illumination from diabolic impulses. In other words, they grasp the religious significance of events. As the synoptic tradition developed not only do we find greater and greater emphasis laid on the importance of invoking Jesus' moral doctrine as the most basic norm for discerning authentic responsiveness to the divine Breath, but the moral demands of new covenant living are stated in even more radical terms.

These insights impose considerable moral constraints on contemporary American Christians. Jesus summons the Breath-baptized to share their goods freely with one another and to bear witness against the forces of antichrist. However, we live in a world in which the arms race and the pursuit of nuclear power and superiority have already brought about the starvation of millions of human beings. We live in an affluent nation that consumes a disproportionate amount of the world's food supply. We also live under an administration that prizes national security over the most basic human rights and enriches the wealthy at the expense of the destitute. If we claim Breath-baptism we must accept its moral and political consequences. We must join in Christian solidarity to denounce those in our society who invoke God's blessing on this nation while grinding the faces of the poor into the dust. The Holy Breath comes to us sinners in either purification or judgment. If we who claim Breath-baptism fail to proclaim and incarnate the mind of Christ and to denounce those principalities whose greed for power oppresses the poor and the needy, how will we ever face the one who said:

> Not every one who says to me, ''Lord, Lord,'' shall enter the kingdom of heaven, but he who does the will of my Father who is in heaven. On that

day many will say to me, "Lord, Lord, did we not prophesy in your name, cast out demons in your name, and do many mighty works in your name?" And then I will declare to them, "I never knew you; depart from me, you evildoers." (Mt 7:19-27)

NOTES

[1]Herbert Scheider, S. J., "Baptism in the Holy Spirit in the New Testament," in *The Holy Spirit and Power*, ed. Kilian McDonnel, O.S.B. (New York: Doubleday, 1975), pp. 35-52. In this essay I indulge in a stylistic conceit. I speak of the Holy Breath and of Breath-baptism rather than of the Holy Spirit and Spirit-baptism. Study of Christian pneumatology has convinced me that the term "spirit" labors under misleading connotations that fail to interpret adequately the biblical terms *rûah* and *pneuma*, connotations I prefer to avoid. The term "breath" seems closer to the original OT term for that aspect of the divinity that we call the Holy Spirit. All Scripture citations follow the RSV except for the substitution of "breath" for "spirit" for stylistic consistency.

[2]C. K. Barrett, *The Holy Spirit in the Gospel Tradition* (London: S.P.C.K., 1947), pp. 25-35; James D. G. Dunn, *Jesus and the Spirit* (Philadelphia: Westminster, 1975), pp. 62-65.

[3]Dunn, *Jesus and the Spirit*, pp. 55-60.

[4]Reginald Fuller, "Christian Initiation in the New Testament," in *Made Not Born*, ed. Aiden Cavanaugh, O.S.B. (Notre Dame: Notre Dame, 1976), pp. 9-10.

[5]Reginald Fuller, "Christian Initiation," pp. 10-14.

[6]Dunn, *Jesus and the Spirit*, pp. 49-53; George Montague, *The Holy Spirit: Growth of a Biblical Tradition* (New York: Paulist, 1976), pp. 244-248.

[7]Günther Bornkamm, Gerhard Barth, and Henry Joachim, *Tradition and Interpretation in Matthew*, trans. by Percy Scott (London: S.C.M. Press, 1963).

[8]Montague, *The Holy Spirit*, p. 307.

[9]Montague, *The Holy Spirit*, p. 266.

[10]John Navone, *Themes of Luke* (Rome: Gregorian, 1970), pp. 158-159, 163.

[11]Navone, *Themes of Luke*, 159-160.

[12]G. S. H. Lampe, "The Holy Spirit in the Writings of St. Luke," in *Studies in the Gospels*, ed. D. E. Nineham (Oxford, Blackwell, 1955), pp. 159-178.

[13]Montague, *The Holy Spirit*, pp. 262-264.

[14]Dunn, *Jesus and the Spirit*, pp. 26-40; Navone, *Themes of Luke*, pp. 256-260.

[15]Dunn, *Jesus and the Spirit*, pp. 49-53.

[16]Montague, *The Holy Spirit*, pp. 257-260.

[17]Montague, *The Holy Spirit*, pp. 260-262, 269; Ernst Haenchen, *The Acts of the Apostles*, trans. by Basil Blackwell (Philadelphia: Westminster Press, 1971), pp. 135-147; Navone, *Themes of Luke*, pp. 163-165; Lampe, "The Holy Spirit in the Writings of St. Luke," pp. 194-200.

[18]Montague, *The Holy Spirit*, pp. 271-273. The spread of the gospel to Samaria results not only from the action of the Breath in the disciples but from the first persecution of the Christians in Jerusalem (Ac 8:1-8). Refugees from that persecution effect the first evangelization of the Samaritans.

Philip the deacon instructs the Samaritans and baptizes them. His ministry is accompanied by signs and wonders. But there is a puzzling absence of charismatic manifestations of the Breath among his converts. Peter and John come down from Jerusalem to pray over the newly baptized, possibly because in the confusion of persecution Philip's Samaritan mission had not been officially commissioned by the Jerusalem community. The two apostles lay hands on the baptized converts. "And they received the Holy Breath" (Ac 8:14-17; Dunn, *Baptism in the Holy Spirit*, pp. 56-66).

This story is a much abused passage in Luke. Both Roman Catholics and Protestant Pentecostals have used it as a proof-text. The former, to establish the existence of confirmation as a separate ritual in the apostolic church; the latter, to prove the inefficacy of water-baptism and its distinction from Spirit-baptism. Both uses of the text lack theological legitimacy. Far from suggesting that a post-baptismal prayer for the descent of the Breath was standard apostolic practice, Luke seems to regard the entire incident as a pastoral anomaly. At the same time, the evangelist clearly recognizes an intimate connection between ritual baptism and the reception of the Divine Breath (Ac 2:38, 9:17-19, 10:44-48), even though he is also unwilling to confine the action of the Breath to cultic moments alone. On Pentecost, the Breath arrives initially with disconcerting spontaneity. And in the baptism of Cornelius and his household, the rite of baptism is administered in acknowledgment that the Pentecostal Breath has descended with the same spontaneity on the first pagan converts (Ac 10:44-48).

In describing the "Pentecost" of the Samaritans, Luke remained, however, quite oblivious of the post-Reformation debates concerning the efficacy of sacramental worship. He seems to suggest deficiency in the first faith of the Samaritans. He notes a morbid fascination with the miraculous in the Samaritan Simon. And he orchestrates the story around Simon in order to illustrate an important point: namely, God's utter sovereignty and freedom in dispensing the Holy Breath. The story climaxes in Simon's attempt to purchase from the apostles the power to confer the Divine Breath on others. He is roundly denounced by Peter, who informs him that he is "trapped in the bitterness of gall and the chains of sin." And Simon, thus rebuked, seems to repent (Ac 8:18-24). Luke has made his point: the Divine Breath can never be purchased. Indeed, the freedom with which the Breath is divinely dispensed stands as an abiding rebuke both to human avarice and to the proud and superstitious desire to control the Breath's activity.

The "Pentecost" of the Samaritans is soon followed by the "Pentecost" of the Gentiles. This time the entire incident is orchestrated from heaven. Before Peter goes to the house of the pagan centurion Cornelius, he is instructed three times in a vision not to consider profane what God has made clean. He then preaches to Cornelius and his household telling them how Jesus was anointed by the Divine Breath, crucified, and how He rose from the dead. The meaning of Peter's earlier vision becomes plain when the Breath descends upon the listening pagans with charismatic manifestations similar to those which accompanied Her descent on Pentecost. Peter orders the Gentiles baptized without circumcision and then justifies his action to the Jerusalem Church by insisting that he had performed it in manifest obedience to God. Here, one notes with interest that Peter does not regard ritual baptism as superfluous, even though the Breath is already charismatically present in his gentile converts (Ac 10:34-11).

[19]Montague, *The Holy Spirit*, pp. 27-29; Haenchen, *The Acts of the Apostles*, pp. 166-175.

[20]Haenchen, *The Acts of the Apostles*, pp. 176-189; George Montague, S. M., "Baptism in the Holy Spirit and Speaking in Tongues," *Theology Digest* XXI (Winter, 1973): 342-361.

[21]Note that Luke does not say "tongues of fire"; he uses the Greek phrase *"glōssai hōsei pyros."*

[22]Montague, *The Holy Spirit*, pp. 291-292; Haenchen, *The Acts of the Apostles*, pp. 230-241.

[23]Dunn, *Baptism in the Holy Spirit*, pp. 74-78; Haenchen, *The Acts of the Apostles*, pp. 327-329.

3

THE GREATER GIFTS

J. Rodman Williams

This paper intends to be an exegetical and theological reflection stemming from the words of Paul in 1 Corinthians 12:31a: *"zēloute de ta charismata ta meizona"*—"but earnestly desire the greater[1] gifts." What are the "greater gifts," the *charismata meizona*, and how do they relate to the life of the church in our time?

Based on Paul's words in 1 Corinthians 12 up to verse 31 two possibilities may be suggested. First, since in the delineation of nine *charismata*[2] (vv. 8-10), he begins with "word of wisdom" and "word of knowledge" and ends with "tongues" and "interpretation of tongues," "the greater" would be those first listed, hence "word of wisdom" and "word of knowledge."[3] Second, since shortly before Paul speaks of earnestly desiring the greater gifts, he declares that "God has appointed in the church, first apostles, second prophets, third teachers, then miracles, then gifts of healing, helps, administrations, various kinds of tongues" (v. 28), the greater gifts would seem to be "apostles" and "prophets" (perhaps also "teachers").

Now the latter understanding may readily suggest itself as Paul's intention both in light of the fact that he has just spoken of "apostles" and "prophets" and since he has also specifically given a prioritized listing: *"first* apostles," *"second* prophets," *"third* teachers." Accordingly, "apostles," "prophets," and possibly "teachers" would be the greater gifts to be desired. However, this interpretation immediately runs into a twofold difficulty. First, the listing is not designated by Paul as gifts *(charismata)* but as "appointments"—"God has appointed[4] in the church. . . ." In the earlier listing (vv. 8-10), the background is: "Now there are varieties of gifts [*charismata*], but the same Spirit"; hence "word of wisdom," "word of knowledge," etc. are specified as spiritual charismata. But in verse 28 Paul is referring to divine appointments (settings, placements) within the church, consisting both of certain offices (prioritized), namely, apostles, prophets, and teachers[5] and certain spheres in which the gifts function, namely, miracles, healing, helps, administrations, various kinds of tongues.[6] Both offices and spheres are divine placements within the church—but they are not charismata.[7] Second, it is quite foreign to Paul's writing, indeed, to the New Testament, to view the offices of apostles and prophets (and teachers) as something to be "earnestly desired." In the language of Ephesians 4 they are divine *domata* (v. 9)—not *charismata*[8]—and the sovereign Lord gives as He wills. They are "callings" of God.[9] Thus it can scarcely be the case that Paul is referring to the appointments listed in 1 Corinthians 12:28 when he adds—"earnestly desire the greater gifts."

What then may we say of the list in 1 Corinthians 12:8-10? As observed, they are designated charismata by Paul, hence might seem more likely to contain the greater gifts, the *charismata meizona*. In other words—to recall our earlier quotation—they would be "word of wisdom" and "word of knowledge" (and possibly the next one or two charisms on the list). But, again, certain difficulties emerge. First, unlike the listing of appointments in verse 28, which contains some specific priorities—"first," "second," "third"—there is no such enumeration in verses 8-10. Of course, it is possible to assume that the gifts in the list first mentioned by Paul would be "the greater gifts" by virtue of their prior listing, but such is only an assumption.[10] Indeed, since Paul speaks of "varieties of gifts"[11] (v. 4) prior to listing them, it would seem that the emphasis falls not on priority but diversity.[12] Second—and here we look beyond, into 1 Corinthians 14:1—Paul will later say, "desire earnestly spiritual gifts, but especially that[13] you may prophesy." If prophecy, or prophesying, is especially to be desired, then it would clearly seem to be of high priority. However, in the listing of the charismata in 12:8-10 Paul mentions prophecy *after* five other gifts. This alone is sufficient evidence to refute any idea that Paul is giving a hierarchical list in this first account.

Before we proceed further, it is to be noted that Paul, immediately after saying, "But earnestly desire the greater gifts," adds: "And I show you a still more excellent way" (12:31b). This translation of the Greek text[14] seems to point another direction in Paul's thought, namely, that rather than encouraging his readers to earnestly desire the charismata, he will show a way far better than striving after these gifts. If such be the case, the whole question of what are the "greater gifts" becomes moot in light of there being a "more excellent way" than zeal for the greater gifts. However, a more precise rendering of the Greek text—if nothing else—points a quite different direction; literally it reads: "And [yet] I show you a way beyond measure."[15] Thus it is that Paul is *not* here setting forth an alternative to desiring the greater gifts: he does not intend to show something better. Rather Paul is declaring that he will show a super-excellent way—"a way beyond measure"—wherein the gifts, including "the greater," are to be exercised.

From this understanding of Paul's words what he has to say in 1 Corinthians 13, the "love" chapter that immediately follows, falls into proper perspective. Verse after verse, from 1 through 13 (the last), Paul is describing the way beyond measure of love. All the gifts—tongues (v. 1), prophecy, knowledge, faith (v. 2)—must be exercised in love; else they are noisy, abrasive, and virtually worthless. Hence, the importance of love cannot be exaggerated. Moreover "love never ends"[16] (RSV), whereas the gifts will pass away when "the perfect" has come (vv. 8-10)—"as for prophecies, they will pass away; as for tongues, they will cease; as for knowledge, it will pass away . . . but when the perfect comes, the imperfect [lit., "that which is in part"[17]] will pass away" (RSV). "The perfect"[18] refers to the perfection of the glory to come, for Paul shortly adds, "For now we see in a mirror dimly; but then face to face" (v. 12). When we are "face to face" with the majestic glory, tongues, prophecy, knowledge—indeed all the charismata—fall away, for they belong to the present age, and are utterly transcended in the *visio dei*. So it is that in the glory to come (as Paul reaches his climax): "faith, hope, love abide, these three; but the greatest of these is love" (v. 13, RSV).

But—to return to our earlier point—Paul is by no means saying that love is a better way than the charismata, hence to be earnestly desired rather than the gifts. To be sure, the gifts will some day be no more, but while they are available in our present life they are much to be desired. However, they *must* be exercised in love, if there is to be genuine edification. Thus, it is not at all proper to say that the concern for gifts should be transcended by the pursuit of love. Indeed, as Paul makes his transition chapter 14, just after saying, "the greatest of these is love," he writes, "Pursue love, yet desire earnestly spiritual gifts."[19] It is not either/or but both/and: with love as the way—the way beyond measure—wherein the gifts find their truly meaningful expression.

Now—going back to chapter 13—we need to mention an additional matter, another error sometimes made: that of viewing the greatest of the gifts as love. We have reflected upon the mistake of considering love as a superior way to the gifts; but we need also to observe that love is in no sense the greatest—or "the greater"—of the gifts. Paul does indeed say that "the greatest [lit., "the greater"[20]] of these is love"; however, it is apparent that he is not talking about the greater among the charismata, but the greater (or greatest) among the triad of faith, hope, and love. Paul is speaking of eternal verities: those realities of faith, hope, and love that "abide" or "remain";[21] he is not referring to gifts, that for all their greatness, pass away in eternity.[22] It should be added that love—neither here nor elsewhere in the Scriptures—is depicted as a gift, or charism. Rather it is a *fruit* of the Spirit (Gal. 5:22—the first mentioned fruit); it is an *effect* of the Holy Spirit's inner presence: "the love of God has been poured out within our hearts through the Holy Spirit who was given to us" (Rom. 5:5); but love is not a charism. Since love is not a gift, it cannot be one of the "greater gifts" about which Paul speaks.

Incidentally, it is not always recognized that this classic chapter[23] on love is set in the midst of a discussion of the gifts. Paul writes to those who know the gifts and who are experiencing them. He urges them to earnestly desire the "greater gifts," indeed "spiritual gifts" in general (1 Cor. 14). Chapter 13 is *not* basically a dissertation by Paul on the Christian life at large, the way of love, and so forth.[24] It is mainly a discourse on the way the gifts are to be exercised. Paul's words (it is apparent from the still larger context) were written to people who were not lacking in any spiritual gift, but who obviously lacked much in love.[25] Hence, the Apostle's words are surely applicable to believers today who need to be encouraged to seek after the charismata and in their every expression to exhibit the spirit of love.

With all this by way of background, we may turn again to Paul's injunction: "but earnestly desire the greater gifts." Since these gifts cannot be identified with the top listing of the *charismata* of 1 Corinthians 12:8-10, nor with the primary placements (the offices) of 12:28-29, and since—according to 1 Corinthians 13—the charismata are not to be superseded by love (or by faith, hope, and love), what, then, are these "greater gifts"?

One answer has already been mentioned—prophecy. For after his injunction to "pursue love" and "desire earnestly spiritual gifts," Paul adds, "but especially that you may prophesy" (1 Cor. 14:1). It is scarcely to be doubted, therefore, that prophesying is to be viewed under the heading of "greater gifts,"[26] if not the greatest—or the "greater of the great," if Paul has only two gifts in mind. And the reason given for desiring to prophesy, Paul shortly thereafter states: ". . . one who prophesies speaks to men for edification and exhortation and consolation" (v. 3). For truly, Paul adds, "one who prophesies edifies the church" (v. 4). Apparently, the measure of a gift, a *charisma*, is the measure of its ability to build up the body of Christ. And nothing can stand higher than prophecy in that regard.

Inasmuch as prophecy is a direct, intelligible communication from God primarily addressed to believers, it cannot be surpassed by any other manifestation of the

Spirit. Prophecy is a "speaking for"[27] God wherein He provides the words and the message; the result is that the whole body, or its various members are built up in the faith. Little wonder that Paul, in reference to seeking the spiritual gifts says, "especially that you may prophesy"; but he also adds later, "desire earnestly to prophesy" (1 Cor. 14:39).

Does Paul give information concerning any other "greater" gift? Unmistakably prophecy is such a gift, what else? The answer is that—in an extraordinary kind of way—speaking in tongues *may* also occupy the top position. Let us follow Paul carefully here. It would seem at first glance that Paul places glossolalia on a rather low level. This might be deduced from the list of charismata in 1 Corinthians 12:8-10, where speaking in tongues is mentioned next to last, or from the list of placements in 1 Corinthians 12:28 which mentions tongues last. However, as we have seen, the listing in verses 8-10 is clearly not a ranking[28] and that in verse 28 is not a gradation of gifts.[29]

Now moving on to chapter 14, where Paul begins to discuss the relationship between prophecy and tongues, there may initially seem to be a lower view of tongues, for, says Paul, "One who speaks in a tongue edifies himself; but one who prophesies edifies the church" (v. 4). Since edification of the church is the purpose of the gifts,[30] and the "greatness" of a gift is measured by its capacity to edify, or build up, the church, and since tongues are said to edify the speaker, the conclusion would seem to be that tongues in relation to the body would have little or no value. Any other gift presumably would rank higher. But let us listen further to Paul, for shortly after the above quoted statement, he declares: ". . . greater is one who prophesies than one who speaks in tongues, unless he interprets, so that the church may receive edifying" (v. 5). *This means in the event that interpretation follows upon tongues the gift of prophecy is not greater.*[31] Indeed, speaking in tongues, then, may be recognized, along with prophecy, as a "greater gift," regarding which there is no higher or greater. Prophecy, for all its ability to upbuild, exhort, and console is not, therefore, greater than tongues. But why? How can tongues with interpretation following compare with such edification?

For an answer to this question we may now turn back to verse 2: ". . . one who speaks in a tongue speaks not to men but to God; for no one understands him, but he utters mysteries in the Spirit"[32] (RSV). Since glossolalia is on the high level of speaking to God, even that of speaking mysteries in the Holy Spirit, if there is an interpretation, the church will be immensely edified. The reason is clear; there will be the *unfolding of divine mysteries.* Paul does not reveal the nature of these mysteries, but by definition they are "hidden things."[33] Such things are declared by the one speaking in tongues, no one understands what he is saying,[34] and only the Spirit can make them known. When this occurs through the gift of interpretation, the church is greatly edified.[35] How could it be otherwise?

It follows that prophecy could not possibly be "greater" than tongues when there is interpretation. The one speaking in tongues is at least on the same level as the prophet,[36] because in both cases there is genuine edification from God, even though the content of the speech may be different.[37] Further, another point now needs to be made: both prophecy and tongues are *direct* spiritual utterances. This has already been mentioned in relation to prophecy—a *"speaking for"* God in which He provides the message. In the case of tongues it is a *"speaking to"* God wherein the Holy Spirit provides the language.[38] Though the human aspect is not denied—persons do the speaking in both cases—it is apparent that in a way beyond any other charismata, prophecy and tongues are operations of divine directness and immediacy.

For all of this it is not hard to conclude that prophecy and tongues are both numbered as "greater gifts" which are much to be desired. However, once again, it needs to be emphasized that the latter only occupies that high level in the body of Christ if interpretation also occurs. When Paul speaks of tongues alone, he states a preference for prophecy: "Now I wish that you all spoke in tongues, but even more that you would prophesy" (1 Cor. 14:5)[39] Moreover, he makes many statements shortly thereafter (beginning with v. 6) about the unedifying character of uninterpreted tongues in the body,[40] and he climaxes with the words, "Therefore let one who speaks in a tongue pray that he may interpret" (v. 13). Paul in none of this is depreciating all tongues,[41] but only tongues that are not interpreted.

Just following his statement that a person who speaks in tongues should pray for interpretation of this speaking, Paul adds, "For if I pray in a tongue, my spirit prays, but my mind is unfruitful. What is the outcome then? I shall pray with the spirit and I shall pray with the mind also; I shall sing with the spirit and I shall sing with the mind also" (1 Cor. 14:14-15).

First, praying in a tongue, praying with the spirit, and singing with the spirit are all references to essentially the same phenomenon: glossolalia, whether spoken, prayed, or sung.[42] What is striking is Paul's very mention of the variety of glossolalic utterance—in speech, prayer, song—which he by no means discounts or devalues; rather, he declares that he will do them all. There is, further, no suggestion that such utterance should be superseded by something other,[43] perhaps higher.

Second, the introduction of the terminology of "praying with the spirit" and "singing with the spirit" are obviously further amplifications of speaking in tongues. Glossolalia is an utterance in prayer and/or song; and since it is done "with the spirit" not the mind, it refers to something other than all communication through the mind (be it word of wisdom, prophecy, teaching, or anything else similar). It is undoubtedly a spiritual utterance in which the Holy Spirit within the human spirit speaks forth through human lips prayer[44] and praise to God. Thus praying with the spirit and in the Spirit (recall 1 Cor. 14:15), singing with the spirit and in the Spirit are actually the same phenomenon. Moreover—and here let us look briefly beyond 1 Corinthians—there is affirmative mention elsewhere of such spiritual utterance. In Ephesians Paul urges his readers to "pray at all times with the Spirit, speaking to one another in psalms and hymns and spiritual songs. . ."[45] (5:18-19). Thus praying in the S(s)pirit and singing in the S(s)pirit ("spiritual songs") are both spoken of very highly. It is to be recognized that in his letter to the Ephesians Paul's reference to praying in the Spirit does not call for interpretation since such praying is for the individual's own edification and strengthening;[46] however, its great importance cannot be minimized: "pray at *all times* in the Spirit." Nor is there any suggestion that "spiritual songs" done by the assembly are to be followed by interpretation; perhaps the point is that such is not needed in the context of "psalms and hymns" which, being sung in the vernacular, are understood by all. Additional references to praying and singing in the Spirit occur in Jude 20—"praying in the Holy Spirit"[47]—and Colossians 3:16—"spiritual songs."[48] These additional statements in Ephesians, Colossians, and Jude—related to speaking in tongues—point further to their great importance. Accordingly, as we return to 1 Corinthians 14:14-15, it is with enhanced recognition of the high significance of glossolalia—whether prayed or sung—for both individual and community.

Third, since Paul is vitally concerned about the edification of the body in the Corinthian situation, he emphasizes repeatedly the urgency of interpretation. What is done in the S(s)pirit, whether prayer or song, is to be followed by prayer and song "with the mind" or "understanding" (KJV). In no way does Paul suggest that spiritual utterance should be eschewed in favor of comprehensible articulation—even though with the former the mind is "unfruitful." Rather, what happens in spiritual utterance is far too important for its being minimized or set aside.[49] However, in the body there definitely should be interpretation that all may be edified.

Now we move on to Paul's next statement—in 1 Corinthians 14:16—where again he stresses both the high value of spiritual utterance and the importance of interpretation: "Otherwise if you bless[50] in the spirit only [i.e., in tongues only], how will the one who fills the place of the ungifted[51] say the 'Amen' to your thanksgiving, since he does not know what you are saying?" We may first recognize here the vital significance of speaking in tongues, in this case as a way of blessing and giving things to God that is superlative "thou verily givest thanks well" [v. 17 KJV].[52] Second, however, once again an interpretation is immediately needed (to return to v. 16) for the "ungifted" person, so that he may be able to participate in the blessing.[53] Thus despite the high value of praising and thanking God in tongues—as Paul continues (in v. 17)—"the other man is not edified." Hence, the Apostle again stresses the need for interpretation that other believers may be edified.

The conclusion—stated quite vigorously—is this: "I thank God, I speak in tongues more than you all; however, in the church I desire to speak five words with my mind, that I may instruct others also, rather than ten thousand words in a tongue" (vv. 18-19). First again is the high valuation placed on tongues ("I thank God"), but in church (where both "gifted" and "ungifted" believers are present) five words that are understood by all are preferable to any number, however many, of words spoken in tongues. This is not a devaluation of tongues as if Paul were saying that speaking with the mind is better[54] or that speaking in tongues does not really belong in church. The basic point rather, (as the whole context shows), is that speaking a multitude of words without interpretation will not edify a congregation with its wide range of experienced and inexperienced believers.

As we look back over the words in 1 Corinthians 14:6-19, it is apparent that Paul is not denying the great value of tongues with interpretation in the assembly (as declared in v. 5). But he is speaking throughout against uninterpreted tongues;[55] they simply do not edify the body.

Therefore, it is not that revelation and knowledge, prophecy and teaching are profitable, whereas glossolalia is not; words with the mind are not better than words spoken in tongues; thanksgiving in understandable speech is not preferable to blessing with spiritual utterance. To be sure, when there is no interpretation given, all these comprehensible operations of speech are far more significant—simply because they *edify all*. But *tongues with interpretation* occurring—which greatly edifies—remains among the "greater gifts."

It would seem proper to say from Paul's discussion of prophecy and tongues that both represent "greater gifts" that are much to be desired. The only difference is that prophecy in its very utterance edifies the assembled body of believers whereas tongues must be followed by interpretation for the same to occur. Nevertheless, one is not "greater" than the other; each carries its own message—and by their functioning together the church may be richly blessed.

We may now add that further evidence that Paul is referring to tongues and prophecy as the "greater gifts" is the fact that in all the discussion of the way of love in 1 Corinthians 13, tongues and prophecy are mentioned first (cf. vv.

1-2 and v. 8),[56] and that in the whole of chapter 14 (vv. 1-40) the only gifts that Paul discusses in detail are prophecy and tongues. In our reflection on 1 Corinthians 14 thus far we have only considered verses 1-19; however, even a cursory glance over the remaining verses of the chapter shows Paul's continuing great concern with these gifts. To be more specific, verses 20-25 are a presentation of the relationship of tongues and prophecy primarily to unbelievers;[57] in 26-33, after a brief mention of "psalm . . . teaching . . . revelation . . . tongues . . . interpretation" (that all should be practiced unto edification), Paul devotes all his attention to the proper ordering of tongues with interpretation and prophecy;[58] and 37-40 contain a final comment on prophecy and tongues.

Let us particularly consider these last verses in 14:37-40. According to the common reading of the passage, tongues and prophecy are mentioned only in verse 39—and in that verse the presumption usually is that Paul suggests a greater desirability for prophecy than tongues ("Therefore, my brethren, desire earnestly to prophesy, and do not forbid to speak in tongues").[59] But let us first note the interesting statement of Paul's in verse 37—then we shall return to verse 39.

Paul begins this passage (v. 37) with the statement, "If any one thinks he is a prophet or spiritual, let him recognize that the things which I wrote are the Lord's commandment." The word translated "spiritual,"[60] *pneumatikos*, is a masculine noun—not an adjective (hence *not* "a spiritual person")—paralleling the noun "prophet," thus literally such a one is "a spiritual." Thus "a prophet or a spiritual" is the literal rendering of the text. But who is "a spiritual?" Some would say "a Spirit-filled" person;[61] however, a prophet is surely "Spirit-filled," and yet he is mentioned in contradistinction to the one designated as a *pneumatikos—prophētēs* or *pneumatikos*. Accordingly, there is a further meaning, namely that Paul is referring to one who speaks in tongues. This is clearly suggested by the parallelism with verse 39 where prophecy and speaking in tongues are specifically mentioned, and in the same order as verse 37 (*prophētēs* first, *pneumatikos* second). Thus the one who is a *pneumatikos* is peculiarly one who speaks in tongues.[62] Hence, climactically in Paul's discourse of chapters 12-14, the speaker in tongues bears the title of *pneumatikos*.[63] In a unique fashion he is a pneumatic, a Spirit-endowed person[64]—not by any means more "spiritual" than others; but *pneumatikos* because through the language of the Spirit, i.e. tongues, he speaks directly to God. If such is the case, this is an additional reason for viewing speaking in tongues as a "greater gift."

But let us proceed to a more careful look at 14:39. Even if it be granted that Paul is referring to prophecy and tongues-speech in verse 37, that a *pneumatikos* is one who speaks in tongues—all of which sounds like a high evaluation of tongues—it might seem here that Paul is finally subordinating tongues to prophecy.

For, to repeat, according to a common reading of the text—"desire earnestly to prophesy, and do not forbid to speak in tongues"—there seems to be a definite lowering of the place of tongues. Does not such an injunction afford positive affirmation for the one, and give only a negative permission for the other? That is to say, speaking in tongues, unlike prophecy is not to be sought after or desired; such is not to be forbidden either.[65] *If* this is what Paul is stating here, it would seem quite out of harmony with any idea that tongues belong to the category of "greater gifts" to be desired. Rather, tongues are perhaps only reluctantly to be permitted. The answer, I believe, to this seeming shift of emphasis, almost to a self-contradiction, rests in a misapprehension of Paul's meaning in this verse—and it stems from the usual English translation, "Do not forbid." However, from another understanding of the meaning of the Greek word, and against the background of what Paul has been stating, the Apostle is much more likely to be saying: "Do not restrain[66] speaking in tongues." It is not a matter of granting negative, perhaps grudging, permission, but of declaring that tongues should not be hindered or checked. In other words, what is often read as negative permission is more likely a positive affirmation. Paul is saying to any who would view tongues as only tolerable, thus not to be sought after, "Let them be spoken!" From this perspective, he is *not* saying prophecy is desirable whereas speaking in tongues is not to be desired. It is rather that any restraint upon tongues needs to be removed so that they may have their proper expression and significance in the body of believers.[67]

Paul concludes with the words: "But let all things be done properly and in an orderly[68] manner" (14:40). Since this final statement is the conclusion of his injunction, "desire earnestly to prophesy, and do not forbid to speak in tongues," it points up Paul's great concern that especially these highly potent *charismata* of prophecy and tongues be properly ordered. As was mentioned, Paul devotes a rather lengthy statement to this matter (14:27-33), specifying in part, "if any speak in a tongue, let there be only two or at most three, and each in turn; and let one interpret. . . . Let two or three prophets speak, and let the others weigh[69] what is said" (RSV). Propriety and orderliness call for both the interpretation of tongues and the weighing or discerning of prophecy.[70] Therefore, while tongues and prophecy are greatly to be desired, of all the gifts they doubtless need the most judicious exercise.

Possibly enough has now been written to substantiate the thesis that Paul's words "earnestly desire the greater gifts" refer to prophecy and tongues.[71] No attempt will be made to summarize the evidence set forth in the preceding pages. However, one point made earlier that indicates their being "greater gifts" needs further emphasis, namely, that prophecy and tongues are uniquely (among the charisms) *direct* utterances relating to Almighty God. In prophecy the words spoken are the speaker's own language, but the message *is given* by the Spirit of God;[72] there is no mental involvement on the part of the speaker.[73] The words are God's message in human language;[74] hence the one prophesying simply speaks it forth. Thus there is direct utterance *from God*. In the case of tongues the directness is even more apparent since the words first spoken (before interpretation) are *not* in the speaker's own language; the *words themselves are given* by the Holy Spirit and addressed directly to God. The interpretation (in the body), as with prophecy, does not actually involve the mind, but sets forth directly in the common language what has been declared in and by the Holy Spirit.[75] Thus, prophecy and tongues represent, as no other charismata,[76] a directness, even an immediacy, of communication between God and humanity. This being the case it seems, again, all the more surely that they are the "greater gifts."

Here we may—leaving Paul for a moment—also be reminded from the book of Acts that in the initial outpouring of the Holy Spirit prophecy and tongues occupy a high place. On the Day of Pentecost speaking in tongues (Acts 2:1-4) and prophecy (Acts 2:14-18) are the primary demonstrations of the Holy Spirit, indeed his direct workings—"And they were all filled with the Holy Spirit and began to speak with other tongues as the Spirit was giving them utterance" (v. 4); "I will pour forth of my Spirit upon all mankind; and your sons and your daughters shall prophesy" (v. 17). It is the Holy Spirit giving persons utterance in tongues; the same Holy Spirit outpoured upon people brings forth prophecy through them.[77] Whatever else will happen on that day (and surely much will, including the salvation of some three thousand persons, and the formation of the first Christian community), and however much the Holy Spirit will be involved in it all (and surely He will: convicting of sin, bringing about faith, enabling *koinōnia*)—the *prior* and *direct* workings are unmistakably tongues and prophecy.[78]

One further note concerning the book of Acts should be made. It is significant that on another occasion in the early mission of the church, there is reference to both tongues and prophecy. Paul had been ministering to some Ephesians with the result that "the Holy Spirit came on them, and they began speaking with tongues and prophesying" (19:6). *What* the Ephesians said is not disclosed; but *that* the primary manifestation of the Holy Spirit's coming was tongues and prophecy is apparent. Again glossolalia and prophecy are shown to be His primary and immediate working.

It would seem to follow from the book of Acts that if prophecy and tongues are ongoing possibilities,[79] they would rank as the most to be desired. For as no other manifestations of the Spirit do they express so directly the presence and power of the Holy Spirit. Of course, this brings us full circle; for Paul clearly speaks of continuing manifestations of the Spirit, he stresses the desirability of all, and he urges the seeking of the "greater gifts," one of which he specifies as prophecy. Our conclusion is based primarily on the inner evidence of 1 Corinthians 12-14, and from a quick review of Acts, tongues surely qualifies for inclusion in "the greater." In sum: prophecy and tongues, in their proper functioning, are gifts of the Spirit greatly to be desired.

A concluding word: this article has been written under the growing conviction that prophecy and tongues are of a potency and value seldom realized in the church. This is said not simply to those who may have difficulty accepting their validity at all (at least for the church today), but also to those who do claim their continuance. It is to this latter group that some closing remarks follow.

My point is this: I believe that we have scarcely begun to realize the *basic* importance of prophecy and tongues. If they are direct, immediate utterances of the Holy Spirit for the body, they should have primacy in all gatherings of assembled believers.[80] This is not in any way to minimize the importance of evangelizing and teaching,[81] of liberality and mercy,[82] or of any of the other ninefold gifts of the Holy Spirit. All just mentioned are gifts of grace,[83] hence of great value, but none of these are quite as powerful and direct expressions of Almighty God as are prophecy and tongues. For what else can correspond to a prophetic "Thus says the Lord"? *If God is truly speaking* therein, then prophecy calls for the highest place and consideration. Again, what else can transcend an utterance in tongues that declares divine mysteries, the hidden things of God? If God's *secret truth* is being declared thereby for His gathered people, there can be nothing else of more importance to comprehend.

It is quite a sad thing that even where the gifts of the Spirit are recognized, and prophecy and tongues are expected, far too often there is a failure both to appreciate their extraordinary character and their proper functioning. There should, on the one hand, be a holy awe in the presence of Him who is now speaking, an eagerness to hear every word spoken, and a yearning to appropriate and act upon whatever is being declared. On the other hand, realizing the human element in all prophetic utterance and interpretation of tongues, there should be a fresh sense of urgency in discerning the truth that is being proclaimed, not hesitating if need be to separate out what is not truly of God, and thereupon earnestly and faithfully seeking to fulfill whatever God has spoken.

It could be a new day in the church when the "greater gifts" are both earnestly desired and truly exercised. May the Lord grant us fresh zeal and determination!

NOTES

[1]*New American Standard Bible* translation (here and throughout the article, unless otherwise noted). The Gk., *meizona*, is rendered as "best" in the KJV, "higher" in the RSV and NEB. "Greater"—also so translated in the NIV—seems closer to the root meaning (*meizona* from *megas*, usually translated "large" or "great").

[2]In v. 4 Paul speaks of "varieties of gifts" or "charismata"—also "varieties of ministries (v. 5) . . . and varieties of effects" (v. 6). Then he adds: "But to each one is given the manifestation of the Spirit. . ." (v. 7). Thus Paul will be setting forth charismata of the Spirit, spiritual gifts, in vv. 8-10.

[3]"Greater" suggests at least two gifts; however, if Paul is giving a hierarchy of gifts in vv. 8-10, the next one "faith," perhaps also next "gifts of healing," might be viewed as in the "greater" category. Actually, from a hierarchical perspective any gift in the list might be viewed as greater than the next one listed.

[4]*etheto*—also "set" (KJV) or "placed."

[5]The parallel with Eph. 4:11 is unmistakable—"He [Christ] gave some as apostles, and some as prophets, and some as evangelists, and some as pastors and teachers." The order—omitting "evangelists" and "pastors"—is the same. Though the word "appointed" is not used, there is clearly a sense that these are set offices. The word "gave" *(edōken)* expresses a completed and fixed action.

[6]The latter listing of spheres is not said to be fourth, fifth, sixth, etc. The Gk. word preceding "miracles" is *epeita*, translated as "then" in NASB, but perhaps better as "after that" (as in KJV). Thus there is succession in the spheres, but not necessarily a prioritized listing. *Epeita* also precedes "gifts of healing," but is not used in reference to the last three spheres, namely helps, administrations, tongues. Hence, this suggests even more strongly that the prioritized listing by no means includes them.

[7]Hence, for example, the *charisma* of "prophecy" (v. 10) is one thing, the office of "prophets" is another. All may prophesy (see Paul's later words "you can all prophesy." [14:31]), thus the *charisma*—but not all are prophets (see Paul's question with implied negative answer: "Are all prophets?" [12:29]). Also there is both the charism of "the effecting [or working] of miracles" (v. 10), and the sphere of "miracles (v. 28). Because God has placed miracles in the church, the workings of miracles can happen: the placement is antecedent to the charism.

[8]Both *domata* and *charismata* are "gifts," but the former refers to gifts of office: they are "for the equipping of the saints for the work of service [or 'ministry']" (Eph. 4:12).

[9]E.g., Paul speaks of himself as "called to be an apostle" (Rom. 1:1; cf. 1

Cor. 1:1; Gal. 1:15); but neither had he "earnestly desired" it, nor does he ever urge anyone else so to desire.

[10]Paul speaks of faith, hope, and love in 1 Cor. 13:13 in that order, but declares that the greatest is love. The first mentioned in this case is *not* specified as the greatest!

[11]Also as we have noted, "varieties of ministries" and "varieties of effects" (or "workings").

[12]RSV translates as "diversities of gifts," KJV—"differences of gifts." The Gk. is *diaireseis charismatōn*.

[13]*mallon de*. KJV translates as "rather that" which gives an adversative sense. Though *mallon de* often carries that connotation (e.g., cf. Eph. 4:28), it may have a supplementary meaning (Thayer: it "marks what has the preference: *more willingly, more readily, sooner*") as in the NASB translation (similarly in RSV, NIV; NEB has "above all").

[14]Almost identical in the RSV. KJV omits "still," NIV has "the most excellent way." All are essentially the same.

[15]*kath' hyperbolēn*—"beyond measure" or "comparison." See, e.g., Gal. 1:13—"beyond measure"; 2 Cor. 4:17—"Beyond all comparison" (also RSV). Thus the translation earlier given, "a still more excellent way" (with parallels in other versions) is quite misleading. According to the *Expositor's Greek Testament "kath' hyperbolēn* . . . is superlative, not comparative; Paul is not pointing out a more excellent way than that of seeking and using the charisms of chapter xii, but a super-excellent way to win them." Though I might differ on the last phrase, "to win them," EGT is surely right in speaking out against the comparative idea.

[16]*piptei*. "Fails" (NASB, NIV; KJV—"faileth"). NEB, as RSV, has "ends." "Ends" is the more likely translation in view of v. 13.

[17]So KJV.

[18]*to teleion*. The attempt on the part of some to identify *to teleion* with the completion of the canon of Scripture hardly needs comment. Such an attempt— which actually is only a device to seek invalidation of the gifts as continuing in the church—is utterly futile.

[19]The word here is not *charismata* but *pneumatika*, literally "spirituals" (as also in 1 Cor. 12:1). However, English translations regularly render *pneumatika* as "spiritual gifts" in light of the context (in both 1 Cor. 12 and 1 Cor. 14).

[20]*meizōn*.

[21]NEB translates: "there are three things that last forever: faith, hope, and love. . . ."

[22]Faith *(pistis)* uniquely functions both as a gift of the Spirit (see 1 Cor. 12:9)

and as one of the eternal verities. However, a fuller discussion (not possible here) would show that faith as a charism is a special faith for healing, working of miracles, etc. The faith that "abides" is eternal faith and trust in the living God.

[23]Of course, there is no chapter in the original letter. Unfortunately, the chapter separation can easily lead to isolation from the overall context.

[24]This is not to say that the chapter has no relevance to the general Christian walk. Quite the contrary, there is much of great edification (note esp. vv. 4-7), regardless of the gifts. But the chapter both begins specifically with the gifts (vv. 1-3), and later continues with them (vv. 8-10). Thus it is clear that however much Paul goes beyond the gifts as he speaks of love, the context is the *charismata*.

[25]See esp. chap. 1. Whereas Paul expresses his thanksgiving to God that the Corinthians were "not lacking in any gift [*charisma*]" (vv. 4-7), he also—immediately thereafter—speaks of "the quarrels" (v. 11) and divisions among them.

[26]Later, Paul uses the word "greater" in describing prophecy as it relates to speaking in tongues: "greater is the one who prophesies. . . . " (1 Cor. 14:5). The Gk. for "greater" is *meizōn*, the same as the *meizona* in "greater gifts."

[27]*pro + phēmi.*

[28]Since prophecy is mentioned sixth, and yet is especially to be desired, the listing of tongues thereafter—actually eighth—does not imply inferiority.

[29]As previously noted, though 28 contains a prioritized listing of offices and a designation of various spheres of charismatic activity, it is not a hierarchy of gifts.

[30]When Paul first discusses the gifts, he speaks of them as "the manifestation of the Spirit for the common good" (1 Cor. 12:7). "The common good" is the edification, or upbuilding, of all in the body.

[31]This is apparent even though Paul speaks (in v. 5) more specifically of the person who is the channel for the gift than the gift itself.

[32]NASB, KJV, and NIV have lower case "s." NAS and NIV give "by the Spirit" as possible renderings (see margins). Since Paul has earlier characterized tongues as a manifestation of Spirit (not *spirit*), I believe that the RSV reading (and NAS, NIV margins) of "Spirit" is better.

[33]*mystērion* is "a hidden thing, secret, mystery . . . not obvious to the understanding" (Thayer), thus mysteries are "hidden things."

[34]"The one who speaks in tongues . . . utters secret truths in the Spirit which he alone shares with God, and which his fellow-man, even a Christian, does not understand"—Bauer, Arndt, and Gingrich under entry on *mystērion.*

[35]It is important to add that mysteries uttered in tongues and made known by the Spirit through interpretation are not "new truths" beyond what are recorded in Scripture. They are rather in line with Paul's prayer that believers may have

"all the riches of assured understanding and the knowledge of God's mystery, of Christ, in whom are hid all the treasures of wisdom and knowledge" (Col. 2:2-3 RSV). In that sense God's mystery is *Christ*, with all the treasures of wisdom and knowledge contained in Him. Hence, a mystery spoken in tongues, when interpreted, will in some sense be a declaration of those treasures both in themselves and in relation to His body.

[36]In EGT the following interesting comment is to be found: "The power to interpret *superadded* to the glossolalia . . . puts the mystic speaker on a level with the prophet: first 'uttering mysteries' (2) and then making them plain to his hearers, he accomplishes in two acts what the prophet does in one" (vol. 2, p. 903). Note especially " . . . on a level with the prophet."

[37]What is revealed in the interpretation of a mystery may not be the same as what is contained in a message that upbuilds, exhorts, and consoles. The two *may* overlap, even at times prove identical, but there is not necessarily an equivalence. Tongues plus interpretation may equal prophecy (as is often said), but equality is *not* equivalency. They are equal in value to the community when properly exercised.

[38]We may recall that in the first occurrence of glossolalia, namely, on the Day of Pentecost, that those assembled "began to speak with other tongues, as the Spirit was giving them utterance" (Acts 2:4).

[39]This immediately precedes the words: "greater is the one who prophesies than one who speaks in tongues, unless he interprets. . . ."

[40]E.g., such is of no more value than a bugle that gives an indistinct sound, and thus prepares no one for battle: also it is but a "speaking into the air" (v. 9).

[41]V. 6 is sometimes read as a devaluation: "But now, brethren, if I come to you speaking in tongues what shall I profit you, unless I speak to you either by way of revelation or of knowledge or of prophecy or of teaching." A first impression could be that tongues are of no profit to the body of believers: there is profit only if one speaks *rather* by revelation, knowledge, prophecy or teaching. However, such a reading of Paul's words seems unwarranted first of all by the fact that they follow immediately from his statement about the need for interpretation "so that the church may receive edifying." Hence what Paul is emphasizing is that speaking in tongues *alone* (i.e. without interpretation following) is of no profit. (It has been proposed by some that Paul's words, "if I come to you speaking in tongues what shall I profit you, unless I speak to you either by way of revelation . . . knowledge . . . prophecy . . . teaching," refer to the great value of tongues plus interpretation, namely, that through the interpretation revelation, knowledge, prophecy, or teaching will occur. If this is Paul's meaning, tongues [with interpretation] unquestionably transcends all other gifts [even

revelation itself] as a channel of their functioning. [See H. M. Ervin, *These are Not Drunken as Ye Suppose* (Plainfield, NJ: Logos International, 1968), pp. 163-65; Ray Hubbard, *Gifts of Grace* (Bromley [Eng.]: New Life Press, 1971), pp. 92-94]. Though I like the strong emphasis on tongues in this view, it really says too much. For Paul is not speaking of tongues' interpretation as bringing revelation, knowledge, prophecy, teaching. This is especially clear in light of Paul's later statement, "When you assemble, each one has a teaching, has a revelation, has a tongue, has an interpretation" [1 Cor. 14:26]. In this verse "tongue" and "interpretation" are set *alongside* "revelation" and "teaching"; the latter do not come by way of interpretation of the former. Thus for all the importance of tongues, it is an overstatement to view their interpretation as bringing about revelation, teaching, etc.)

[42]As reference back to v. 13 makes clear.

[43]This emphasizes all the more that Paul did not mean earlier (recall v. 6) that there is no profit in tongues unless one also speaks by way of revelation, prophecy, etc.

[44]NEB rather than rendering 1 Cor. 14:14a as "if I pray in a tongue, my spirit prays" (as NASB and many others similarly) translates the latter phrase as "the Spirit in me prays." The NEB correctly catches the deeper meaning.

[45]*ōdais pneumatikais.* "Pneumatic odes," songs given by the Spirit.

[46]We may recall 1 Cor. 14:4—"One who speaks in a tongue edifies himself. . . ."

[47]"But you, beloved, building yourself up on your most holy faith; praying in the Holy Spirit. . . ." The focus here is also on personal edification through tongues.

[48]Identical with Eph. 5:19—"psalms and hymns and spiritual songs." An interesting comment on "spiritual songs" (in Col. 3:16) is made by a footnote in the Jerusalem Bible stating that they "could be charismatic improvisations suggested by the Spirit during liturgical assembly"(!) Accordingly, I would add, such "improvisations" are "singing in the Spirit."

[49]As observed earlier, "mysteries in the Spirit" are being uttered. See next paragraph for further significance of tongues.

[50]*eulogēs.* The better translation may be "praise" (as in NIV and NEB). In any event it is directed to God and contains the note of thanksgiving (as the continuation of the verse shows).

[51]*idiōtou*—"unlearned" (KJV); "those who do not understand" (NIV); "outsider" (RSV—mg. "him that is without gifts"); "the plain man" (NEB). The *idiōtai* seem to represent those who are not unbelievers but are "outsiders" to spiritual gifts ("unversed in spiritual gifts"—NASB Margin). Incidental note:

perhaps the *idiōtai* are represented today by believers unfamiliar with and unversed in charismatic experience.

[52]The KJV is quoted here because most other translations produce a misimpression. "For you are giving thanks well enough" (NASB), "you may give thanks well enough" (RSV, similarly NIV), "your prayer of thanksgiving may be all that could be desired" (NEB)—all sound like a grudging admission of the value of this blessing of God in the Spirit. The KJV is on target, since the Greek text literally reads: "For you indeed give thanks well *(sy men gar kalōs eucharisteis)*."

[53]One might wonder why Paul here singles out the "ungifted" as not being edified by uninterpreted tongues. Would that not be true of all believers present? The point, however, is that tongues described here are peculiarly expressions of blessing and thanksgiving to God. The "gifted" among believers would know what is going on, hence could very well say an "Amen" to such an uninterpreted expression; but the "ungifted," not comprehending, would be quite at a loss to do so.

[54]Sometimes the words of Paul, "I desire [or 'would rather'—RSV, NIV, NEB] speak five words with my mind," are understood to mean, "It is *better* to speak comprehensively." However, Paul never (here or elsewhere) deemphasizes the extraordinary value of glossalalic utterance.

[55]Undoubtedly the Corinthians were out of order in this regard. In the midst of the passage Paul writes: ". . . since you are zealous of spirits [lit. *'pneumata'*], seek to abound for the edification of the church." The Corinthians being "zealous [or zealots—*zēlotai*] of spirits" signifies zealous for spiritual realities in general (not simply spiritual gifts—which are *pneumatika* [see earlier note] and for which Paul urges them to be zealous.). Being thus zealous, they should be all the more concerned to abound in what edifies the church. Interpretation of tongues (which Paul discusses immediately thereafter) (v. 13) is urgent if this is to happen.

[56]The order in vv. 1-2 is tongues, prophecy, knowledge, faith; in v. 8 it is prophecy, tongues, knowledge (incidentally, "knowledge" probably refers to "word of knowledge" in 12:8; "faith" to the gift of faith in 12:9).

[57]The concern about unbelievers *(apistoi)* in the church assembly goes largely beyond Paul's earlier concern about the "ungifted" *(idiōtai)*. The question now is an additional one: *not* how do tongues and prophecy edify the believer, but what are their effects on the unbeliever? Tongues, Paul says, are a sign (of judgment) for the unbeliever, but not so for the believer; prophecy on the other hand can bring an unbeliever (also an "ungifted" person) into a profound experience: "But if all prophesy, and an unbeliever or an ungifted man enters, he is convicted by all, he is called to account by all; the secrets of his heart are

disclosed; and so he will fall on his face and worship God, declaring that God is certainly among you" (vv. 24-25).

[58]The parity of tongues with interpretation and prophecy is further suggested by the fact that Paul directs that there be "two or at most three" speakers in tongues, "two or three" who prophesy. The high importance of both is also implied in that Paul does not speak of two or three with "word of wisdom," "word of knowledge," etc. This again suggests that Paul views tongues and prophecy as the "greater gifts."

[59]Similarly in KJV, RSV, NIV, NEB, and many others.

[60]Also in KJV, RSV.

[61]E.g., Thayer—in references to *pneumatikos*—"one who is filled with and governed by the Spirit of God." BAG—in regard to *pneumatikoi*—"spirit-filled people."

[62]Attention may be called to Hermann Gunkel's seminal work, *The Influence of the Holy Spirit*, trans. by Roy Harrisville and Philip A. Quanbeck II (Philadelphia: Fortress Press, 1979), in which he says forcefully: "In 1 Cor. 14:37; *pneumatikos* in contrast to *prophētēs* . . . clearly denotes *glossolalia*" (p. 31). A. T. Robertson likewise views the *pneumatikos* as the speaker in tongues: "The prophet or the one with the gift of tongues" (*Word Pictures in the NT*, IV, 185. [I owe this quotation to Howard M. Ervin's *These Are Not Drunken as Ye Suppose*, p. 114]).

[63]It is interesting to observe that Paul begins 1 Cor. 12-14 thus: "Now concerning *pneumatikōn*. . . ." The word "gifts" is usually added; however, it could be "matters" or "things," or even "persons," i.e., *pneumatikoi*. I am inclined to the usual translation of "gifts"; however, there is undoubtedly some attractiveness in thinking that Paul at the outset is primarily concerned with those who speak in tongues (for a helpful discussion of 1 Cor. 12:1 see Ervin's *These Are Not Drunken*, chap. 14).

[64]Rudolf Bultmann writes similarly: "Since Paul can say, 'If anyone thinks that he is a prophet or one Spirit-endowed . . .' he presupposes a usage of speech according to which the ecstatic [*sic*] speaker in tongues (*in the context it can mean only him* [italics: mine]) is the 'Spirit-endowed' par excellence. . . ." *Theology of the New Testament*, Vol. 1, trans. by Kendrick Grobel (New York: Charles Scribner's Sons, 1951), p. 158.

[65]In regard to speaking in tongues *from this perspective*, a good rule of thumb would indeed be: "Seek not, forbid not."

[66]The Greek word is *kōlyete*. The proper translation for *kōlyō* often is "forbid." However, "restrain" or "check" is far more likely in this context. We may note the use of *kōlyō* in another place, 2 Pet. 2:16, where only "restrained" or

"checked" makes good sense: "a dumb donkey, speaking with the voice of a man, restrained (ekōlysen) the madness of the prophet" (KJV translates ekōlysen as "forbid," but such unfortunately only confuses the meaning; RSV and NIV, like NASB, translate as "restrained"). Incidentally, BAG refers to 2 Pet. 2:16, and the translation as "restrained," in the context of discussing 1 Cor. 14:39 (see article on kōlyō). In line with this (and the overall context), I repeat that "do not restrain speaking in tongues" is surely Paul's meaning. Weymouth's New Testament in Modern Speech is one of the few versions that translates in similar fashion thus: "Do not check speaking with tongues." Also see Moffatt's New Translation: "Do not put any check upon speaking in 'tongues.' "

[67]It is interesting to observe that Paul writes similarly about prophecy in 1 Thess. 5:20—"do not despise prophetic utterances." A restraint upon speaking in tongues and a despising of prophecy are both serious handicaps for the body of Christ. Incidentally, in words just preceding "do not despise prophetic utterance," Paul says: "Do not quench the Spirit" (v. 19). It is quite possible that this first exhortation concerns speaking in tongues (e.g., Gunkel writes: ". . . in 1 Thess. 5:19 pneuma is set next to prophēteia as the capacity for speaking in tongues" [The Influence of the Spirit, p. 31]); if so there is a close parallel between 1 Cor. 14:39—". . . desire earnestly to prophesy and do not restrain speaking in tongues"—and 1 Thess. 5:19-20—"Do not quench the Spirit; do not despise prophetic utterances."

[68]euschēmonōs—"decently" (KJV, RSV, NEB), "in a fitting way" (NIV). "Becomingly" is another good translation (cf. Rom. 13:13; 1 Thess. 4:12).

[69]diakrinetōsan—"judge" (KJV); "pass judgment" (NASB); "exercise judgment upon" (NEB). "Weigh" (RSV and NIV) avoids any negative impression that may be contained in the idea of judging or judgment. "Discern" is another helpful translation. Since prophecy is "in part," not everything said may be a word from the Lord; thus there is particular need for weighing, judging, discerning.

[70]It is probably not without significance that in the listing of the nine charismata of the Spirit in 1 Cor. 12:8-10 that the sixth and seventh relate to prophecy and the "discernings" [diakriseis—from the same root as diakrinetōsan in 14:29] of spirits," the eighth and ninth to tongues and interpretation of tongues. Though "discernings" (weighing, judging) may refer to more than prophecy, it surely has a connection therewith. Thus prophecy needs discernment even as tongues need interpretation. In accordance with this is the climactic listing of the nine gifts in 12:8-10—and to the same matters Paul returns in 14:27-33.

[71]Or, as in the prior observation: "prophecy with discernment" and "tongues with interpretation." The shorthand for this is simply "prophecy and tongues."

[72]Bearing in mind that prophecy is "in part," or partial; hence not everything said may come from the Holy Spirit (thus the need for discernment).

[73]"Word of wisdom" and "word of knowledge," on the other hand, are gifts in which the mind while anointed by the Holy Spirit is fully involved. In these two gifts, or manifestations of the Holy Spirit, the Spirit inspires the utterance of wisdom and knowledge which is given by the speaker. But no such "word of wisdom" or "knowledge" comes forth with the directness of a prophetic "Thus says the Lord."

[74]"Human language" includes a person's natural way of speaking, his own inflection and tone, even his peculiarities of speech. The Holy Spirit while speaking directly does not reduce the human instrument to a mere automaton.

[75]As with prophecy, since the interpretation comes through a human vessel it may likewise be "in part." This could mean that because of human limitations only a part of the message is given, or that the interpretation of it contains elements which are not fully consonant with what is spoken in the tongue.

[76]The other spiritual charismata (after word of wisdom and word of knowledge and before prophecy and tongues), namely faith, gifts of healing, and working of miracles are of course not in the realm of communication. They are supernatural powers but not supernatural utterances.

[77]It is significant to note that the same Greek word *apophthengomai*, is used in Acts 2:4 and Acts 2:14 for communication regarding both tongues and prophecy. The word for "utterance" in 2:4 is *"apopthengesthai"*; likewise in the preface to the words concerning the outpouring of the Holy Spirit the text reads: "Peter . . . declared to them," the word for "declared" being *apephthenxato*. English translations do not carry the full force of the Greek word, *apophthengomai*, which contains the note of *inspired speech*. According to BAG, in Greek literature, the word is used "of the speech of the wise man . . . but also of the oracle-giver, diviner, prophet, exorcist, and other 'inspired persons.' " Against that background the New Testament usage of the word signifies speech inspired by the Holy Spirit. In the one case it was speech in tongues, in the other it was speech in prophecy— both given directly from the Holy Spirit.

[78]Gunkel writes in his *The Influence of the Holy Spirit* that in "the Pentecost narrative . . . the Spirit *directly* [italics mine] works only glossolalia and prophecy. . . ." (p. 16). This, I believe, is a correct statement.

[79]In regard to prophecy, the words of Peter (quoting Joel)—"your sons and your daughters shall prophesy. . . ."—clearly point to such a possibility. Also there is continuing prophetic activity recorded in various places in Acts. There is, however, no reference as such to continuing of tongues beyond the initial events (in Acts 2, 19; also see Acts 10:46). In the latter case we need to turn to other

portions of the NT—as we have previously done—which imply continuance. Mark 16:17—not previously mentioned—"they shall speak with new tongues"—underscores an ongoing reality.

[80]Of course, I do not mean by this that words spoken in prophecy and tongues stand above Scripture, for the Scriptures are normative, decisive, and unerring; whereas, as observed before, prophecy calls for discernment, and tongues need interpretation. Accordingly, in both prophecy and tongues the human element is present. Neither gift in its exercise can be normative, nor can it have the assurance of being free of all error. However, in spite of this, through prophecy and tongues, the living God, *whose written word is in holy Scripture*, speaks in and to His people today.

[81]As in Eph. 4:11—two *domata* among five (or four—if "pastors" and "teachers" are the same office).

[82]As in Rom. 12:8—two charismata among seven.

[83]Whether *domata* or *charismata*.

4

ASPECTS OF WORSHIP IN 1 CORINTHIANS 14:1-25

Ralph P. Martin

INTRODUCTION

First Corinthians 14:1-25 is a difficult passage, but at least the main headings are clear. Paul is talking about three parts of early Christian worship as these items contribute to the total picture of the events which went on when the primitive believers gathered for corporate worship. Here is our first vital clue. Paul is not addressing the inner meaning of what the worship of God should be to the individual, except only incidentally (14:2, 4, 28). The scope of his vision—and so the intent of his admonition—is related to the congregation at public assembly.

The closest parallels we have to Paul's descriptions of Corinthian worship are drawn from Jewish worship in the synagogue. As far as we can piece together the format of synagogue worship, three elements stand out: the praise of God, the reading and exposition of Scripture, both enclosed within a framework of united prayer. Though there is some current discussion on how far our knowledge of Jewish worship in the first century AD extends, the primary emphasis does seem clearly to fall on *praise*, whether of the "berakah" (lit. "blessing" God) type or the "hodayah" which means more properly thanksgiving to God for his mercies. There is also an "anamnesis" type of prayer by which the goodness of Israel's God is "remembered" and his saving favors to the nation and individuals relived. Side by side with praise there was a central place given to Scripture, both read and applied, but with the reading in public worship accorded precedence over the rabbis' homily. Paul F. Bradshaw sums up:

These considerations [of the various, yet essential ways the Hebrew scriptures were read on the basis of a *lectio continua* on set days in the calendar] . . . point to the conclusion that the ministry of the word was not seen as in integral element in the act of worship but rather as an occasional appendix to it, made simply for the sake of convenience, because the congregation happened to be gathered together already.[1]

On the basis of his study, he writes of three elements in the daily devotion of every pious Jew, reflected in synagogue worship: the orderly and continuous study of the Scriptures, the *shema* (or confession of faith), and the *tefillah* (or daily prayers). If we confine our interest to 1 Corinthians 14, it is apparent that some links are there, but also there are major differences. In particular, Paul's writing is confronting a scene of unbridled enthusiasm and absence of "order." To anticipate our conclusion, it seems that Paul wants to inject some semblance of "control" and "order" (14:32, 33, 40) into this situation. His discussion reflects his cultural bias derived from the synagogue as well as his concern to keep worship within set limits that promote "reverence" (14:25). His rubrics or signpost words are therefore a necessary preamble to our understanding of his mind.

PAUL'S CONTROLS

1. We remind ourselves—because this is the theme to which Paul continues to return in 14:1-40—that we are looking at *the church gathered for and practicing worship in the public assembly.* Consider the following:

"In the church" *(en ekklēsia)* (v. 19)
"In the church" *(en ekklēsia)* (v. 28)
"When/if the whole church comes together" *(synelthē)* (v. 23)
"When you come together" *(synerchēsthe)* (v. 26)
"It is disgraceful for a woman to speak in the church" *(en ekklēsia)* (v. 35)

And with an alternative translation:

God is not a God of disorder but of peace, as in all the congregations *(en pasais tais ekklēsiais)* of the saints (v. 33).

2. The central motif, given this context of the entire assembly met together, is not surprisingly *one of "upbuilding" (oikodomē)*, which Paul goes out of his way to insist on, both negatively (14:17: "the other person is not edified") and more emphatically in a positive manner:

The prophet speaks [unlike the tongue-speaker who builds up himself, v. 4a] . . . to the congregation for its . . . strengthening (lit. *oikodomē*, upbuilding)

(v. 3) and builds up the community (v. 4b [The latter course is clearly preferred.]).

Paul qualifies his demotion of the glossolalic who speaks "in private"; but if there is a corresponding interpretation given to what is now obviously a tongue offered "in public," then the desired effect of worship is secured: "so that the church may be edified" (v. 5).

> "Excellent gifts," Paul comments, carry this hallmark: they build up the church (v. 12).
>
> Whatever contributions are brought to the service, their value stands under this banner: "all of these must be done for the strengthening (oikodomē) of the church" (v. 26).

Paul's teaching on *oikodomē* can hardly be exaggerated, and several students have noted the stress on the well-being and growth of the entire fellowship, as opposed to the Corinthians' desire to turn the church into a gnostic conventicle of private individuals, each concerned with his or her own inalienable experiences and heedless of the corporate dimension (what we could surname "body life") as *a Pauline distinctive.* Failure to observe the designation "one body, one Spirit" (1 Cor. 12:12, 13) had led to much mischief at Corinth; and this fault was never more glaring and tragically obvious than at public worship and at the Lord's Supper table (1 Cor. 11:17-34).

3. Yet one more apostolic injunction was called for at Corinth, in light of the chaotic conditions that prevailed at the worship gathering. We note the excesses of speech (12:1-3) and the irreverent and disgraceful behavior at the meal-rite (11:20-22, 27-34). It is therefore to be expected that Paul will issue *a call to good order, self-control, and a disciplined way of conducting the worship:*

> No blasphemous outcry, such as "a curse on Jesus" (12:3) emanates from the Holy Spirit's activity.
>
> Speaking, praying, and praising "with my spirit" is good (14:15, 16), but these exercises must be firmly kept under the control of—as they are complemented by and conjoined to—speaking, praying and praising "with my mind." "My spirit" is an ambiguous phrase (C. K. Barrett notes the possibilities); it appears to mean "my spiritual gift" that leads to the various exercises; hence I have the responsibility, Paul insists, both to employ the gift yet not to abuse its privilege by allowing it to get out of hand and lead me into a trance-like state where I cease to be held accountable for what takes place. The interpretation is supported by *(i)* the way Paul writes somewhat disdainfully of "my mind" as being "unfruitful" (i.e. inactive and not producing any good) when the speaker is exercising a glossolalic gift; *(ii)* the encouragement to *seek* exactly those gifts which serve the church's well-

being suggests a Christian's active participation (so plainly in v. 32: "the spirits of the prophets are subject to the control of the prophets"). He or she is responsible to seek the health-producing gifts, and thereby to turn from what is only self-gratifying and maybe destructive of the *koinōnia* of the church; *(iii)* the criterion that a person must calculate what will be the effect on others. If worship gets out of hand, the onlooker will dismiss Christians as people "demon-possessed" (v. 23: not simply "deranged" but positively demonically controlled); and *(iv)* the plain warnings of verse 43: God is not a God of "anarchy" (*akatastasia,* a word otherwise meaning insurrection, Luke 21:9 or civil disorder, 2 Cor. 6:5).

The apostle's exhortation stands at the close: let "everything be done in a fitting and orderly way" (14:40).

THE POSITIVE CONTRIBUTION OF PAUL'S TEACHING

From the foregoing—and before we get to the detailed discussion of this chapter—three "principles" to define and regulate Christian worship in a "healthy" church emerge.

1. There is clearly for Paul the need for *the Spirit's control.* Granting the freedom of the Holy Spirit to inspire both the praying and the praising (v. 14-16), Paul is careful to insist that worship should not get out of hand (v. 32) and so allow an open door to anarchy. The reason for this warning is given in verse 23: "so if the whole church comes together and everyone speaks in tongues, and some who do not understand [or, some inquirers] or some unbelievers come in, will they not say that you are out of your mind?" This lamentable effect on the outsider is to bring worship into disrepute; on the other side, nonecstatic gifts or ecstatic gifts which promote the building up of the church—and so touch the outsider as a direct consequence—are, in Paul's esteem (as E. Schweizer understands it)[2] "the real yardstick for estimating the value of ministries." Here is a good clue for the exegesis of 14:22 whose "plain" sense is often taken to say the opposite.

2. As a consequence what counts above all is *social responsibility in worship.* We do not worship as separate units who "happen" to be in the same place, sitting in adjacent seats or nearby pews, and singing the same hymns as we go through the motions of worship together. We are there as "one body" (1 Cor. 12:12, 13)—and this oneness is also the Spirit's gift.

E. Schweizer[3] has also written trenchantly of the failure of much modern worship precisely because it does not lead to and so express fellowship-in-worship.

> It is completely foreign to the New Testament to split the Christian community into one speaker and a silent body of listeners.

3. There is a *special ministry* in corporate worship which gives it a dignity

and decorum different from our worship as individuals, family members or even
as parts of subgroups in the Christian society. We may concede that what this
chapter (1 Cor. 14) depicts is the coming-together of a house congregation (v.
26), yet it must not be overlooked that, for all their divisiveness and cliquishness,
the Corinthians *did* unite in a common liturgical meeting (as J. Héring observes),[4]
and Paul repeatedly stresses here the idea of "the *entire* church" assembling
together.

The fact of "the church of God at Corinth" meeting in one place lends to its
worship an importance—and so a style and ethos—that cannot always be true of
smaller units of believers when they meet in fellowship, Bible study, prayer and
for the purposes of mutual enrichment, called today "sharing." There is, in a
public service, a desired blend of the formal with the intimate, that never descends
to the level of what is no better than the matey bonhomie or the casual or even
flippant, so losing the sense of the majesty and mystery of God whom we adore
and the sense of the numinous that both awakens our healthy "awe" and speaks
to reassure our salutary fear. So Richard John Neuhaus reminds us:[5]

> Worship is the perilous enactment of God's *sacramentum* with us, and ours
> with him. When we speak of worship as "celebration," we must know that
> we are not celebrating our securities and satisfactions. We are celebrating
> the perilous business of love—of that supreme love that did not and does not
> turn back from the cross.

For all the apparent features of 1 Corinthians 14 that could be summed up under
the heading of spontaneity and freedom, we can cite counterbalancing emphases
that caution us against confusing "spontaneity" with "eccentricity" or
"familiarity" with "chumminess" (Neuhaus's terms). The upshot of this way
of viewing worship is put in simple language that speaks to a pressing modern
pastoral problem: With all the stress today on worship as "encounter" (and 1
Cor. 14 is usually the proof-text for such a designation), there is need to recall
and to hold constantly in view that "worship chiefly has to do not with encountering
one another but with encountering God."

Proclaiming/Prophesying

We are now ready to tackle the three areas where Paul applies these ideas.
First, verses 1-12 are devoted to the subject of "prophesying," or as it may be
suggestively rendered, "proclaiming."

At the close of his tribute to "love" Paul places the expected injunction: "Make
love your aim" (lit. "pursue" *[diōkete]* the love I have been just describing, or—if
my reconstruction of 13:13b is possible—"set your sights on God's love" in a

way parallel to Paul's call in Philippians 3:12, 14: "I pursue the prize of God's call" and [in a negative sense] of Gentiles' not seeking the divine righteousness as in Rom. 10:3). At all events, "Pursue love" or even more tellingly "Follow the way of love" goes back to 12:31 and represents the answering call to Paul's earlier promise: "I show you a still better way." Clearly that *is* the path of love, and Paul intends his readers to lay the counsel to heart and practice it in their lives. The first readers needed such an admonition in the light of the confusion over "spiritual gifts" that reigned at Corinth.

Paul's total answer has been in terms of the more excellent *charismata* which, however, are valueless or worse until they are accompanied and directed by love. *Charismata* is evidently Paul's word and it puts all the emphasis on the divine character *(charis)* of the gifts *(charis-mata)*. We would suggest that spirit-gifts *(pneumatika)* is the Corinthians' terminology; they had enquired about these manifestations and sought Paul's ruling (12:1). Interestingly in chapter 14 *charismata* drops out, and Paul picks up their terms, probably actually citing their statements only to correct them. As M-A. Chevallier puts it,

> In order to correct on theological grounds the Corinthian idea of pneumatika,
> Paul has brought in the idea of the charismata, the graces which God gives
> by his Spirit for the life of the community.[6]

I think there may be two places where this literary device is seen:

(a) "You are striving for *pneumatika*" (as in 12:31a) is a quoted insertion from the readers' own position, since both the verb *(zēloute)* and noun, as we observed, reflect their ambition. Paul quickly modifies the statement with an adversative, "but rather *(mallon)* that you may prophesy." Chevallier gives a special value to Paul's word "but" *(de)* which plays the part, he submits, of an ordinal number: "first, love: and *then* the *pneumatika*." He is using the criterion of what is excellent to set the *pneumatika* in their rightful order; but as Conzelmann notes, the test is no longer that of *agapē*, it is *oikodomē*, that which builds up the community life. *Oikodomē* is thus the chapter's keyword (Senft).

(b) At 14:12 we are actually told that this was the Corinthians' position: "So it is even with you: since you are eager to have spirit-gifts" *(pneumata)*—a concession Paul quotes but proceeds straightway to revise in the words following: "try to *excel* in gifts that build up the church" ("excel" is *perisseuēte*, a verb that suggests that which is gained as an enrichment [1 Cor. 8:8] and may reflect Paul's comment on the Corinthians' watchword, "it is for our best" [1 Cor. 6:12; 10:23]). What Paul thought of as being for the church's chief good is their "upbuilding"; and how he conceived that desired end to be reached is contained in 14:1-25.

So he highlights "prophesying" (14:3), a spirit-gift which aims to bring God's truth to bear on human lives with a view to their *understanding* and *growth*. He sets the gift of *prophēteia* over against "tongues" in four ways, outlined by John Goldingay,[7] which we may indicate with some modifications:

(a) Tongues cannot be directly understood by human beings, whereas prophecy can (14:2-3a, 7-11). In glossolalia, at least in this section which seems to refer to the use of tongues in private devotion when the communion of an individual with God is so intimate and profound that no earthly language can be the vehicle of its expression (cf. Rom. 8:26, 27; 2 Cor. 12:2-4), the speaker in a rapture utters words which are not immediately intelligible. "The glossolalist speaks *to* God rather than *from* God."[8] "Communion" with God is of the essence of the experience, rather than "communication" with God, a term otherwise preferred by J. D. G. Dunn.[9]

In prophecy, however, there is no such barrier to instant communication: "the prophet, although inspired, speaks in a comprehensible language and, without interpretation, can have a beneficial effect on the meeting," J. Héring remarks.[10] The exact nature of this type of public speaking is spelled out in verse 3: it is a ministry which builds up, and exhorts, and comforts. These verses offer a thumb-nail sketch of the role of "prophets" in the Pauline communities; the essence of the prophetic ministry is its immediate intelligibility, and its resultant capability of speaking a word "to the situation of need in the assembly" (J. D. G. Dunn who remarks that the distinguishing mark of prophecy over against glossolalia is not inspiration but intelligibility).[11] Paul gives three illustrations to contrast ecstatic "tongues" with inspired "prophecy": (i) from ancient musical practices (v. 7); (ii) from military parades (v. 8); and (iii) from simple conversation which can only be carried on effectively if the speakers understand each other (v. 9-11). Flute and harp give different sounds to make harmony and melody; the trumpet blast sounds to call the troops to battle (Judg. 7:19-23) and demands a response; human speech is meaningful as it communicates the thoughts of the speakers. In all, the point of the analogy is the same, though we may pinpoint the nature of various responses as *pleasure*, when music is harmonious (Mozart's *Musical Joke*, K.522, is the exception to prove the rule); *obedience*, as the army gets the signal to advance; *satisfaction*, as a person derives fulfillment from both speaking to a friend and hearing the friend's conversation. There are sounds which take on meaning as they make sense. So it is with Christian speaking: unless the hearers catch the drift of what is being said and understand it, they will dismiss such noises as those of a "gibberish talker" (Conzelmann) whose words seem none other than "bar-bar" (*barbaros*, v. 11). And that is both a waste of time, and a travesty of the worship situation when "words" should convey meaningful truth.

(b) Tongues benefit the speaker, while prophecy serves to benefit the whole company (v. 3b-6, 12). We should not minimize, as Paul grants, the way "tongues" do fulfill a role in private worship. W. J. Hollenweger[12] notes that "tongues speaking" is evidently of two types: "hot," i.e. involving ecstatic utterances that can easily border on frenzy and unrestrained outbursts (as in 12:1-3 perhaps); and what he calls "cool," i.e. a more mystical experience that can readily be controlled, a point derived from 14:28 which informs us that Paul expected a glossolalic to be able to keep his/her utterance under restraint. Evidently Paul's own use of glossolalia was of the second type (14:18) and his advocacy "do not forbid speaking in tongues" (14:39) is in regard to the same species of glossolalia. And we may appeal to 12:30 which is Paul's emphatic declaration that "not all speak in tongues" as being explained by this distinction he makes between "tongues" that are acceptable (14:5, 13, with the necessary qualification) and those that are not, since the latter type promote only confusion (14:23) and must not be given free rein—certainly not among the excitable Corinthians who were (apparently) also falling into theological error by treating "tongues of angels" (13:1) as a proof of their realized eschatology, with its promise of a celestial life already begun on earth.

Prophecy, on the contrary, has no such attendant risks. It is above all "a sign for believers" (14:22). The exercise of this gift of prophecy plays a multifaceted role, as Paul understood it (the list is one of the intelligible gifts, all virtually synonymous with prophecy: so Barrett). Primarily it "builds up" the congregation so that it can function as a mature body of Christ (14:5, 12). The objects of the verb of 14:3 tell us as much. There is equally another side to prophecy. It confirms believers in the faith they profess, and in particular it imparts a peculiar form of "God-consciousness" as the divine presence is known in such a dramatic way that even the unbeliever or casual visitor to the assembly is immediately struck with holy fear and forced to acknowledge that "God is really among you" (vv. 24, 25). J. D. G. Dunn draws the extended conclusion from this scene that "prophecy edifies because it does not exalt man but humbles him, making him aware that he stands before God in all his vulnerability."[13] Just how this is accomplished, on the human level, is difficult to say. Evidently the prophets' words were charged with a "numinous" power that pierced the shell of complacency; and possibly, with Käsemann, we should see this "unmasking" of the unbeliever as effected by the uttering of the so-called sentences of holy law (e.g. 1 Cor. 3:17, 14:38, 16:22a) of the order "destruction to the destroyer"—except that these words were first directed to the professed believers as a rebuke and overheard by the outsider.[14] The judgment that came on Ananias and Sapphira (Acts 5:11) may be instanced, since as a result, we are told, "great fear seized the whole church *and all who heard about these events*" (v. 11).

(c) This section demands a separate heading since it is concerned not so much with prophesying as with praying (14:13-15). The gist of Paul's treatment is that whereas the exercise of "tongues" involves the Spirit, both to impart the glossolalic gift and to enable that utterance to be interpreted (whether by him/herself or by another [v. 27]), there is a type of praying which is *both* "in the Spirit" *and* "with the mind"—a description that exactly fits the prophetic ministry which "speaks . . . intelligible (lit. "with my mind") words" (v. 19).

Paul touches here on what we may call, in modern terms, the psychology of prayer. "If I pray in a tongue, my spirit prays—or perhaps 'the Spirit in me,' referring to the work of the Holy Spirit within the believer (C. K. Barrett considers the various options in interpreting a cryptic phrase, *to pneuma mou*)—but my mind is *unfruitful*" (v. 14). The last word implies that the human intellect in this kind of ecstatic praying lies dormant, contributing nothing to the process of articulating thoughts into words. Here is perhaps the central place where Paul tells us what he believed glossolalia to be. It suggests an enraptured fellowship with God when the human spirit is in such deep, hidden communion with the divine Spirit that "words"—at best broken utterances of our secret selves—are formed by a spiritual upsurge requiring no mental effort.

His next phrase is slightly enigmatic: *ti oun estin*; "What then is it?" C. K. Barrett renders: What is to be done then? suggesting a state of affairs needing to be put right. "If I pray in a tongue, part, and that a most significant part, of my nature remains out of action. This is not good for me, and it is not good for the community I ought to serve." So Paul proceeds to qualify the use of glossolalia: "I will pray with the spirit (the personal pronoun is dropped, as Barrett notes, but most translators retain it), but *(de)* I will pray with the mind also *(kai)*. These two qualifications, at first sight insignificant, are important: one sets up a contrast ("but . . .") and the other adds in another component which Paul deemed to be vital to a proper understanding of prayer. Rational prayer takes precedence over irrational utterances, especially in the congregational assembly. The reason is not far to seek. It lies in the effect on the outsider, as we have seen (vv. 23-25); and "strange sounds" have a detrimental consequence on interested non-Christians who visit the Corinthians at their worship.

The upshot of Paul's discussion is to do two things: *(i)* to curtail the use of tongues to private praying presumably at home (14:28: "let him speak *to himself*"), when no interpreter seemingly is needed. The glossolalic "utters mysteries with his spirit" (or "in the Spirit," v. 2) and "build himself up"—a verb which suggests to M. E. Thrall[15] a note of condemnation or at least disdain of this practice: "To regard it (glossolalia) as the gift supremely to be desired is a form of selfishness," because it forgets the ever-insistent need for the *charismata* to build up the church of "the other person" (v. 17) who may overhear my "private" communion. More likely what Paul is opposing is an understanding of worship as a private exercise in which individuals seal themselves off from others and concentrate exclusively on their own personal experiences.

Paul therefore wants *(ii)* to insist on "interpretation" when "tongues" occur in the assembly, for precisely this reason. For him worship takes on its true character when it is corporate, or at least expressed in a way that is related to the growth and enrichment of the entire body. His purpose is probably polemical, namely in resisting the notion of the "church" as a gnostic conventicle made up of persons each with his or her own privatized religious exercises and ambitions.

PRAISING

All that Paul said about "praying" in spirit and with the mind is repeated and applied in reference to the offering of praise (v. 15). The vehicle of praise is a type of singing, "a kind of *charismatic hymnody*" (J. D. G. Dunn's phrase)[16] that includes both singing in tongues and singing with intelligible words. The setting of this verse is difficult to pinpoint and it is just as uncertain whether Paul has in mind singing that is spontaneous or the use of a pre-composed "hymn," which seems required at 14:26 since a person brings such a composition to the meeting. The evidence for charismatic singing is seen elsewhere, e.g., Ephesians 5:18f.: "Do not get drunk with wine . . . be filled with the Spirit. Speak to one another with psalms, hymns and spiritual songs. Sing and make music in your heart to the Lord." In the parallel text of Colossians 3:16 the use of "spiritual songs," i.e. songs inspired by the Spirit, is set in a context of the didactic ministry ("the word of Christ . . . teach . . . counsel one another with all wisdom"), though we suggest that this emphasis denotes a shift from the Corinthian scene with its acceptance of a more spontaneous, unstructured format of worship (even in 14:26 which Paul is probably reporting and seeking to correct, as has been maintained). The singing at Corinth may have been expressed in enraptured cries or acclamations (not always acceptable to Paul, as we see from 1 Cor. 12:3). Yet the stress on "thanksgiving" in 14:16, 17 suggests a more extended type of praise, perhaps borrowed from the Jewish *hodayah* ("I thank thee") form.

Even such a personal aspect of worship as this "singing in the Spirit" has to be safeguarded, according to Paul. What is offered in song is intended to be "understood" (v. 16) even by an ordinary person, who is here presumably to be equated with an "inquirer" whose Christian status is not yet accepted but who is a "catechumen" (like Theophilus, Luke 1:4?). That person must be able to know what is being said or sung so that he may respond with the affirmation, "Amen" to the thanksgiving.

The inference is that Paul expected Christian praise to be meaningful and not simply—as it seems to have been at Corinth—the effusion of emotional, subrational outbursts, whether in an ecstacy of joy or in the releasing of pent-up feelings in shouts of nonsense syllables, or "primal numinous sounds" vocalizing the collective memory of a group (Williams).[17] Paul's allusion to "five intelligible words" spoken to build up the church (v. 18) qualifies his concession that he too knew the gift of glossolalia, presumably in his "mystical" experiences such as the one recorded in 2 Corinthians 12 (Conzelmann), or it may be his argument *ad hominem*, conceding the phenomenon of "tongues" at Corinth for the sake of making a corrective point. It is noteworthy, as Cyril G. Williams notes,[18] that in the New Testament "there is no concrete evidence of glossolalia," i.e. no glossolalia speech is reported as such. The call to adult maturity in "thinking" is to offset the "childish" practice of tongues-speaking (perhaps a reference back to 13:11, "when I was an infant [*nēpios*, lit. "not able to speak"], I spoke [*elaloun*, the verb *lalein* means to speak in a tongue in this Corinthian context, says M.-A. Chevallier][19] like an infant"). At all events, the apostle's conclusion stands out clearly in verse 20: "do not be children *(paidia)* in your thinking . . . but in your thinking be mature" *(teleioi).*

(d) The section in verses 21-25 is especially difficult to exegete. Its plain teaching if verse 22 is central is that "tongues" are less desirable than "prophecy" because they affect "unbelievers" in quite different ways, and Paul has in his mind's eye a situation where the "unbelievers" *(apistoi)* are present in the congregational worship.

Paul recalls to his readers the Old Testament passage (Isa. 28:11, 12) in which Yahweh threatens to punish his rebellious people Israel by foreign invaders (in this case the Assyrians) whose strange language will mystify the Jewish nation (cf. Isa. 36:11ff.). Because the Jewish kingdom remained obstinate to the prophet's warning and pleading in God's name, they would be judged by suffering a foreign invasion and being hardened in their unbelief (Isa. 6:9-13). In the Old Testament context these strange "tongues," spoken by the Assyrian enemies, confirmed unbelieving Israel in their unbelief and so acted deleteriously.

Paul now takes over this reference to Isaiah 28 which, I suggest, is found not only in the cited text of verse 21 but also in verse 22 where he offers a midrash, or interpretative comment, on the Old Testament quotation. The midrash on "men of strange tongues"/"lips of foreigners" applies the effect of speech on the unbelieving people of Israel; and this midrashic application is then related to

Isaiah's "prophecy" (in v. 22) which has a good effect. "Tongues" is taken in its Old Testament sense of Assyrian foreign languages which confirmed (by God's judgment) Israel's apostasy, whereas Isaiah's prophetic ministry was beneficial to the remnant of Israel which believed (Isa. 8:16). We can observe a precedent for this Pauline use of the Old Testament[20] in 2 Corinthians 3:16, 17; and Philippians 2:15 (the reference to ethnic Israel as a "crooked and depraved generation" becomes in Paul's hands a transferred—or midrashic—allusion to the pagan world around the Israel of the church). The novelty of this way of exegeting 1 Corinthians 14:21, 22 is to remove the references to "tongues" and "prophecy" from the Corinthian scene—whereas, as the references stand they appear to say exactly the opposite of what Paul elsewhere in this chapter intends. *His* position is rather:

> "Tongues" build up believers, albeit in a private capacity (14:2, 4).
> "Prophecy" builds up the church, but also has a signal and salutary effect
> on the non-believer (14:23-25).

An alternative proposal is to stress the use—by Paul, granting now that verse 22 has the Corinthian problems in view—of "signs." That term *(sēmeion)* is understood by some commentators in the sense of what the charismatic gift is intended to do, rather than as a witness to what is already a fact. We may also point, with J. Héring, to the present participles used: "those coming to faith" *(tois pisteuousin)* in the two places where verse 22 in translation normally reads "believers." Then the sense will be:

> Ecstatic utterance (tongues) is not intended to be something which produces
> belief in Christianity. It is a phenomenon which leaves non-Christians in their
> unbelieving state. Prophecy. on the other hand, is intended not to confirm
> unbelievers in their unbelief but to encourage conversion to the Christian
> faith.[21]

The net effect is to praise the superiority of "prophecy" which is a sign "in the sense that it produces believers," i.e. those coming to faith (cf. Bruce). "Tongues," on the contrary, serve[22] only to alienate strangers and lead to the travestied conclusion that "madness" (= demonic possession) reigns in the Christian assembly.

The apostle's concern is for believers to speak the prophetic word that, even if not directly aimed at "unbelievers" (cf. 14:3) will have a salutary operation. E. Schweizer finds here a litmus test of authentic worship, namely the impression it leaves on the "outsider" or casual visitor as well as the value it promotes in helping believers and catechumens.[23]

Verse 25 is one of the most dramatic descriptions of early Christian worship we have. "Prophecy" carries a judgment-power. Whether it acts on the Corinthians as professed believers (who evidently were demeaning its role and shutting their ears to such prophets as exposed their failings like ancient Israel sadly apostate; hence they were incurring divine displeasure, as in 10:1-22; 11:34) or on real "unbelievers" who "drop in" to view the service of worship, the consequence is the same. "Prophecy" acts as a divine judgment, revealing a person's secret thoughts and confronting him or her with the truth that humbles and saves. The entering unbeliever's prostration (as an act of obedience in Gen. 17:3; Luke 5:12; Rev. 7:11; 11:16, a creaturely awareness of frailty in the presence of the numinous) and his/her acknowledgement, "God is really among you" are, for Paul, of the essence of true "worship" (*proskynēsis*, parallel with the Old Testament picture of worship as "bowing down," the verbal *histahawah*).

The key phrase is "God is *truly among you*" (*ontōs . . . en hymin*). Clearly *en* cannot mean "in" you, for that would be exactly what the gnostic Corinthians would hold true of themselves as "men and women of the spirit" (*hoi pneumatikoi*, imbued with *pneuma*). The total phrase is taken, not from 1 Kings 18:39 (as some suggest) but from Isaiah 45:14, or more tellingly, Zechariah 8:23, "Let us go with you, for we have heard that God is with you." In other words, what was predicted of the end-time, namely the turning of the Gentiles to Israel in an acknowledgement that Israel's God was "truly" to be found among his people, is now a present reality. Worship, for Paul, shares that eschatological quality of confronting the gathered company with the divine presence in such a way that what is fervently hoped for as the final victory of God's reign is already shared, at least in part and as a token, in the present as an experienced reality.[24]

In this light we are perhaps meant to read Paul's concluding statement, buttressed by scriptural citation, as a polemical counterposition to what was being urged at Corinth. In their enthusiasm and preference for the more individualistic spirit-gifts (*pneumatika*), some Corinthians were claiming that *their* type of worship brought the future into the present. Paul retorts by partly agreeing that in worship we do glimpse and experience heavenly realities ("God is really here"), though never to the exclusion of the fullness of worship reserved for the future fulfillment of eschatological hope. Our worship as our knowledge is "in part" (1 Cor. 13:12). Yet, Paul goes on, what we do have now is that expression and experience of worship which brings us face to face, not with *our* spiritual ecstasies and emotional exaltation, but with God, before whom the most fitting posture is to bow down and confess that he, by his Spirit, reads our secret thoughts and convicts us of our frail humanity and utter dependence on him. It is the function of the *charismata*, properly exercised in love and with an eye on the needs of the community, to lead worshippers to that goal.

*This article, first offered as a paper at the November 18-20, 1982 annual meeting of the Society for Pentecostal Studies, has also appeared as a chapter in Dr. Martin's latest book *The Spirit and the Congregation: Studies in 1 Corinthians 12-15* (Grand Rapids: Wm. B. Eerdmans Publishing Company, 1984).

NOTES

[1]P. F. Bradshaw, *Daily Prayer in the Early Church* (London: Alcuin Club/SPCK, 1981), p. 20.

[2]E. Schweizer, *Church Order in the New Testament* (SBT 32; London: SCM Press Ltd., 1961) ET 1961, p. 185 (22f).

[3]E. Schweizer, "Worship in the New Testament," *The Reformed and Presbyterian World* 24 (1957): 295 (reprinted in his *Neotestamentica. German and English Essays 1951-1963* (Zurich: Zwingli Verlag, 1963).

[4]J. Héring, *The First Epistle of Saint Paul to the Corinthians*, ET (London: The Epworth Press, 1962), pp. 4, 112, 114. This attendance of the entire church in one place is an important factor when social conditions at the Corinthian agape and eucharist are considered. It tends to get overlooked in G. Theissen's essay, "Social Integration and Sacramental Activity: An Analysis of 1 Cor. 11:17-34," *The Social Setting of Pauline Christianity* ET (Philadelphia: Fortress Press, 1982), pp. 145-174.

[5]R. J. Neuhaus, *Freedom for Ministry* (San Francisco: Harper & Row, Publishers, 1979), pp. 125, 127, 128 for following citations in the text.

[6]M.-A. Chevallier, *Esprit de Dieu, Paroles d'Hommes* (Neuchâtel: Editions Delachaux et Niestlé, 1966), p. 172.

[7]J. Goldingay, *The Church and the Gifts of the Spirit* (Bamcote, Notts.: Grove Books, 1972), pp. 18-21.

[8]J. W. MacGorman, *The Gifts of the Spirit* (Nashville: Broadman Press, 1974), p. 81.

[9]J. D. G. Dunn, *Jesus and the Spirit* (London & Philadelphia: SCM & Westminster, 1975), p. 245. On the "type" of speech referred to in ch. 14 see C. G. Williams, *Tongues of the Spirit, A Study of Pentecostal Glossolalia and Related Phenomena* (Cardiff: University of Wales Press, 1981), ch. 2. He argues cogently for "ecstatic" tongues. The coincidence of reported glossolalia with a known language is explained, with Felicitas D. Goodman, *Speaking in Tongues: A Cross-Cultural Study of Glossolalia* (Chicago: University of Chicago Press, 1972), pp. 148-151, as a matter of statistical probability, namely that glossolalia

sounds will, given enough examples, bear resemblance to meaningful words in some human language: cf. Williams, op. cit. pp. 183-189.

[10]J. Héring, *First Corinthians*, p. 145.

[11]J. D. G. Dunn, *Jesus and the Spirit,* p. 229.

[12]W. J. Hollenweger, *The Pentecostals* (Minneapolis: Augsburg Publishing House, 1972), p. 344.

[13]J. D. G. Dunn, *Jesus and the Spirit*, p. 232 (printed in italics).

[14]E. Käsemann, "Sentences of Holy Law in the New Testament," *New Testament Questions of Today*, ET (Philadelphia: Fortress Press, 1969), pp. 66-81.

[15]M. E. Thrall, *I and II Corinthians* (CBC, Cambridge: The University Press, 1965), pp. 99. See H. Wayne House, "Tongues and the Mystery Religions of Corinth," *Bibliotheca Sacra* 140 (1983): 135-150, for the comment that in verse 4 Paul's statement is conciliatory, "merely conced[ing] a point here for argument." H. Chadwick, "All Things to All Men," *New Testament Studies* 1 (1954-55): 261-275, has effectively shown that this was Paul's strategy in handling the delicate situation at Corinth.

[16]J. D. G. Dunn, *Jesus and the Spirit*, p. 238.

[17]Cyril G. Williams, *Tongues of the Spirit*, p. 231.

[18]Williams, Ibid., p. 213. The nursery-words of Isa. 28:10 (Heb. *saw la-saw, qaw la-qaw*) is not glossolalic speech, even if the following verse is cited by Paul.

[19]M.-A. Chevallier, *Esprit de Dieu, Paroles d'Hommes*, p. 149 n.4. This estimate is true only if we qualify it. *Lalein* is used of the prophetic speech but there is then a direct object of the verb (14:3); where there is not, *lalein* means a glossolalic utterance.

[20]On Paul's use of the OT here see E. E. Ellis, *Paul's Use of the Old Testament* (Edinburgh: Oliver and Boyd, 1957), pp. 107-112 who suggests the presence of a fragment of Christian anti-Jewish polemic. This understanding is seen in J. M. Sweet, "A Sign for Unbelievers," *New Testament Studies* 13 (1966-67): 240-257.

[21]M. E. Thrall, *I and II Corinthians*, p. 100.

[22]The verb "to be" in 14:22 ("Tongues are—*eisin*—for a sign") could very well carry the exegetical sense: "Tongues represent, stand for."

[23]E. Schweizer, *Church Order in the New Testament*, pp. 101-103 (7 1, m).

[24]In a way similar to Paul's appropriation of Zech. 14:9 in reference to the universal "Lord," identified with the exalted Jesus: see D. R. de Lacey, in *Christ the Lord: Studies in Christology Presented to Donald Guthrie*, ed. H. H. Rowdon (Downers Grove: Inter-Varsity Press, 1982), esp. pp. 196-203.

5

MINISTRY AND THE MINISTRY: THE CHARISMATIC RENEWAL'S CHALLENGE TO TRADITIONAL ECCLESIOLOGY

James D. G. Dunn

I

It has been my privilege and pleasure to talk or lecture about the charismatic renewal on many occasions since the middle '60s to a wide variety of groups. I usually conclude such talks by focusing on the main points of challenge which the renewal poses to the wider church. For me this challenge can be summed up in the two words, "experience" and "ministry." By "experience" I mean the rediscovery that when we talk of the Spirit in biblical terms we are talking also about the inspiring, transforming, and empowering *experience* of the grace of God in the life of the believer and of the church. The charismatic renewal has challenged us to recognize the importance (not exclusive importance, but importance) of the emotional and non-rational in a fully integrated faith and life, to give place to these less structured and less predictable elements in our worship, and to take seriously the third article of the creed—"I believe in the Holy Spirit, the Lord, the *Life*-giver." In other writings, books and articles, I have elaborated and emphasized the importance of this point, of the Spirit as the experienced Spirit, particularly with reference to the Spirit of prophecy and the dangers of false prophecy.[1]

However, hitherto I have not given so much attention to the other main challenge which I believe the charismatic renewal poses to the wider church—the challenge summed up in the word "ministry."[2] The invitation to address the annual meeting of the Society for Pentecostal Studies gives me the opportunity to do so now, and I am happy to share my further, though still tentative, reflections on what in many ways is the more challenging subject. We might simply note in passing that this transition from focus on "experience" to focus on "ministry" is not wholly coincidential. It reflects also the transition which has taken place in the renewal movement itself—from what I tend to think of as the "neo-Pentecostal" phase in the 1960s, when the keynotes were "baptism in the Spirit" and "speaking in tongues," and the categories used were those of classical Pentecostalism, to the "charismatic renewal" phase proper, where the keynotes have been "charisma" and "community," and where those involved in the renewal within the older denominations have more and more tried to understand the renewal in terms of their own tradition and as a force for renewal of their own traditional forms and structures.[3]

Ministry is a focal point of challenge for the simple reason that *the renewal's rediscovery of the charismatic dimension of ministry puts a large question mark against what has become the traditional conception of "the ministry."* Let me explain what I have in mind. An important aspect of the charismatic renewal, as of classical Pentecostalism earlier, is its rediscovery of what Paul meant when he spoke about the body of Christ.[4] In 1 Cor. 12 and Rom. 12 in particular, Paul envisages the local church as the body of Christ, as a charismatic community, where each member, by definition, has a function within the body, a role within the community of faith. To define the church as Christ's body is to define each member as a functionary within that body, and is to define each member as a charismatic in that sense. To put it another way: by *charisma* Paul means any function, word or action, which contributes to the corporate life of the believers in any place. *Charisma* means, by definition, manifestation, embodiment of grace *(charis)*. Consequently, any and every word, any and every act in and through which the Spirit of God brings the grace of God to concrete expression is, in Paul's terms, a charism. The point then is that in Paul's vision of the body of Christ—the charismatic community—*charisma cannot be restricted in terms either of the "who" or the "what."* "Charisma" is not given to a select few; "to *each* is given the manifestation of the Spirit" (1 Cor. 12:7). And "charisma" is not reserved for a particular set of clearly defined gifts; *whatever* word or act mediates grace to the believing community is "charisma". The force of the point becomes clearer when we further recall that for Paul *charisma* is synonymous with *diakonia*, ministry (1 Cor. 12:4-5). If we merely substitute "ministry" for "charisma" in the previous sentences the challenge of the charismatic renewal's rediscovery of these Pauline emphases begins to take shape: "ministry" is not given only to a few, but to *each*; "ministry" is not confined to a particular set of clearly defined functions but describes *every* word or act of grace to the believing community.

I do not say, incidentally, that classical Pentecostalism or the charismatic renewal have necessarily been wholly successful in giving expression to this wider experience and expression of ministry within their own ranks. I have, for example, elsewhere criticized classical Pentecostal expositions for confining the range of charisms too narrowly by treating the list of 1 Cor. 12:8-10 as a definitive rather than representative list.[5] And you will be more familiar than I with the too often crippling rather than liberating effects of some of the very authoritarian structures which have emerged within the wider renewal movement. But at least the renewal has drawn our attention once again to these important chapters in Paul, as did classical Pentecostalism earlier. And in their attempt to take these chapters seriously Pentecostals and charismatics have at least attempted to express a theology of ministry which in principle recognizes its proper range and diversity (both the "who" and the "what"). Whether their own structures of ministry which have evolved—no doubt often for good pragmatic reasons—need to be challenged by their own theology of ministry is for them to decide. My brief here is to speak of the renewal's challenge to the wider church.

Over against this Pauline concept of *all* member ministry, of ministry as *every* expression of grace, we have to set what has become the traditional conception of *the* ministry within the older churches on both sides of the Reformation. (I leave aside Eastern Christianity, the Orthodox churches, for lack of space and expertise). The fact that the phrase "the ministry" has become so familiar and established within Christian circles makes my point for me, for it reflects the long established presumption that when Christians talk of "ministry" they are to all intents and purposes talking about the role of "the ordained ministry," the clergy. In saying this I do not forget the important Reformation reaffirmation of the priesthood of all believers. On the contrary, my point is precisely that the priesthood of all believers has been confined in effect to the realm of personal piety, the right of the head of the household to conduct family prayers as its highest expression. It has not been allowed to encroach upon the realm of corporate worship; outside the churches of the radical Reformation, the central act of priesthood, presiding at the Lord's Supper, has remained a reserved area, unaffected in practice by the assertion that priesthood belongs to all believers.

Nor am I unaware that in recent decades the effective restriction of ministry to "the ministry" has become something of an embarrassment to the older churches. I am well aware of the pains taken in official church documents of the past twenty years or so to emphasize that, of course, ministry belongs also to the laity, of course, ministry belongs to the whole people of God. But in fact what this has meant is that ministry has been subdivided into two grades or classes or castes—the ordained ministry and the ministry of the laity—the two set alongside each other in uneasy juxtaposition with only the sketchiest or rather incoherent attempts to explain their relationship to each other. The ordained ministry has been assumed as the fixed point, and the task has been to discover what is the ministry of the laity in distinction from that of the clergy, what, we might say, is *left* for the ministry of the laity after the ordained ministry has been defined. The basic divide between clergy and laity has remained fundamental and largely unquestioned at any depth—despite the embarrassing fact that "laity" properly denotes the whole people of God *(laos)*, clergy included. The concept of charism has been drawn in, but only as a kind of sop to the laity, not as an alternative concept of ministry which might actually call in question the axiomatic distinction between clergy and laity and the hierarchical structure built upon it.

My point can be easily illustrated from various ecclesiastical documents of the past twenty years. For example, despite all the welcome reforms of the Second Vatican Council, consider the unyielding tone of the Council's statement on the church at the point which concerns us:

> There is an *essential difference* between the faithful's priesthood in common and the priesthood of the ministry or the hierarchy, and not just a difference of degree. . . . In the person of Christ he (the priest) makes the eucharistic sacrifice and offers it in the name of the whole of God's People. The faithful . . . practice their priesthood in the reception of the sacraments, in prayer and thanksgiving, the witness of a holy life, self-denial and active charity.[6]

Not altogether surprisingly, the Anglican-Roman Catholic International Commissions (ARCIC) echoed this dogmatic assertion in their statement on "Ministry and Ordination" in 1973:

> Christian ministers . . . share through baptism in the priesthood of the people of God. . . .Nevertheless their ministry is not an extension of the common Christian priesthood but belongs to *another realm* of the gifts of the Spirit. . . . Ordination denotes entry into this apostolic and God-given ministry (pars 13-14).[7]

Rather more disturbing was the realization that this more Catholic conception of an ordained ministry which is "essentially different" in kind from the ministry of the whole people, seems to have been echoed in *The Report of the Churches' Council for Covenanting*, which recently sought (unsuccessfully) to draw together the Church of England, the Methodist Church, the Moravian Church and the United Reformed Church in England:

> The responsibility of the ordained ministry is to enable the whole Church to be fully the visible body of Christ. . . . The ordained minister is a representative figure portraying to the Christian community Christ's *Lordship* and care of his people. . . . Ordination denotes entry into the apostolic and God given ministry.[8]

The same point can be illustrated from a different angle by the World Council of Churches statements on *Ministry*. The earlier one begins by assuming the category of "the ordained ministry" as a starting point, though in an effort to diminish the "quantum leap" from "the ministry of the whole people of God" to "the ordained ministry" it defines the latter alternatively and rather awkwardly as "the special ministry." When it goes on to describe "this special ministry" we find that functions like "assembling the community," "proclaiming and teaching the Word of God," "presiding over the liturgical and sacramental life of the eucharistic community," and "coordinating and uniting the different gifts in the community" have been drawn into the definition, presumably on historical grounds (this is how "the ordained ministry" actually developed), but with little or no attempt to provide a theological justification for treating such functions as the prerogative of "the ministry."

> The minister, who participates, as every Christian does, in the priesthood of Christ, and of all the People of God, fulfills his particular ministry in strengthening, building up and expressing the royal and prophetic priesthood of the faithful through the service of the Gospel, the lending of the liturgical and sacramental life of the eucharistic community, and intercession.[9]

But if "the minister" "participates, as every Christian does, in the priesthood of Christ," why are the ministerial functions which follow "*his particular* [priestly] ministry"?

In its revised text on *Ministry* the World Council starts by underlining more emphatically "the calling of the whole people of God," but the rest is devoted to "the ordained ministry"—more than 90% of the whole document![10] It is difficult to avoid the impression that the first section, far from being the starting point and foundation for the whole, is more in the nature of an afterthought, tacked on to meet fears of prelacy. To put it so is probably unfair to the authors, who, I have no doubt, sincerely wish to take "the calling of the whole people of God" with the utmost seriousness. But what effective difference has the first section made to the other 90%?—not very much.[11] The real issues dealt with in the text are those relating to the ordained ministry. The ministry of the whole people of God can be given scanty treatment because it is unproblematic and raises so few questions and controversies, whereas one would have thought that any attempt to explore and explain the diversity of ministries, the theological rationale of "special ministries" within that diversity, and the relation of ministry to special ministry, was bound to raise many issues which would require a more careful treatment. Is it unfair to conclude that ministry so lightly treated is in effect ministry lightly regarded?

Indicative of the same blind spot in most traditional ecclesiologies is the recently published final comment of the Churches' Council for Covenanting.[12] In picking over the bones of the lately deceased Covenant scheme in England, the report notes how little time has been spent in the Covenant proposals on the part that lay readers, local preachers, lay preachers and elders would play. In a scheme carefully designed to draw the churches together into common ministry, the role of lay ministry has simply been taken for granted! and the impression given that only the ordained ministry really counted. What such an oversight (and its unfortunate results) actually reveals is that the role of lay ministry has *not* actually been thought through at a theological level, particularly in its relation to the ordained ministry. Lay ministries have developed in a pragmatic way rather than on the basis of clearly articulated and worked out theological principles; furthermore, underlying the problem of the disputed validity of some ordained ministries is the far more fundamental problem of the divide between ordained and lay ministries.

A final illustration comes from my own background. There is a strong strand of thought within the Reformed tradition which regards the minister as alone the authoritative mouthpiece of the Word of God within a congregation. The minister is as the Old Testament prophet; his exposition of Scripture is as the Old Testament prophecy. And the idea that all might prophesy is dismissed as a temporary provision for the apostolic age (Acts 2:17-18; 1 Cor. 14:1, 39). Far from recognizing that the age of fulfillment has come with Christ and with Pentecost, we still sigh with Old Testament Moses, "Would that all the Lord's People were prophets, that the Lord would put his Spirit upon them" (Num. 11:29). Or again, as a student studying for the ministry of the Church of Scotland (Presbyterian) I was often puzzled by what seemed to me, and still seems to me, a strange theological double-think. I was instructed that there was no essential difference between the minister and his fellow elders of the Kirk Session. They were all ruling elders, but he was also a preaching elder. This meant that there was no theological reason why only the minister should preside at the Lord's Supper. The fact that only he did preside was merely a matter of good order. What I could not understand, then or now, is how "good order" would be threatened if, for example, the Lord's Supper was conducted by a well-known ruling elder, highly respected in church and community for his Christian witness. I have asked the question more than once, but never received a satisfactory answer. Perhaps Milton was right after all, that "new Presbyter is by old Priest writ large."[13] And now that I am a practising Methodist, what do I find?—a church which, if truth be told, is in large degree embarrassed by that tradition from its Primitive Methodist past whereby local or lay preachers could conduct communion—a church which, despite the fact that the Deed of Union denies to the ordained ministry "a priesthood which belongs exclusively to a particular order," nevertheless assumes that the direction of Holy Communion "belongs exclusively" to the ordained ministry when an ordained minister is present. Should I then, perhaps, reword Milton's line to fit my new situation: "The new ministry is but the old priesthood writ large"?

What does the charismatic renewal say to such ecclesiastical traditions? There is, I believe, a serious danger that the main challenge of the renewal at this point will be sidetracked and largely dissipated. There is a danger that the charismatic renewal's rediscovery of the diversity and universality of charisms among believers will be seen merely in terms of the ministry of the *laity*.[14] An emphasis on the diverse charisms of the people of God can be used neatly to supplement the established teaching about the ordained ministry, to fill out the rather scanty treatment of the ministry of the whole people—to supplement but not to challenge that established teaching, to fill out but not to call in question that basic division, the "essential difference" between clergy and laity. And yet that, it seems to me, is precisely the challenge and question of the charismatic renewal—to rethink our traditional conceptions of ministry and the ministry from the bottom up, to rework our whole theology of ministry, not on the basis that the ordained ministry is a given, an established fixed point, but from first principles where any concept of "special ministry" truly grows again from a thoroughly thought out understanding of the ministry of the whole people of God as the basis. The attempt to graft a concept of the ministry of the people on the established root of the ordained ministry has not really worked. Now it is time to reaffirm that the root of all ministry is the charismatic Spirit given variously to members of Christ's body, to recognize that our starting point is the new covenant of the Pentecostal Spirit and not an old covenant institution of priesthood.

How might this challenge of the charismatic renewal to traditional ecclesiology be developed? Permit me, if you will, to spend the rest of my paper elaborating some of the theological and hermeneutical issues which must feature in any fundamental rethink of ministry—bearing in mind that I address these issues from the perspective of a New Testament specialist rather than of a dogmatician or philosophical theologian or expert in pastoralia and mission.

II

One of the principal factors in subdividing a category of "the ministry" within the broader category of ministry in general is *ordination*. The theology and practice of ordination lies at the heart of the distinction between clergy and laity, between "the ministry" and "ministry." Thus, for example, Anthony Harvey asks, "What is it that makes a Christian minister what he is?" His answer begins, "We shall, of course, regard *one* qualification as essential: the man *(sic)* must have been ordained."[15] It is ordination which constitutes the "essential difference" between the ordained ministry and the ministry of the whole people of God. It is ordination which gives "the minister" his ecclesiastical authority, which gives him exclusive right to preside at the Lord's Supper, which is the fulcrum point on which disputes about women ministers, valid orders and apostolic succession turn. Such a crucial rite one would think out then to be a focal point in ecumenical discussion, in attempts to reexamine and reexpress the theology of ministry. But here too, indicative of the present state of affairs, it is often simply assumed that the *theology* of ordination can be taken for granted as common ground among the churches, with the real discussion limited to divergence of *practice*. In the two World Council of Churches statements of ministry, for example, the treatment of ordination comes at the end, *after* the exposition of ordained ministry, where the fact of a "special ministry" singled out by ordination has been simply assumed from the start.

At one level, of course, the justification for ordination is simple and can be (and is) stated briefly. Jesus appointed twelve men as apostles (to special ministry). The practice of laying on of hands in some kind of ordination can be found already in the very earliest days of Christianity in the setting apart of the seven in Acts 6, and of Barnabas and Paul in Acts 13, and it clearly constitutes an ordination, (cf. 1 Tim. 4:14 and 2 Tim. 1:6—"the gift of God which is in you through the laying on of hands.") As early as Paul's letter to the Philippians we see the emergence of "bishops and deacons" (Phil. 1:1). Still within the first century we see the first appearance of the (implied) distinction between clergy and laity (*klerikos* and *laikos*) in Clement of Rome (1 Clem. 40:4-5). And already in Ignatius of Antioch we see presidency of the eucharists restricted in relation to the bishop (*Smyrneans* 8:1). But hidden within and obscured by such brief expositions are usually a number of question-begging assumptions and some doubtful theology. Let me explain what I mean.

a) First, a preliminary point—*the danger of a doubtful methodology* invites the danger of approaching our foundational documents with a methodology which predetermines the results we will find. Expressed more provocatively—this is the danger of finding what you are looking for! because your question to the text forces the evidence of the text into the categories posed by you, or, more seriously, because your object in coming to the text is to find justification for your presuppositions, your already established position. For example, any theological student worth his/her salt knows that if he or she comes to the letter of 2 Peter with the aim of defending Petrine authorship, he or she is bound to order the arguments and evaluate the evidence in accordance with that aim—playing up what favors Petrine authorship, playing down what counts against it. One also knows, or should know, that the sounder exegetical method is to let the text speak for itself, so far as that is possible, to let the evidence read in the light of its own historical context point to its own conclusions. So, too, with our question regarding ordination and "the ministry." If we come to the New Testament looking for evidence of the threefold ministry (bishop, presbyter and deacon) we will find it—because we will inevitably tend to push what may actually be more diverse and more ambiguous evidence into one or other of these categories. A classic case in point is the way in which the appointment of the seven in Acts 6 has been read as the beginning of the diaconate, with the seven regularly described as "deacons" in older treatments, even though the word "deacon" nowhere appears in the text.[16] So our starting question should be not, Where can we find evidence of "the ministry" or of ordination in the New Testament?, but, What do we learn from the New Testament about ministry in the first two generations of Christianity?

b) A second concern is over *the way in which the Old Testament is used in traditional ecclesiology*—more or less as though Christians still belonged under the old covenant and not under the new. The search for types and patterns of God's dealings with humanity within the Old Testament too quickly forgets the eschatological dimension which is fundamental to the New Testament, the sense that in and through Christ God has done a new thing, has begun a *new* phase in his dealings with humankind. Thus models and patterns can *not* simply be transferred from the old dispensation to the new. Yet many of the classic expositions on which traditional ecclesiology has been built seem to ignore this very basic point—for example, Clement with his implicit distinction between *klerikos* and *laikos* analogous to the Jewish distinction between priest and people (Isa. 24:2; Hos. 4:9), Hippolytus with his repeated likening of the bishop to a high priest (*Traditio* 3, 34), and Cyprian who was "one of the first to have a clear predilection for the Old Testament priestly sacrificial terminology."[17] But, how can we forget that the whole idea of a particular order of priesthood is essentially Old Testament in character, by which I mean Old Testament in *contrast* to New Testament? Of course the New Testament does talk of Christians as priests (1 Pet. 2:5; Rev. 1:6; 10; 20:6), but in these cases the thought is precisely of *all* Christians as priests, not of a distinct body *within* the Christian community.

How often do we need to be reminded that in the churches of the New Testament there was *no* distinct order of priesthood? That in the New Testament itself there is *no room* for a distinct order of priesthood within the congregations of the new covenant? On the contrary, it is precisely the New Testament writers' point, variously expressed, that the new covenant has removed the need for such an order (e.g. Matt. 23:8-10; John 4:21-4; Rom. 12:1; 2 Cor. 3:7-18).[18] It has always puzzled me how it is that churches which so readily ascribe primary authority to the Scriptures can ignore a basic element in New Testament teaching so completely. The subsequent link between the idea of the Lord's Supper as a sacrifice and of the celebrant as a priest is understandable on historical and sociological grounds, but from a theological perspective it signals a loss of the New Testament eschatological perspective, a reversion to categories and functions rendered obsolete by Christ's institution of the new covenant. For all the difference it has made to classical ecclesiology the letter to the Hebrews might well never have been written—for it is precisely the central assertion of that letter, that sacrifice and priest belong to the old age of shadow and promise and have been wholly superseded by the new age of reality and fulfillment, which has been so disregarded in traditional ecclesiology. Christians tend to look askance at Mormon misunderstanding and abusing of Hebrews in seeking justification for the orders of Aaronic and Melchizedek priesthoods within the Church of Latter Day Saints. But traditional Christian assertions of a distinct priesthood within the body of Christian believers are equally foreign to the argument of Hebrews.

c) The one way which might seem to escape the obvious force of Hebrews's argument has been *the appeal to Christ himself as the model of Christian priesthood.* The Aaronic priesthood has been rendered obsolete, but not priesthood as such, for Christ is a priest in the order of Melchizedek. It is this priestly role of Christ, so the argument goes, which is reflected in the church's ministry. Thus in the passages quoted above: according to Vatican II, the priest makes the eucharistic sacrifice "in the person of Christ;" and in the language of the Report of the Churches' Council for Covenanting, "The ordained minister is a representative figure portraying to the Christian community Christ's Lordship and care of his people." But the justification for confining such participation in Christ's priestly or kingly role to a particular group of the faithful is wholly lacking from within the New Testament. The argument of Hebrews really leaves us no choice: either we say Christ's priesthood is unique to Christ—since only he "has neither beginning of days nor end of life" (Heb. 7:3); or we may regard it as participated in by all—since *all* may now "draw near" and enter into the Holy of Holies, the very presence of God, and not just priests (Heb. 10:19-25). There seems to be no third option. On the contrary, to argue that there is (still) a particular order of priesthood, which shares in Christ's priesthood in a distinctive way, would surely have been regarded by the writer to the Hebrews as a falling back into the era of shadow and imperfection. Even to argue for a special priesthood of the ordained ministry on the grounds that they "represent" the priesthood of the whole people is to ignore the fact that such representative capacity is primarily a characteristic of the superceded Aaronic priesthood (Heb. 5:1-4); under the new covenant it still provides no justification for a distinct priesthood other than the priesthood of Christ himself.

Alternatively, if we return to the Pauline imagery of the body of Christ, the point is that it is the whole community which is the body. Even in the developed ecclesiology of Eph. 4, the point of verse 16 is that all members and organs of the body depend directly on Christ the head and all depend equally on each other, not simply on a group of "higher organs" within the body (other than Christ). We might simply contrast the classic treatment of R. C. Moberly on *Ministerial Priesthood*, which distinguished between ministry and laity by identifying the ordained *alone* as the organs of the body,[19] as though Paul or the writer to the Ephesians had been concerned to distinguish between "members" and "organs," with the members "functioning" merely as passive recipients of the grace mediated to them only through the organs! Such a distinction between "members" and "organs," with the members "functioning" merely as passive recipients of the grace mediated to them only through the organs! is *eis*egesis not *ex*egesis and distorts the whole point of Paul's body of Christ metaphor.

d) But does Paul not give prominence to particular ministries, *special ministries*, within his churches? Even within the egalitarian body of Christ there are first apostles, second prophets, third teachers, and so on (1 Cor. 12:28), apostles, prophets, evangelists, pastors and teachers for the equipment of the saints, for the work of ministry, for building up the body of Christ (Eph. 4:11-12). Are these not functions of "the ministry?"

The role of the *apostles*, in particular, as a distinct category of ministry from the very beginning of Christianity, is bound to provide an important precedent for any concept of ordained ministry, as we may see once again in the two World Council statements. The problem is that apostles were seen from the first as a unique group: as witnesses of the risen Christ appointed by the risen Christ they were a closed circle (Acts 1:21-2; 1 Cor. 15:8—"last of all"). If their other function as church founders is emphasized (1 Cor. 9:2), we should presumably have to accept the corollary that we are dealing with a much wider group than merely the Twelve plus Paul (1 Cor. 15:7—"all the apostles"), including such as Andronicus and Junias (Rom. 16:7), the second of whom may have been a woman—Junia, or even, according to some manuscripts, Julia! Furthermore, if church founding is the criterion of apostleship, we are still left with the choice either of confining the apostolic role to the apostolic age (founders of the Church), or of recognizing church founders in every age as apostles, whether Paul in the first century or Simon Kimbangu in the twentieth. And still we do not have a precedent for "the ministry" today. Alternatively, if passing on the apostolic tradition is the mark of apostleship, that is not a function exclusively of apostles as such, since presumably teachers also are charged with that task (e.g. Gal. 6:6)—apostolicity attaches to the tradition more than to the function of passing it on.

What of the other "special" ministries of Paul? There can certainly be no question that Paul expected certain individuals to be recognized as having such ministries. Most frequently mentioned are prophets and teachers, but the list of Rom. 12:6-8 envisages other regular ministries, including exhorting, sharing, caring and giving, and in 1 Thess. 5:12 Paul speaks of "those who labor among you, who care for you in the Lord and admonish you." But two points of importance have to be borne in mind here. First, these regular ministries were no different in kind from specific acts of ministry to which *any* member might be called; they were not confined to a particular group within the community. There were prophets, but at Corinth at least, all were encouraged to prophesy (1 Cor. 14:1, 39), and there seem to have been women who prophesied (11:5) even though not prophets (cf. 14:29-36). There were teachers, but Col. 3:16 encourages all to teach and admonish one another; and according to Acts 18:26 Apollos was instructed more accurately in the faith by Priscilla and Aquila (the wife evidently playing the leading role!). In 1 Thess. 5:14 all the brethren are exhorted to do what those commended in verse 12 were already doing. Indeed, according to the next few verses, the whole community is responsible for testing a prophecy—a function which *Lumen Gentium* in a piece of tendentious and bad exegesis confines to the bishops![20] In other words, precisely that priestly distinction in kind or function which is given by ordination is lacking in Paul. Not only are there no priests in Paul's ecclesiology, but also there are no special ministries confined to a few (the apostles excepted).[21]

The second point is simply to note the way in which traditional ecclesiology has tended to concentrate a wide range of functions upon the ordained ministry. The World Council revised text is not at all atypical in defining ordained ministers "as heralds and ambassadors . . . as leaders and teachers . . . as pastors" (Par. 10—the earlier draft added ". . . as intercessors"). The inevitable result is to sustain that model of *monoministry* which has been one of the greatest hinderances to the mission of the whole church. The point is that these were originally all different ministries, *not* different functions of the one ordained ministry. In Paul exhortation could evidently be a ministry in itself, "helpful deeds" and "giving guidance'' were different charisms from prophesying and teaching, healing or speaking in tongues (1 Cor. 12:28). In the older denominations we still expect ''the minister'' to combine with himself/herself the roles of pastor, teacher, preacher, evangelist, chairman, administrator, organizer (to name but a few!). But since God only occasionally gifts an individual with more than one or two of these charisms, the effect of ordination has been to stifle the diversity of ministry and thus to diminish and sometimes even cripple the vitality of Christ's body. If unity depends on diversity functioning as such, then is it any surprise that unity has been so difficult to bring about, since a proper diversity is lacking? To rephrase the same question more starkly, since ordination has so stifled diversity, is it any wonder that the ordained ministry has been the chief stumbling block on the road to unity?

e) What in particular of *the close link between the Lord's Supper and the ordained ministry?* It is no secret that in early centuries the reemergence of a concept of priesthood went hand in hand with the developing concept of the eucharist as a sacrifice, as we have already noted[22]—a quite understandable association of ideas in that age: only as a priest can an individual offer up a sacrifice. Not surprisingly, as we have also already noted, the church of Rome continues to affirm this link quite explicitly—''the priest makes the eucharistic sacrifice.'' Rather more surprisingly, however, is the fact that the churches of the Reformation, which protested vigorously against the idea of the Lord's Supper as a sacrifice (other than as a ''sacrifice'' of praise and thanksgiving), have nevertheless retained the concomitant idea of the celebrant as a priest, by continuing to insist that only the ordained can officiate at the sacrament of holy communion. It is difficult to see how any church which thus systematically restricts the administration of the Lord's Supper to the ordained can escape the charge that their ordained ministry forms a distinct priesthood within the body of believers. When a presbyter or minister has exclusive right to preside at the central celebration of a congregation's communal life then Milton's charge cannot be escaped—new presbyter *is* old priest writ large.

But however much this priest-sacrifice model of the eucharist can be traced back to the early centuries, it must remain significant that it cannot be traced back into or be justified from our common canonical documents, the New Testament. The ''breaking of bread'' in Acts 2:42 and 46 took place in the houses of the first believers. If that ''breaking of bread'' regularly included what we now isolate as the eucharistic elements, as is quite probable, then we should note that there is nothing to show that this breaking of bread was exclusively the prerogative of the apostles. On the contrary, the subject of ''breaking bread'' is the quite general ''they'' of ''all who believed;'' those who broke bread together were the disciples in general. So, too, in the one passage which deals with the Lord's Supper as such in the New Testament (1 Cor. 11:17-34), what is particularly striking is the *lack* of any specified leader of the common meal or established function of presidency. Were there such, Paul must either have appealed to him (or her) in 1 Cor. 11 to correct the abuses of the common meal, or have appealed to the community to follow the celebrant's lead. The only plausible explanation of this silence in 1 Cor. 11 is that there was no such established role or function confined to a particular figure.[23] In that case we are on firmer ground if we simply assume that the common meal with its eucharistic elements was naturally presided over by the host in whose house the church met (cf. Acts 18:7; Rom. 16:23). And because his (or her) authority was that of host and not of priestly celebrant, it was not he or she but the congregation as a whole which had to be held responsible for maintaining orderly behavior at these meals. The same would be true of the other, no doubt often quite small churches which met in particular houses. Almost certainly such gatherings would involve common meals including recollection at least on some occasions of the Last Supper. And almost certainly insofar as anyone presided at these meals it would have been the host (such would have been the convention of the day, as now)—probably Priscilla or Aquila in their house church (Rom. 16:5; 1 Cor. 16:19), and presumably Nympha herself in her church at Colosse or Laodicea (Col. 4:15)— further examples of women being involved in a ministry which was subsequently confined to an all male ministry set apart from other ministry by the rite of ordination. In short, there is no precedent or justification in the New Testament for a theology or practice of ordination as something indispensable before one can conduct holy communion, no precedent or justification for a concept of ministry which restricts conduct of the eucharists to the ordained ministry.

 f) If we think finally of New Testament precedents for ordination itself, the case for "the ordained ministry" is no better off. In Acts 6 and 13 the laying on of hands is indeed a setting apart for ministry—though we might simply note that in the first case, according to the most grammatical sense of the Greek, it was the multitude of believers who did the laying on of hands (6:6), and in the latter, Paul's apostolic (that is, in this case, missionary) authority was given through the hands of their fellow prophets and teachers (13:1-3). The more important point, however, is that these ordinations, as they may properly be called, were evidently *short-term* ordinations. Of the seven ordained "to serve tables" we only hear more of two, in neither case persevering in their appointed ministry—Stephen as an apologist (6-7), and Philip as an evangelist (8; 21:8). Their ordination evidently was not regarded as a life-long appointment. Similarly in the case of Barnabas and Paul. What the laying on of hands of Acts 13:3 signified was their being set apart as missionaries of the church of Antioch—a commissioning which lasted for what we now think of as the first missionary journey (during which time they were apostles + missionaries of Antioch—Acts 14:4, 14). Thereafter Paul and Barnabas went their own ways (15:39-41), with Paul, at any rate, becoming an independent missionary based chiefly in Corinth and then in Ephesus (18-19). Another passage sometimes treated as an allusion to ordination yields precisely the same point: in 2 Cor. 8:19 Paul speaks of "the brother who has been appointed (cheirotonētheis) by the churches to travel with me in this gracious work." The point is clear: "The gracious work" is Paul's collection for the Christians in Jerusalem—an appointment precisely defined and limited in time and scope—a short-term ordination. Even with 1 Tim. 4:14 and 2 Tim. 1:6 we should not jump too quickly to the conclusion that here we have a concept of ordination for a life-long ministry. The passages could mean that, and the possibility that that is what the writer had in mind is quite strong. But what precisely the charism (singular) is which Timothy has been given "through the laying on of hands" is not clear. And we should recall that in the Pastorals Timothy and Titus are still represented as Paul's emissaries—apostolic delegates not successors to Paul, and agents of Paul more than ministers within the churches of Ephesus and Crete. In short, if we look to the New Testament for a basic theology and practice of ordination it is a different and broader concept of ordination than that maintained in traditional ecclesiology.

The Pastorals of course do bear testimony to a more clearly structured conception of ministry, where the previous diversity of ministry within the Pauline churches seems to have become more circumscribed and focused upon the evidently more established ministries of bishop (or bishop-elder) and deacon (1 Tim. 3:1-13; Tit. 1:5-9). And to that extent, at least, the subsequent idea of "the ordained ministry," as an official ministry distinct within and from the more amorphous ministry of the whole church, is founded within the New Testament. But the Pastorals should not be given primacy over the other New Testament writings when it comes to formulating a theology of ministry. What has happened in effect is that classical ecclesiology has taken its lead from the clearer outlines of the Pastorals, and largely ignored the more obscure or different ecclesiologies of other New Testament writings. But should the Pastorals be allowed to reduce the canonical weight of 1 Corinthians and Romans? Even if the Pastorals were written by Paul and reflect his changed attitude as death drew near, are we to conclude that he would have wished to withdraw his vision of the body of Christ as charismatic community in his earlier letters? Are we to say that the late Paul would not have approved the canonization of his earlier eccesiology? That is surely too bold a conclusion to draw from the more amenable eccesiology of the Pastorals. But the alternative is to recognize as also canonical a broader concept of ministry than that which begins to take shape in the Pastorals, to recognize as also normative a different theology of ministry from that defined in terms of ordination.

Less clearly defined, but just as challenging in their impact, are the different ecclesiological emphases which become evident outside the Pauline corpus— particularly the type of individualistic piety and what may not unfairly be called the conventicle or convention Christianity of the Johannine writings (Gospel and Epistles), and the picture of a church that lives through and out of prophecy which emerges from the Revelation of John the seer (cf., e.g., Rev. 11:10; 12:11; 19:10; 22:9).[24] And outside the New Testament canon, alongside Ignatius, we may simply set the alternative of the *Didache*, in which peripatetic prophets and travelling missionaries/apostles still appear as a different model of ministry alongside the local bishops and deacons (Did. 11:13; 15:1). All that this means is that there were *other* ways of ordering church and ministry in the earliest days of Christianity and in the New Testament than that which foreshadowed the clear distinction between clergy and laity, that *other* concepts of ministry can look to the New Testament for validation with just as much justification as those who cherish a high doctrine of ordination, and that a true ecumenicity cannot insist on a particular doctrine of ordination or concept of "the ordained ministry" as the starting point when a church seeks to rethink its ministry or reform its ecclesiology.

<h3 style="text-align:center">III</h3>

On the basis of such a radical requestioning of traditional concepts of the ministry and of ordination from the New Testament roots upwards, and thinking in practical and realistic terms, how, in conclusion, might the charismatic renewal express its contribution to an ecumenical rethink on ministry?

a) It must surely start from the fundamental point, *the recognition that every member of the body of Christ has some ministry*, whether to others, on behalf of the community of faith, or within the community of faith. If we take Paul seriously when he teaches that the health of the body depends on each member functioning properly, then a proper concern of corporate church life must be the discovery and recognition of all these ministries, and the encouragement and support of individuals in their ministry. This will require a truly broad perspective to recognize the full diversity of these ministries; for one thing, ministry should not be defined so as to include only the "activists" in a congregation or only those who contribute to its public worship. What would such a recognition and its corollaries mean for a church's corporate life, for its structures of fellowship and other gatherings, for its times of worship? That would be an agenda for many meetings of house church or synod. We may perhaps recall that the development of such specialist ministries as industrial chaplaincy was often accompanied by muddled thinking which assumed that the church was not represented in the world of industry until ordained ministers were appointed to such chaplaincies. What value this put upon the ministry and witness of the laity may be imagined. Conversely, the proper recognition of the responsibility of all believers in one form of ministry or another could do more to mobilize the witness of the church than almost anything else.

b) Secondly, *there must surely be an insistence that there is no difference in kind between one ministry and another.* Here the challenge to the Catholic tradition is at its sharpest; but we should not flinch from posing that challenge, if our concern if for the church's health and faith. If Paul is right in 1 Cor. 12 and Rom. 12, ministry has always to be seen more as a function than as an expression of official status. There are of course, different functions, exercised by different people. Some of these functions are more important for the corporate life (as prophecy should have been more important than speaking in tongues in the Corinthian assembly—1 Cor. 14). But *each* is a *charisma*, an expression of God's free grace, and ministry properly exercised is the opposite of hierarchical status and authority (cf. Mark 10:42-5). This is not to deny the pragmatic sociological point that any large organization needs its full-time professionals to maintain it, and that some hierarchical structure is almost inevitable. But however much we may recognize the need for professionalism in organization, on questions of ministry per se, the distinction between professional and amateur is surely to be avoided. For if we take Paul seriously, the essence of ministry is openness to the Spirit to be a medium of grace to others. Training and experience can help facilitate (or hinder!) that openness, but they do not constitute the ministry itself; so that the temptation to make them a basis for distinction in status should be resisted as far as possible—as also the tendency to concentrate several ministries in one individual to the disregard of those ministries in others. Such policy may be appropriate to the model of the profession business; it is not appropriate to the body of Christ. Here, too, the identification of areas of need and opportunity in and around a particular church, and how they might be met and with what priority and through which member(s), is an agenda too little followed by churches whose tradition has been to ''leave it to the minister—that's what he's paid for!''

c) In the rethink of ordination in particular *its function as an act whereby the community of believers recognizes the call of one of its members to a particular ministry should be given primary place.* And given that all members have some ministry, the theology of ordination should include the recognition of this diversity of ministry. Ordination should not be confined to a life-long commitment, but should be equally expressive of a congregation's commendation of a short-term commitment. It should certainly not be confined to the recognition of male ministry, but should be the congregation's identification with ministry of whatever kind through whatever member. This of course need not require an endless round of "ordination services": a community's recognition can be expressed briefly or more elaborately, and the longer the commitment or the more strategic its task the fuller in expression will most congregations want their act of recognition to be. So long as the emphasis is always present that whether the ministry envisaged be long or short, more strategic or less, the actual ordination in each case is just the same in kind and essence, the community owning and commending the one no less and no more than the other. To put the point more plainly and provaca- tively: until we count "ordination" of Sunday School teachers and distributors of church flowers as no different in essence from "ordination" of elder or bishop, we cannot claim to be functioning as the body of Christ.

d) A final thought on the issue which seems for good or ill to be so tightly bound up with the concept of "the ministry" and the theology of ordination— viz, the Lord's Supper, the Eucharist. If we accept that presiding at the eucharist is not a charism distinct from the rest, that God's Spirit brings such grace to expression through all believers, then we should insist as a fundamental theological expression of the body of Christ that the conducting of holy communion must not be confined to a particular group within the diverse ministries of the community of faith.[25] This should not be misrepresented as a recipe for chaos or disorder;[26] the churches of the radical Reformation show clearly enough that an invited preacher, lay as well as ordained, can conduct the Lord's Supper without any deterioration of "good order." For other traditions to deny that such a sacrament is a sacrament of the universal church can hardly be counted as other than a presumption abhorrent to the mind of Christ, an example of Pharisee-like arrogance antipathetic to the Spirit of grace. This single step of allowing the sacrament of the Lord's Supper once again to be the natural expression of fellowship wherever groups of believers come together, even when "the minister" is not present, could be one of the most liberating steps in renewal and growth. Apart from anything else, it would allow house churches properly speaking to become as much an integral part of the local church's life as they were in the beginning, and might thus be the key to liberating the full potential of the house church for richer forms of ministry within itself and its locality.

These then are some of the ways in which the challenge of the charismatic renewal could begin to impinge on the older churches. It is a challenge which is overdue, both in its making and in its being heard by the older denominations. If my paper today helps to express this very important challenge and to gain it a wider hearing, I will count my visit to this Conference as time and effort well spent and more than ordinarily worthwhile.

*This paper was delivered at the Twelfth Annual meeting of the Society for Pentecostal Studies held November 18-20, 1982 at Fuller Theological Seminary.

NOTES

[1]See e.g. my "Rediscovering the Spirit (2)," *Expository Times* 94 (1982-3): 9-18.

[2]Though see my "Rediscovering the Spirit (1)," *Expository Times* 84 (1972-73): 42f.; also J. D. G. Dunn, *Jesus and the Spirit,* (London/Philadelphia: Westminster/SCM, 1975), particularly chaps. 8 and 9.

[3]I may refer particularly to the recent World Council of Churches report, *The Church is Charismatic: the World Council and the Charismatic Renewal* (Geneva: World Council of Churches, 1981).

[4]What follows is drawn in summary fashion from the more detailed exposition in *Jesus and the Spirit*, chaps. 8 and 9.

[5]Dunn, *Jesus and the Spirit*, p. 256.

[6]*Lumen Gentium* 10 (my emphasis).

[7]Anglican-Roman Catholic International Commission, *The Final Report*, CTS/SPC 1982, p. 36 (my emphasis).

[8]*Towards Visible Unity: Proposals for a Covenant*, 1980, pp. 45-6 (my emphasis). Note the presumably deliberate near quotation from the ARCIC statement cited above.

[9]*One Baptism, One Eucharist and a Mutually Recognized Ministry*, Faith and Order Paper No. 73, World Council of Churches, 5th printing 1978, p. 35.

[10]*Baptism, Eucharist and Ministry*, Faith and Order Paper No. 111, World Council of Churches 1982.

[11]Cf. par. 32, where the flexibility introduced by the concept of charism (some permanent, some temporary; men and women) is not allowed to extend to the ordained ministry, despite the assertion that it, too, is a charism.

[12]*The Failure of the English Covenant: An Assessment of the Experience of the Churches' Council for Covenanting*, 1982.

[13]John Milton, *On the New Forcers of Conscience under the Long Parliament*.

[14]Cf. again par. 32 of the World Council's revised text (above n. 10).

[15]A. E. Harvey, *Priest or President?*, (London: SPCK, 1975), p. 41.

[16]Cf. those cited in *Jesus and the Spirit*, p. 404 n. 100, and the somewhat more discriminating discussion by R. B. Rackham, *Acts*, (Methuen, 1901), [14]1951, p. 86.

[17]E. Shillebeeckx, *Ministry: A Case for Change* (London: SCM Press 1981), from who these references are drawn (pp. 48, 70).

[18]It is precisely in the same spirit that Paul can describe his own ministry as

"priestly service" (Rom. 15:16)—not because he in particular is a priest and other believers are not, or because his ministry is priestly in character as distinct from the ministries of other believers, but because all ministry in the new age of the Spirit, his included, has a significance which in the old era attached only to the ministry of priests.

[19]R. C. Moberly, *Ministerial Priesthood*, 1897 2 1910, reprinted (London: SPCK, 1969), p. 68.

[20]*Lumen Gentium* par. 12. Cf. the World Council's revised text: "The authority of ordained ministers must not be so reduced as to make them dependent on the common opinion of the community. Their authority lies in their responsibility to express the will of God in the community" (commentary on par. 16). This rather begs the question of how the will of God is to be discerned within and by the community.

[21]Despite the fact that "bishops" and "deacons" became the established titles for two of the orders of the ordained ministry it can hardly be assumed from Phil. 1:1 that this was already the case in the church at Philippi or that the functions of the bishops and deacons at Philippi were confined to them alone. The fact that 50-100 years later neither Ignatius nor Polycarp know of any bishop's office in connection with Philippi should not be overlooked.

[22]See above, p. 89.

[23]It can hardly be assumed that Stephanas in particular was expected to preside at the meal, as 1 Clem. 42:4 might later imply, since all that is said of Stephanas is that he and his household had (lit.) "appointed themselves to" some unidentified ministry (1 Cor. 16:15).

[24]For fuller details see my *Unity and Diversity in the New Testament* (Philadelphia/London: Westminster/SCM, 1977), pp. 116-21.

[25]One of the most interesting features of ecclesiastical discussions of the last ten years is the growing advocacy of the view that lay presidency of the eucharist is both permissible and desirable (rather than depriving believers of the sacrament because of a shortage of priests)—by such writers as the Anglican A. E. Harvey [*Priest or President?* (London: SPCK, 1975), p. 63] and the Roman Catholic Edward Schillebeeckx in his bold and valuable study of *Ministry: Leadership in the Community of Jesus Christ* ET (New York: Crossroad, 1980). What they would argue for as an answer to the shortage of priests should be insisted on as a matter of first theological principle. One of the most important sections of the World Council's revised text on Ministry is its commentary on par. 13, where it notes, "These tasks are not exercised by the ordained ministry in an exclusive way. Since the ordained ministry and the community are inextricably related, all members participate in fulfilling these functions. . . . Any member of the body

may share in proclaiming and teaching the Word of God, may contribute to the sacramental life of that body. The ordained ministry fulfills these functions in a representative way, providing the focus for the unity of life and witness of the community.'' Excellent! All that is needed now is the recognition that there is no good theological reason for confining such representative capacity exclusively to the ordained ministry.

[26]Contrast Harvey: ''Without this provision (or ordained ministers) there can be no order'' (*Priest*, p. 64).

6

DEBUNKING SOME OF THE MYTHS ABOUT GLOSSOLALIA*

H. Newton Malony

Recently, a young man was observed muttering to himself as he examined various titles on the shelves of a bookstore. He would run his fingers over the title of the book in a gingerly manner then touch his forehead lightly with the volume. This would be followed by incomprehensible muttering. It soon became apparent that the youth was praying in a strange language. It was glossolalia—the pietistic utterances of those who feel they are expressing their faith in a manner similar to first-century Christians at the Day of Pentecost (cf. Acts 2) and in the Corinthian Church (see e.g., 1 Cor. 12 and 14).

Events like this, plus many other similar experiences, have led many to presume that glossolalic persons were abnormal at worst or eccentric at best. Such questions as the following have been posed: Are glossolalics psychologically different from others? Do glossolalics tend toward greater preoccupation with emotional experience than others? Is the experience of glossolalia one in which persons go into a trance and lose consciousness? In what manner could glossolalia be considered a valid Christian experience?

In an effort to answer these questions a programmatic study of these issues has been in process at the Graduate School of Psychology, Fuller Theological Seminary since 1971. For the past decade graduate students under the direction of this author, a clinical psychologist and United Methodist minister, have completed a variety of experiments designed to determine the parameters of glossolalic phenomena. This essay is a report of this research.

WHAT IS GLOSSOLALIA?

Although most persons are acquainted with glossolalia, a brief summary of its meaning is in order. The literal definition of the term is "gift of tongues." In the Christian tradition it referred originally to phenomena which occurred on the Day of Pentecost. The author of Acts reports that as the faithful were gathered together in prayer after the death and resurrection of Jesus, the Holy Spirit swept over them with mighty power and they all began to speak in the languages of the world. None of them had any background in these languages, so the ability to speak in them was understood as due to the power of the Holy Spirit. The explanation given for this miracle was that it occurred so the good news of Jesus could be spoken to the nations.

As the church became established in the cities of the Roman Empire, glossolalia came to be thought of as evidence that the Holy Spirit was present in one's life. In the tongue-speaking noted in the church at Corinth the utterances did not seem to be recognizable languages and the problem of interpreting the meaning of the words became an issue. Further, tongue-speaking was suggested to be only one of the indications that a person was baptized with the Holy Spirit.

Since New Testament times, glossolalia has continued to be a part of numerous Christians' experience, although it long ago ceased to play a major role in Catholic, Orthodox or Protestant Christianity. Nevertheless, contemporary Christianity includes several smaller denominations for whom all gifts of the Spirit, and especially speaking in tongues, are the central concern. These well-established Pentecostal churches have been joined in the last half of this century by a neo-Pentecostal revival within major religious groups. Thus, there is a vital and increasingly accepted facet of Christianity that expresses its faith in this manner, even though no research has proven these utterances to be understandable in the syntax or semantics of any extant language.

WHO BECOMES GLOSSOLALIC AND WHY?

Since by no means all Christians speak in tongues the questions of who does and why become important. A number of personal and situational variables have been, or should be, considered. Psychopathology was early suggested as the prime concomitant of glossolalia (R. A. Knox, *Enthusiasm* [Oxford: Clarendon Press, 1950]). While several authors[1] postulate such a relationship, Hine[2] concluded there was none.

Glossolalics have been found to be well adjusted to their social environments[3] and able to control their thought processes outside the experience in a way dissimilar to schizophrenics who also spoke in tongues.[4] While evidence of interpersonal uncertainty was reported in other research utilizing psychological tests,[5] still no signs of psychopathology were observed. In fact, Gerrard[6] indicated that an analysis of MMPI profiles suggested glossolalics were better adjusted than members of a conventional denomination. Only Kildahl and Qualben,[7] among contemporary investigators, reported evidence for lower ego strength and higher suggestibility.

Pattison[8] suggested there was an interesting relationship between social expectancy and psychopathology in glossolalia. He proposed that in religious groups where glossolalia was the norm, speaking in tongues would not be psychopathological but that in groups where it was not expected the reverse would be true.

He further reported that there were class differences in his research. Overt psychopathology seemed to be present more often among lower class glossolalics than among middle and upper classes. This accorded with the insight of Boisen,[9] among others, that glossolalia functioned as a status symbol among the isolated and dispossessed.

Hine[10] termed this the disorganization-deprivation theory. Where society was fluid and changing and where a group of people were not succeeding in moving up the socio-economic scale, there glossolalia would be expected to be a compensatory act designed to overcome isolation and lack of status. Boisen,[11] Johnson,[12] Lanternari,[13] and Pattison[14] all concluded that in marginal socio-economic groups certain religious expressions served as substitutes for lack of achievement.

Another interesting tendency reported by Hine[15] was an inclination for second generation glossolalics to speak in tongues less frequently than their parents who tended to come from denominations where it was devalued. It has also been suggested that in middle class groups glossolalia meets group goals rather than personal needs. It is more a matter of social conformity than of compensation for loss. Therefore the functional meaning of tongue-speaking seems to be more critical among those for whom the experience is a more radical departure from social expectancy.

A three dimensional model including the presence of psychopathology, the group expectancy of glossolalia and social class was conceived as the basis for our investigations. Figure 1 illustrates this model.

Thus, where people were glossolalic we hypothesized they would be more likely to be psychopathological if they were from the lower class in a group where glossolalia was not the norm. They would be less likely to be psychopathological if they were members of the middle-upper class in a group where glossolalia was the norm.

In the first study, based on this model, the incidence and frequency of glossolalia

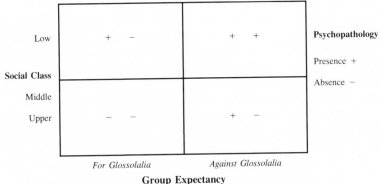

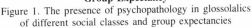

Group Expectancy

Figure 1. The presence of psychopathology in glossolalics
of different social classes and group expectancies

were correlated with the personality variables among youth who were members of a religious group where glossolalia was the expected norm (middle to upper class Assemblies of God youth attending a summer camp). Over ninety percent of the youths (ages 14-17) reported they spoke in tongues. Demographic data regarding family background, initial glossolalic experience, conversion, etc. were also assessed. These data were studied via analyses of variance in which high and low frequencies of glossolalia were the independent variables. No relationship was found between introversion or extroversion (using the Eysenck Personality Inventory) and the incidence or frequency of glossolalics to feel more internally or externally controlled (as measured by Rotter's I-E Scale[16]).

These results lent some support to our presumption that there would be no evidence of psychopathology among those in the middle to upper social classes where glossolalia was the norm. Of related interest was the finding of a significant tendency for high-frequency glossolalics to be more intrinsic in their orientation to religion than either nonglossolalics or low frequency glossolalics (as measured by Allport's EIRO scale). This suggested to us that they were more likely to perceive religion as meeting individual personal fulfillment than status needs in their lives. Demographically, glossolalia was related to having been converted, frequency of church attendance and the religious activity of parents. It was not related to sex or an index of socio-economic class, i.e., the salary of the father. While it most often began in a group setting, it was more frequently used in private devotions.

A second study was undertaken to replicate the data on intrinsic orientation toward religion plus relate glossolalia to religious beliefs and an index of religious activity, social action. Sample weaknesses in the first study were also corrected.

This interest in whether glossolalia resulted in new behavior (such as participation in social action projects) was prompted by Gerlack, et al.,[17] who saw glossolalia as a sign that the personality was being radically reorganized and a person was willing to risk new behavior. Again, the investigation was conducted among persons of similar social background who had all been exposed to similar religious experiences where glossolalia was the expected norm. Forty Assemblies of God youths who went on a social action trip to Mexico were compared to forty youths who did not go. High and low frequency glossolalics in each group were also compared. The data were subjected to analysis of variance. The earlier lack of relationships between socio-economic class and sex was confirmed as was the tendency for glossolalics to be more intrinsic in their orientation toward religion and for glossolalia among youths to be related to glossolalia among parents. There was a significant tendency for youths who participated in the social action project to be more glossolalic, thus giving support to the hypothesis about the behavioral effect of the phenomena. Further, although there was no differences in beliefs about God's nearness and accessibility, there was a significant tendency for more frequent glossolalia to be related to a negative and sinful view of humanity. Those who participated in the social action project were more pessimistic in their view of humanity than those who did not participate.[18]

In a more direct test of our model, we compared the physiological changes which occurred during the experiences of upper and lower class glossolalics.[19] Early in the 1900s investigators had proposed that glossolalia was a regressive psychological state involving automatisms, loss of conscious control, fugue states and dissociations resembling hypnotic trance. Later Pattison[20] proposed that there were different types of glossolalia with varying degrees of cortical control. Those with less control he called "serious" and those with more control he termed "playful." We hypothesized that those in the lower social class, from a religious tradition where it was not expected, and who frequently spoke in tongues, would show physiological changes (i.e., be more hysterical and suggestible). We suspected that those in the middle-upper social classes from traditions where glossolalia was the norm, and who spoke infrequently, would not show such changes. The former we labeled "Process" glossolalia (cf. Pattison's "serious") indicating it was a *personal* inner process probably reflecting psychological compensation for lack of status. The latter we labeled "Act" glossolalia (cf. Pattison's "playful") indicating it was a social *act* designed to reflect group conformity.

Changes in brain wave activity and heart rate were assessed as glossolalics prayed in English and prayed in tongues. Contrary to expectation there were no significant differences between Act and Process glossolalics.

Initially this led us to conclude that our model was in error. This still may be so. However, we are more inclined to think that the lack of results was due to the problems we encountered in convincing people to come to pray in a psychophysiological laboratory and the errors we made in assigning persons to socio-economic levels. In regard to the first we may have utilized a very biased sample of persons. They seemed to be neo-Pentecostals for whom glossolalia appears to be predominantly under voluntary control. We need to assess the phenomenon among traditional Pentecostals for whom glossolalia reportedly is much more likely to be experienced in uninvited possession. Further, the instrument used in determining social class assessed occupation and education. In one case, this formula placed an unemployed graduate student in the lower social class—an obvious error of measurement. A more rigorous standard is needed. However, if the results of this study are accepted as conclusive, the inference that glossolalics are different psychologically at the time of the event must be reconsidered.

Perhaps our most conclusive study to date was concerned with personality changes that might result from the experience of becoming glossolalic.[21] As early as 1908 Lombard[22] had suggested that glossolalia was a "rejuvenating" experience that had some positive impact on persons. As noted earlier, although the presence of psychopathology in the glossolalic experience had been postulated, little evidence had been found for this dynamic except in the research of Kildahl and Qualben[23] and Wood.[24] We reasoned that the "normality" observed in such studies as Gerrard and Gerrard[25] and Vivier[26] could perhaps have been accounted for by the impact of speaking in tongues on personality integration. In other words, they might have been abnormal before the event but have become mentally healthy afterwards.

Heretofore there had been no published studies on personality changes resulting from glossolalia that included assessment prior to the experience. This study attempted to study the effects of this phenomenon by measuring persons in "Life in the Spirit" seminars on personality and attitudinal variables pre-, post-, and three months after the seminar. These seminars (in Roman Catholic and Episcopal churches in New Mexico and California) were twelve week-long study groups designed to introduce persons to the gifts of the Holy Spirit. Persons who became glossolalic were compared to those who were already glossolalic and to those who did not become glossolalic. None of the groups was psychopathological at pre-testing time. Although persons who did not become glossolalic were highest in depression, hostility, and anxiety at the beginning of the seminar, all groups were similar at the time of follow-up. All persons changed in the direction of personality integration. However, those who became glossolalic did not change more than those who did not. the results were interpreted primarily as a function of attending the seminar rather than of the glossolalic experience.

We even compared the participants in the seminars to the standardized norms for the several personality tests we used and found them to be not significantly different on any measure from the average prior to the experience. Thus, we concluded that tongue-speaking Christians appeared to be normal both prior to as well as after they became glossolalic. Most surprising to us was the finding that being a part of the group had as much impact as speaking in tongues.

Finally, our most recent study extended the investigation of physiological changes during speaking in tongues by comparing "body auras" in glossolalic and non-glossolalic Presbyterians.[27] Matched pairs (on sex, marital status and years in the church) were measured via the Kirlian (negative photography) method in resting, prayer-in-English, and prayer-in-tongues conditions. Thorough analysis of variance procedures among conditions and between group comparisons were made. No significant differences in such measures as size and color of aura were observed. The hypothesis that change in auras should be different in various kinds of persons and among emotional conditions was not confirmed. No evidence for significant physiological change during the phenomenon was observed. Trance state was not evident.

CONCLUSIONS

Our research is ongoing. We are still asking some of the basic questions concerning individual differences among persons who speak in tongues and concerning the nature of the phenomenon itself. We are well aware of the significant variety in traditions, setting, and types of glossolalia and intend to replicate our study of socio-economic class and group expectancy.

However, our conclusions to date are as follows:

1. Speaking in tongues appears to be a concomitant of pietistic revivals throughout Christian history.
2. Contemporary glossolalic expression can be observed in both traditional and in neo-Pentecostalism and varies greatly in terms of group expectancy, setting and frequency.
3. Where tongue-speaking is expected, the vast majority of youth are glossolalic by age seventeen. More frequent glossolalics do not differ psychologically from less frequent glossolalics but they do appear to participate in more projects of social action.
4. Frequent glossolalia evidenced by persons in the lower social class from a background where it was not the norm does not appear to differ in kind from that practiced infrequently by upper to middle class persons in traditions where it is expected.

5. There is no indication that glossolalics go into trance during the experience.
6. Persons who speak in tongues do not appear to be mentally unhealthy either before or after the experience.

NOTES

*This article was published previously in *The Journal of the American Scientific Affiliation* 34 (1982), pp. 144-148.

[1]W. LaBarre, *They Shall Take up Serpents: Psychology of the Southern Snake-Handling Cult* (Minneapolis: Univ. of Minn. Press, 1962); K. Thomas, "Speaking in Tongues," Unpublished paper. Berlin Suicide Prevention Center, 1965; J. N., Lapsley, and J. H. Simpson, "Speaking in Tongues," *Pastoral Psychology*, 15 (1964): 16-24, 48-55.

[2]V. H. Hine, "Pentecostal Glossolalia: Toward a Functional Interpretation," *Journal for the Scientific Study of Religion* 8 (1969): 211-226.

[3]A. Alland, "Possession in a Revivalist Negro Church," *JSSR* 1 (1961): 204-213.

[4]A. Boisen, "Economic Distress and Religious Experience: A Study of the Holy-Roller," *Psychiatry* 2 (1939): 185-194; A. Kiev, *The Study of Folk Psychiatry in Magic, Faith and Healing: Studies in Primitive Psychiatry* (Glencoe: Free Press, 1964), pp. 3-35.

[5]W. W. Wood, *Culture and Personality Aspects of the Pentecostal Holiness Religion* (Paris: Mouton, 1965); S. C. Plog, "Preliminary Analysis of Group Questionnaires as Glossolalia," Unpublished data, University of California at Los Angeles, 1966.

[6]N. L. Gerrard and L. B. Gerrard, "Scrabble Greek Folk: Mental Health, Part II" Unpublished Report, Department of Sociology, Morris Harvey College, Charleston, West Virginia, 1966.

[7]J. P. Kildahl and P. A. Qualben, "A Study of Speaking in Tongues," Unpublished data, 1966.

[8]E. M. Pattison, "Behavioral Science Research on Glossolalia," *Journal of the American Scientific Affiliation* 20 (1968): 73-86.

[9]A. T. Boisen, *Religion in Crises and Custom: A Sociological and Psychological Study* (New York: Harper, 1955).

[10]V. H. Hine, "Pentecostal Glossolalia: Toward a Functional Interpretation," *JSSR* 8 (2, 1969): 211-226.

[11]A. T. Boisen, *Religion.*

[12]B. Johnson, "Do Holiness Sects Socialize in Dominant Values?" *Social Forces* 39 (1961): 309-316.

[13]V. Lanternari, *The Religions of the Oppressed* (New York: A. F. Knopf, 1963).

[14]Pattison, "Behavioral Science," pp. 73-86.

[15]Hine, "Pentecostal Glossolalia, pp. 211-226.

[16]H. N. Malony, N. Zwaanstra, and J. W. Ramsey, "Personal and Situational Determinants of Glossolalia: A Literature Review and Report of Ongoing Research," Paper presented at the International Congress of Religious Studies, Los Angeles, September, 1972.

[17]L. P. Gerlack and V. H. Hine, "The Charismatic Revival: Processes of Recruitment, Conversion, and Behavioral Change in a Modern Religious Movement," Unpublished papers, Univ. Minnesota, 1966.

[18]H. N. Malony, N. Zwaanstra, and J.W. Ramsey, "Personal and Situational Determinants of Glossolalia."

[19]R. C. Pavelsky, A. D. Hart, and H. N. Malony, "Toward a Definition of Act and Process Glossolalia: Social, Physiological and Personality Determinants," Paper delivered at the Annual Meeting of the Society for the Scientific Study of Religion, Milwaukee, 1976.

[20]Pattison, "Behavioral Science," pp. 73-86.

[21]A. Lovekin and H. N. Malony, "Religious Glossolalia: A Longitudinal Study of Personality Changes." JSSR 16 (4, 1977): 383-393.

[22]M. E. Lombard, "Essai d'une classification des phenomenes de glossolalie," Archives de Psychologie 7 (1908): 1-51.

[23]J. P. Kildahl and P. A. Qualben, "A Study of Speaking in Tongues," Unpublished data, 1966.

[24]W. W. Wood Culture and Personality.

[25]N. L. Gerrard and L. B. Gerrard, "Scrabble Creek Folk."

[26]L. Vivier, "Glossolalia," Unpublished Ph.D. dissertation, Department of Psychiatry, University Witwatersand, 1960.

7

ORIGEN'S TREATMENT OF THE CHARISMATA
IN 1 CORINTHIANS 12:8-10

Cecil M. Robeck, Jr.

Origen was born about AD 185 most probably in Alexandria, Egypt. While he was still a young child his parents converted to Christianity, and as a consequence he was reared in a family of "ardent neophytes."[1] As a boy he showed great promise in the study of Scripture, and he was appropriately schooled in it. His father, Leonides, was martyred under the edict issued by Septimius Severus at the beginning of the third century (AD 202-3) during the same persecution which claimed the lives of Perpetua and Felicitas in Carthage.[2] Leonides' death left Origen at age seventeen with the responsibility of providing for his mother and six younger brothers. Within a year, Origen had been appointed by his bishop to head the catechetical school in Alexandria.[3]

Alexandria has been described as the "cultural capital of the Hellenistic world,"[4] boasting of at least two major libraries and a museum. As a resident and student in Alexandria, Origen would have been exposed to some of the most brilliant and versatile thinkers of the past and present. He studied not only Scripture, but also the writings of such philosophers as Plato, Aristotle, Pythagoras, and the Stoics, as well as such Christian thinkers as Clement of Alexandria, and the Gnostics Heracleon, Valentinus, and even Marcion. Perhaps because he had been reared in this type of intellectual climate, Origen was at pains to make the gospel appealing to the thinking mind. Drawing upon his philosophical studies, he made good use of them in his theological work.

Origen's teaching ministry came in two parts. From AD 203-231 he served the bishop of Alexandria as the teacher of new converts. He was ordained, however, in Caesarea about AD 231. Because the bishop of Alexandria did not concur with the decision to ordain him, Origen moved from Alexandria to Caesarea where from AD 232-253 he oversaw and taught at a Bible college. He died in AD 255 at Tyre in Phoenicia. Throughout his ministry and especially in the years at Caesarea, Origen wrote prolifically. The sermons which he preached almost daily were transcribed, and his commentaries were multitudinous.

It was from these latter years that Origen's comments on spiritual gifts most frequently appear. His remarks regarding the charismata listed in 1 Corinthians 12:8-10 appear in a variety of his works, from his early work *On First Principles* to his commentaries on various portions of Scripture, to his treatise *On Prayer* or his *Exhortation to Martyrdom*, and ultimately his apology *Against Celsus*. Yet his comments regarding many of these gifts were very much a part of his concept of the "spiritual significance" of Scripture.

At times, Origen interpreted Scripture in a literal, historical fashion. But his most significant contribution to the interpretation of Scripture was his use of the "allegorical" method by which he so often attempted to reach beneath the surface of a rigid literalism to pick out a figurative, spiritual meaning which he believed to be hidden there. He argued that the Church as a whole believed this type of exegesis to be legitimate for the Law, for "the whole law is spiritual," but he noted "the inspired [spiritual] meaning is not recognized by all (*On First Principles*, Preface, 8)."

Origen seems to have followed Clement's lead (*The Stromata* 5.4) in that he also believed that this spiritual or hidden meaning was not unrelated to the literal meaning. There was, indeed, a connection between them, and it was important to learn what the spiritual meaning was since the better educated "had need of a spiritual food to attract them to the Christian banquet table."[5]

In general, however, Origen's interpretation of these charismata appears to have been straightforward and in some cases quite literal. He taught that God's grace-gifts are given on the basis of need (*On First Principles* 2.7.3). They are distributed by the will of God. Even though one may question why specific individuals do or do not receive certain of these grace-gifts, Origen argued, God distributes them wisely (*On Prayer* 16.2). He held that spiritual gifts are bestowed through the ministry of Christ and the working of the Father " . . . in proportion to the merits of those who become capable of receiving it."[6] While God is the ultimate source of these charismata, it is the Holy Spirit in whom every manner of gift is present (*On First Principles* 2.7.3). Indeed, it is the Spirit who provides the building blocks or the raw material *(hylēs)* for these gifts which the Father activates *(energoumentēs)* and the Son superintends *(diakonoumentēs)*.[7]

These gifts are granted only to Christians, and not all Christians at that, but rather, to those who "have been deemed worthy of advancing to this degree through the sanctification of the Holy Spirit. . . ."[8] In a sense, then, Origen condoned a doctrine of a second work in which the Christian who had been sufficiently sanctified was granted through God's grace, the appropriate charismata (*Homily on Numbers* 3.1; 6.3). Regardless of the gift or gifts received, Origen enjoined his readers to remember Paul's exhortation, "Do not quench the Spirit" (1 Thess. 5:19) for the divine fire can at times be extinguished even among Christians.[9] Gifts can be lost to sin (*Homily 9 on 1 Samuel* 28), yet nothing upholds the righteous like the charismata (*Selections on Psalm* 37:17).

Origen's treatment of the charismata mentioned in 1 Corinthians 12:8-10 follows an hierarchical structure, a fact which is surely not unrelated to his concern to reach the intellectual audience of his day. While Paul seems to have listed various charismata in a fairly indiscriminate order as is evidenced by his several catalogs (Rom. 12:7-8; 1 Cor. 12:8-10, 23, 29) as well as by his random mention of various gifts, Origen understood Paul's catalog in 1 Corinthians 12:8-10 to be a list of grace-gifts from higher to lower rank. He taught that the word of wisdom took precedence over the word of knowledge, but that both of these were superior to faith.[10] But it is at this precise point that Origen's understanding of Scripture begins to impinge upon his definition of the various gifts under discussion. His definitions are themselves related to his "spiritual" understanding of the text, and they are directed toward the acceptance of an intellectual audience.

The word of wisdom and the word of knowledge were singled out as God's greatest gifts.[11] Origen came to call these the "intellectual gifts *(ta logika charismata)*"[12] which were also thought of as virtues. These gifts could be sought through prayer and those who did so prayed rightly. He regarded the task of seeking these gifts to be a continuous one, and he encouraged his readers to seek them regularly for it was in this way that they would continue to receive more insights of wisdom and knowledge (*On Prayer* 25.2).

Origen understood the word of wisdom to be somewhat intuitive or transrational *(theorēma)* in nature, in that it was divinely revealed.[13] False prophets during Origen's day claimed to have received a "word of the Lord *(Kyriou rhēma)*" or a word of wisdom *(sophia logos)*."[14] By reverse logic it would seem that such a word would have been expected from those who were genuine prophets as well. According to Origen, however, those who claimed to be prophets were not the only ones to have experienced this gift, although he seems to have limited its expression to the extraordinary people "whose ability is superior and stands out among all those who are adherents of Christianity."[15] Here it is that Origen works with what one might call the roles of nature and grace.

Celsus had charged that Christianity was composed of the uneducated, the ignorant, and the enslaved, as well as those who were not educated in Greek learning. Origen responded by noting that even the most naturally ignorant of Christians did not act like the "educated" Greeks and address lifeless objects such as idols or images made by the hands of human beings. Rather, these "ignorant" Christians had been delivered by grace from the true lack of education or ignorance which would condone such a practice. But, he went on to say that it is "the most intelligent *(phronimōtatois)* who understand and comprehend the divine hope."[16] Thus, while it appears that all Christians may be able to distinguish the falsity of human wisdom when it is compared with the truth of the divine wisdom, it is the naturally intelligent who receive the grace of the divine wisdom and are thereby able to use the gift of the word of wisdom most fully.

These gifts known as the word of wisdom and the word of knowledge are given to a few who through them, come to understand the "hidden meaning" or the "spiritual significance" of Scripture.[17] It is this "inspired" meaning of the Scriptures which have been composed by the divine Spirit, and only those "who are gifted with the grace of the Holy Spirit in the word of wisdom and knowledge" are privy to its significance. As such, these people are fit to teach the true meaning of Scripture.[18]

According to Origen, the gift of faith leads initially to salvation, thus it is widespread *(Against Celsus* 6.13). Like the words of wisdom and knowledge, faith as a gift from God is granted to supplement a person's previously existing natural faith which has been obtained through the exercise of free will. To this, the gift of faith is added, thereby raising the individual's natural faith to new heights *(Commentary on John*, Fragment 11 on 1:16). When these two faiths are united, that individual's faith is then to be considered as perfect or complete.[19] The result of this increased faith is faithfulness *(Commentary on Jeremiah* 8.5 on 10:13).

As we work our way down the list of gifts in 1 Corinthians 12:8-10, we find that Origen was not unaware of the presence of miracles and gifts of healing in his own day. Origen described these gifts as being in a lower place *(en tē katōterō)* than the gifts of the intellect,[20] attributing to Paul the listing of these gifts according to their relative value, since Paul " . . . values reason above miraculous workings. . . ."[21] Yet, these miraculous workings still had value. Of primary importance was the fact that they had in times past served as proofs of the apostolic message of the gospel.[22] While these wonders no longer appeared in the numbers or with the frequency that they had in previous years, Origen on several occasions acknowledged their continued presence among those who lived according to the will of the Logos, those who had been purified by the Logos and the actions which resulted from his teachings, namely Christians.[23]

Among these signs and wonders, these miracles and healings, were mentioned several specific types. Origen listed healing of "serious ailments *(chalepōn symprōmatōn)*, mental distraction *(ekstaseōn)* and madness *(manion)* and countless other diseases *(kai allōn myriōn)* which neither men nor demons had cured." Yet, through faith in Jesus, Origen argued, many were the Greeks and barbarians who had received the ability to do these things. They did so in simplicity, invoking the name of the supreme God, or of Jesus, together with his "history *(historias)*."[24] Precisely what this "history" was is unknown, but Chadwick has noted and I think rightfully so, that it was probably some phrase such as "crucified under Pontius Pilate,"[25] an appeal to His historical sojourn as God incarnate.

It is interesting to note that among the ailments healed are mental distraction *(ekstaseōn)* and madness *(manion)*. Origen's friendship with his former student Firmilian, bishop of Caesarea in Cappadocia would surely have ensured that Origen, like Cyprian had heard of the ecstasy of certain Montanists,[26] as well as attempts by church leaders to exorcise demons from these ecstatics.[27] The term *manion*, however, was often, although not always, associated with the Delphic oracle, demon-inspired persons, and false prophets.[28] As such, the subject of exorcism is an important one on which to touch briefly.

Origen knew of many Christians who performed exorcisms. They were not educated in the art of exorcism nor did they serve an apprenticeship to learn how one might command a demon to leave his host. In fact, Origen argued, in contrast to the intellectuals who sought the spiritual meaning of Scripture, it was generally the "uneducated people" who did this type of work.[29] They did so not with any sophisticated "magical art" or "sorcerer's device." Instead, they did so through simple prayer, employing such adjurations *(horkōsesis haplousterais)* as the uneducated might be apt to use, most probably a simple plea in the name of Jesus.[30]

One of the most interesting gifts to be mentioned in Origen's works is the gift of prophecy. Those who exercised this gift were said to be inspired by the Spirit *(On First Principles,* Preface, 4) and enabled by God's grace to prophesy *(Homily on Luke* 4). As such, those who prophesied, argued Origen, should be able to benefit first and foremost from the activity. This concern by Origen that the Holy Spirit did not violate the individual and that the place of ecstasy in genuine prophecy if any, was moderate, seems on the one hand to be aimed at the Montanists and on the other at the Pythian oracle. In the latter case, Origen noted how the Pythian priestess was led ". . . into a state of ecstasy *(ekstasin)* and frenzy *(manikēn)*" so that she lost possession of her consciousness.[31] Origen's contention was that this type of activity, prophetic though it claimed to be, was not from the Holy Spirit, but was rather, demonic in origin. Thus, the genuine prophet would possess the clearest vision at the precise moment when God was in communication with him (*Against Celsus* 7.3), a vision which would allow the prophet to declare the Spirit revealed profundities of Christian doctrine (*On First Principles* 6.17). Once again his definition was dictated by his understanding of the proper interpretation of Scripture.

Origen believed that it was in the province of all Christians to receive the gift of prophecy based upon Paul's exhortation to the Corinthians that they should seek the higher gifts.[32] His concern seems to have rotated around the value of prophecy in biblical interpretation, and its ultimate effect upon the spiritual welfare of the congregation, and he encouraged his readers to strive toward that end.

His understanding of prophecy is somewhat developed and in many cases quite literal as one searches through his notes on 1 Corinthians 12-14. Not everyone was a prophet, he wrote; those who were were exhorted to take turns exercising their gift. It was thought to be a strength if their messages were given this way, particularly in the presence of unbelievers.[33] The one who prophesied held a high position in the Church by upbuilding the Church with the gift. However, a person who spoke with tongues which was then immediately interpreted for all to hear was not to be seen as holding a lower position than the prophet.[34]

According to Origen, prophecy was a system of revelation which made known previously concealed knowledge to the person who was in the Spirit (*Homilies on Luke* 4 on 1:17). Revelation *(apokalyspsis)* was thought to occur when the mind *(ho nous)* put aside everything fleshly *(sarkikēn)*, submitted to the power of God *(dynamei theou)*, and came to know nonearthly things *(exō ginetai tōn gēinōn)*. It could include knowledge of the formation of the world, of the working of the elements, or of the times. It might also include the knowledge of things to come.[35]

If during worship a prophet should receive such a message, Origen declared that the prophet should remain silent until the proper moment. His rationale was that the spirit of the prophet was subject to the prophet, but that the souls of the prophets were those things by which true prophecy was given.[36]

While Origen argued that all were not prophets, he did indicate that every, male or female, had the potential ability to prophesy.[37] Even with this possibility, however, he believed that in the Church, it was not the role of women to prophesy.[38] He recognized the fact that God used the four virgin daughters of Philip to prophesy (Acts 21:9), that Deborah was a prophetess (Jud. 4:4), and that Miriam, the sister of Aaron the priest led the women (Ex. 15:20-21). But, he argued, while God chose to use these women, they were never allowed to speak in the tabernacle or in the temple as were Isaiah or Jeremiah. For a woman to speak in the congregation, he concluded, was dishonoring and shameful.[39]

The passage which is most fruitful with respect to Origen's understanding of the gift of prophecy in a literal sense, however, is found in his work *Against Celsus*. Celsus, a neo-platonist skeptic had claimed to have had some first-hand knowledge of prophets in the region of Phoenicia and Palestine a not insignificant fact in light of the fact that Origen resided there when he responded to Celsus' writings. Within his own work Celsus apparently incorporated a composite example of some of the types of oracles he had heard in his travels there.

Origen's skepticism of Celsus truthfulness is not to be undervalued at this point. He chided Celsus first for not specifying who prophesied, whether they be alien to Judaism or Christianity, or whether they be Jews who prophesied in a manner similar to previous prophets (*Against Celsus* 7.8). Next, he rebuked Celsus for mentioning that he had heard "several kinds *(pleiona)*" of prophecies, but he had failed to record any of them. Origen's conclusion was that Celsus failed to do so because he had had no such experience.

Yet, according to Origen's account of Celsus' work, Celsus must surely have had some knowledge of which he wrote. His concern was that there were many *(pollois)* who prophesied in Phoenicia and Palestine, although he knew none of them by name. They prophesied within temples and outside in public places. Some were itinerants who, according to Celsus, begged their way from place to place, whether it be in the city or on a military reservation. According to Celsus, they did not need much encouragement to prophesy, and when they did they "appeared" to be moved in some divine way. They pretended *(ageirantes)* to be under divine control, appearing to give genuine prophetic oracles. What they actually gave, Celsus argued, was something which they had themselves contrived to fool the unwary who heard them (*Against Celsus* 7.9).

Celsus' account of their message is interesting to say the least. He remarked that it was customary for them to say such things as:

> I am God (or a son of God, or a divine Spirit). And I have come. Already the world is being destroyed. And you, O men, are to perish because of your iniquities. But I wish to save you. And you shall see me returning again with heavenly power. Blessed is he who has worshipped me now! But I will cast everlasting fire upon all the rest, both on cities and on country places. And men who fail to realize the penalties in store for them will in vain repent and groan. But I will preserve for ever those who have been convinced by me.[40]

Several points may be noted from the description left by Celsus' record of prophetic activity. First, he began by quoting what appear to be "messenger formulas." "I am God" is one, perhaps a "first person" restatement of the familiar "Thus saith the Lord." Others were said to indicate a son of God, or to point toward a divine Spirit. Whether or not these claims were Christian cannot be established beyond doubt in the final analysis, for these forms appeared from time to time in other religions as well. However, that they were Christian seems to be the case for several reasons. First, Celsus was arguing against Christianity in his work and the inclusion of non-Christian prophetic activity would have done nothing for his case. Second, there is nothing in these statements which would disqualify them from being Christian. Indeed, as Chadwick has pointed out, these Messenger Formulas, if that is what they may be called, are followed by a "parody of perfectly good ante-Nicene Christian preaching of a rather enthusiastic type."[41] Furthermore, the fact that these messenger formulas appear in the first person does no harm either, if one assumes the passive role of the prophet who speaks for God, and such first person messenger formulas have adequate precedent within the Jewish tradition.[42]

In addition to the sayings which Celsus preserved is found the description of certain activities of these "prophets." They were said "to pretend to be moved as if giving some oracular utterance." Also, they were said to add to the oracles "incomprehensible *(agnōsta)*, incoherent *(paroitstra)*, and utterly obscure *(pantē adēla)* utterances the meaning of which no intelligent person could discover." Celsus' judgment of this fact is that these words had no meaning, but were pure nonsense, conjured up by the so-called prophet to allow the interpretation to fit the expectations of those who would be taken in by such an activity.[43]

This passage has been understood by many scholars to be a reference to the activity of speaking in tongues.[44] But in light of Origen's ensuing comments, this would not seem to be the case. Origen provided two facts which make it appear once again that the subject was really prophetic utterance. First, Origen accused Celsus of adding these statements as a footnote to dissuade his own readers from investigating Christianity or Christian prophets any further.[45] Second, and more forcefully, Origen provided a model whereby he himself spoke of a prophetic activity in which the ideas that went beyond immediate comprehension were said to be expressed in riddles, allegories, and dark sayings, in parables or proverbs *(Against Celsus* 7.10). Such sayings, he argued, had been found in his own exposition of Isaiah, Ezekiel, and the minor prophets. Furthermore, he was open to the possibility that God would eventually provide the "intelligent" with the necessary understanding (perhaps through a word of wisdom or knowledge?) in the future.[46] Such argumentation points clearly to the fact that should the prophets Celsus saw have said them, Origen was prepared to understand them in the sense of prophetic oracles.

In light of this discussion, the actual oracles recorded by Celsus and preserved by Origen point to a prophet or prophets who spoke in Celsus' day (AD 178), not like the ancient prophets (*Against Celsus* 7.11), but rather, as Christian prophets, perhaps of an ecstatic type.[47] Their message was consistent with the New Testament message, particularly that which is found in the Gospels.[48] Thus, the passage may be typified as pointing to the existence of prophets in Origen's day.

Origen argued, too, that the gift which was given to the Church to help it distinguish true from false prophecy was a charism known as the discerning of spirits. In his *Homilies on Exodus*, Origen concluded that it was by this great gift that the Church could recognize the mouth opened by the devil. Indeed, it was only by this gift of the Holy Spirit that Christians could reveal or disclose the difference between God's words and those of the devil. As Origen put it:

> That is why, among the gifts which the Spirit distributes one may find the "discernment of spirits." It is thus by a grace-gift that one discerns the Spirit, as the Apostle elsewhere wrote, "Prove (test) the spirits to see if they are of God" [1 John 4:1]. In the same way as God opens the mouth of saints, I believe that he opens also their ears to hear the divine words.[49]

The gift of tongues received treatment in several of Origen's works. Paul had remarked in 1 Corinthians 14:18 that he spoke in tongues *(glōssais lalō)* more than the Corinthian Christians he was addressing. Origen argued that this was a reference to the fact that Paul had received the gift of speaking in the languages of all nations.[50] Such a statement may show that Origen's position on the subject of speaking in tongues came as a result of interpreting 1 Corinthians "in light of Luke's account of Pentecost."[51] On the other hand it may indicate that Origen's thinking on the subject of tongues was affected by the prior background of the confusion of tongues at Babel, or by the Sinai tradition.[52] In this particular instance Origen's understanding of the gift of tongues appears to have been an example of xenolalia, defined in this case as an ability given by God through the grace of the Holy Spirit to bridge the language barrier for the purpose of cross-cultural preaching.[53] In so defining it, however, Origen seems once again to have been working with his "spiritual" interpretation of the subject, providing a definition which enabled others to communicate revealed spiritual truths cross-culturally.

Such a definition for speaking in tongues, then, carries with it the implicit understanding that the gift of interpretation of tongues involves mere translation. This idea comes clear in another of Origen's works in which he notes that tongues cease when the speaker in tongues finds someone with whom s/he is able to converse.[54] A foreign tongue remains foreign until one knows the language as one's own (cf. *Homily on Exodus* 13.2).

Yet, this understanding of tongues appears not to have been Origen's only idea of the gift. At times he discussed the topic of "praying in the Spirit" without necessarily relating it to speaking in tongues (e.g. *On First Principles* 2.8.2), but in his discussion of Romans 8:26, he linked praying in the Spirit explicitly with speaking in tongues.[55] It is impossible to know from the text whether or not tongues in this form of prayer should be understood as xenolalic in form, or whether it should be taken as true glossolalia. What is known, however, is that Origen must have held that prayer in tongues existed in his day, and it was thought to be beneficial in that it was through this type of prayer that the Spirit interceded exceedingly before God. Since Christians are greatly helped when they understand how they pray, however, and Origen balanced his statements on praying in tongues by noting that they should also pray using words which were intelligible to themselves, this type of prayer is spiritual, too, "for neither can our understanding pray unless the Spirit prays first, as it were in its hearing. . . ."[56]

On the subject of manifestations of speaking in tongues in a public meeting place, Origen seems to have followed Paul's lead closely . The one who speaks in a tongue speaks to God.[57] Those who stand by the person who speak in tongues generally do not understand what is heard.[58] Thus, an uninterpreted tongue does not edify a congregation. To insure that the congregation is edified, it is important that the utterance be interpreted.[59]

In some ways it is unfortunate that most of Origen's discussions regarding the gifts of 1 Corinthians 12:8-10 are limited to his later works when his understanding of Scripture was so interrelated with his allegorical method. Such a treatment of gifts which showed up as early as his work *On First Principles* became more rigid as time elapsed. As a result, many of his definitions for these gifts revolved around his understanding of the spiritual interpretation of Scripture.

On behalf of the intelligent, those to whom he wished primarily to address himself, Origen assured that the word of wisdom and the word of knowledge would come when the Holy Spirit saw that they merited these gifts. Those who had knowledge and wisdom could, through prayer, receive more. These enhanced gifts would then provide the divinely given insight into the spiritual meaning of the text of Scripture and its applications. Many would come to believe the gospel through a combination of the gift of faith and their own free will, and in Origen's day there was still evidence of healings and miracles which testified to the validity of the gospel proclaimed.

The prophet was thought to be the primary spokesperson who proclaimed the insights gained through the words of wisdom and knowledge, and since God gave this gift of prophecy through the mouth of the prophet He would also supply by His Spirit the gift of discerning of spirits so that the listener might hear and be able to distinguish the voice of God through the prophet from other voices.

The gift of tongues, defined as xenolalic in nature paralleled the gift of prophecy, but its primary purpose was understood as proclaiming the spiritual significance of Scripture in another human language so that others might come to faith. Those who heard the words spoken in a tongues were then interpreters of those words.

Origen's definitions for these gifts followed a sophisticated and complex understanding of Scripture and its interpretation. What appears to have been the case is that his definitions were based largely on his own allegorical or spiritual interpretation of Scripture. Origen knew of the manifestation of the spiritual gifts mentioned in 1 Corinthians 12:8-10, but much of his work involved the exposition of what he saw as the spiritual significance of these grace-gifts over against their literal presence. His apologetic was of a different order. As such, when using Origen's treatment of the charismata of 1 Corinthians 12:8-10 to build a case for the continuance of these grace-gifts into the middle of the third century Alexandria and Caesarea, it is important to remind ourselves of precisely what Origen meant when he mentioned them. That they existed in his day and that he would have defined them in a manner similar to his contemporaries need not be questioned. But, Origen's primary concern seems to have been a concern to relate all of these gifts to the proper understanding of Scripture, an understanding which encouraged him to write about them in a manner which brought "spiritual" meaning to his intellectual audience.

NOTES

[1]Eugene de Faye, *Origen and His Work* (New York: Columbia University Press, 1929), p. 23.

[2]On the evidence for this edict see W. H. C. Frend, "Open Questions Concerning the Christians and the Roman Empire in the Age of the Severi," *Journal of Theological Studies* 25 (1974): 340-343.

[3]The best brief summary on this school and its significance may be found in Jean Daniélou, *Origen*, trans. Walter Mitchell (New York: Sheed and Ward, 1955), pp. 9-13.

[4]Napthali Lewis, *Life in Egypt under Roman Rule* (Oxford: Clarendon Press, 1983), p. 25.

[5]Rene Cadiou, *Origen: His Life at Alexandria*, trans. John A. Southwell (London: B. Herder Book Co., 1944), p. 39.

[6]Origen, *On First Principles* 1.3.7. ". . . *gratia quae dignis praestatur.*" Latin text from J. P. Migne, ed. *Patrologiae Cursus Completus*, Series Graeca, Tomus 11 (Paris: Petit-montrouge, 1857), 154, denoted hereafter Migne, *PG* 11:154. English Translation of *On First Principles* used throughout is G. W. Butterworth, *Origen On First Principles* introduction by Henri de Lubac (1936, 1966;

Glouchester, MA: Peter Smith, rpt. 1973), p. 37. Cf. *On Prayer* 11.2.

[7]*Commentary on John* 2.6. Migne, *PG* 14:129.

[8]*On First Principles* 1.3.8; *Commentary on John*, Fragment 44 on 3:27.

[9]*Homily on Genesis* 15.3; *On First Principles* 2.10.7.

[10]*Commentary on John* 15:53; *Against Celsus* 3:46; 6:13. Benjamin Drewery, *Origen and the Doctrine of Grace* (London: The Epworth Press, 1960), pp. 61, 64, 197.

[11]*Commentary on Matthew* 3; Drewery, *Origin and the Doctrine of Grace*, p. 61.

[12]Origen, *Against Celsus* 3.46. Greek text from Paul Koetschau, ed. *Die Griechischen Christlichen Schriftsteller der Erste Drei Jahrhunderte* (Leipzig: J. C. Heinrichs'sche Buchhandlung, 1899) Erster Band, 243, denoted hereafter as Koetschau, 1:243. English Translation of *Against Celsus* used throughout is Henry Chadwick, *Origen: Contra Celsum* (1953, rpt. 1965; Cambridge: University Press, 1980), p. 160.

[13]Origen, *On Prayer* 25.2. Migne, *PG* 11:497. See on this word G. W. H. Lampe, ed. *A Patristic Greek Lexicon* (Oxford: The Clarendon Press, 1961), p. 647 who suggests that the word refers to a "speculation," "vision," a mystery of the faith received in a "contemplative experience" which is not accessible to the ordinary faithful.

[14]*Exhortation to Martyrdom* 8; Migne, *PG* 11:576.

[15]*Against Celsus* 6.13; Chadwick, *Origen: Contra Celsum*, p. 327.

[16]*Against Celsus* 6.14; Koetschau, 2:84; Chadwick, *Origen: Contra Celsum*, p. 327; Cf. *On First Principles*, Preface, 3.

[17]*On First Principles*, Preface 8; Butterworth, *Origen On First Principles*, p. 5; Cf. *On First Principles* 2.7.2.

[18]*Against Celsus* 1:44; *Commentary on Matthew* 15.37; 16.13. These gifts appear to be ones by which the exposition of the spiritual meaning of Scripture is made known. Cf. *Homily on Joshua* 8.1.

[19]*Commentary on Romans* 4.5; *Homily on Luke* 39.

[20]*Against Celsus* 3.46; Koetschau, 1:242.

[21]*Against Celsus* 3.46; Chadwick, *Origen: Contra Celsum*, p. 160.

[22]*Against Celsus* 1.2; Cf. 2 Cor. 12:12; Heb. 2:3-4.

[23]*Against Celsus* 1.2; Cf. 1.46; 2.8; 7.8.

[24]*Against Celsus* 3.24; Chadwick, *Origen: Contra Celsum*, p. 142; Koetschau, 1:220.

[25]Chadwick, *Origen: Contra Celsum*, p. 10, n. 1. Cf. Justin Martyr, *Apology* 2.6; *Dialog with Trypho* 30 and 76; Irenaeus, *Against Heresies* 2.32.4.

[26]Firmilian, in AD 256 addressed an epistle to Cyprian in which he mentioned a woman who "in a state of ecstasy announced herself as a prophetess and acted

as if filled with the Holy Spirit." *Epistle* 75 (74). The woman was said, however, to be demon possessed, and the incident was said to date from AD 234.

[27]Eusebius, *Ecclesiastical History* 5.16.8, 17; 5.18.13; 5.18.3.

[28]Plutarch, *The Obsolescence of Oracles* 435 A-E (46); 438 A (51); Cf. LXX Jer. 14:14; Ezek. 13:7-8; Plutarch *Moralia* 758 E; Plato *Timaeus* 71 E, 72 A-B; Acts 16:17-18; Hermas, *Mandate* 11.2, 4.

[29]*Against Celsus* 7.4; Chadwick, *Origen: Contra Celsum*, p. 398.

[30]Justin Martyr, *Apology* 2.6; Irenaeus, *Against Heresies* 2.32.4-5; Tertullian, *The Scorpion* 1.3; Mark 16:17; Acts 16.18.

[31]*Against Celsus* 7.3; Koetschau, 2:155; Cf. Plutarch, *The Obsolescence of Oracles* 438 A-B (51).

[32]1 Corinthians 12:31; 14:1; *Homily on Exodus* 4.5.

[33]Claude Jenkins, "Documents: Origen on 1 Corinthians," *Journal of Theological Studies* 10 (1909): 32; Fragment 48 on 1 Corinthians 12:8-10 and 27-28, denoted hereafter Jenkins, 32, Fragment 48.

[34]Jenkins, 36, Fragment 54.

[35]Jenkins, 36, Fragment 55; trans. mine.

[36]Jenkins, 40, Fragment 70.

[37]Jenkins, 41, Fragment 73.

[38]Jenkins, 41, Fragment 74.

[39]Jenkins, 42, Fragment 74.

[40]*Against Celsus* 7.9; Chadwick, *Origen: Contra Celsum*, p. 402; *"egō ho theos eimi ē theou pais ē pneuma theion. hēkō de; ēdē gar ho kosmos apollytai, kai hymeis, hōi anthrōpoi, dia tas adikias oichesthe. egō de sōsei thelō; kai opsesthe me authis met' ouraniou dynameōs epanionta makarios ho nyn me thēskeusas, tois d' allois hapasi pyr aiōnion epibalō kai polesi kai chōrais. kai anthrōpoi, hoi mē tas heauton poinas isasi, metagnōsontai matēn kai stenaxousi; tous de moi peisthentas aiōnious phylaxō."* Koetschau, 2:161. See on this passage my article, "Origen, Celsus, and Prophetic Utterance," *Paraclete* 11:1 (Winter, 1977), 19-23.

[41]Chadwick, *Origen: Contra Celsum*, p. 403, n. 6.

[42]The first person appears in many Old Testament prophecies, e.g. Isa. 45:5-16, 18; 46:8-9; 48:17, etc., and in a messenger formula in Jer. 32:27.

[43]*Against Celsus* 7.9; Chadwick, *Origen: Contra Celsum*, pp. 402-403; Koetschau, 2:161.

[44]R. Leonard Carroll, "Glossolalia: Apostles to the Reformation," in Wade H. Horton, ed. *The Glossolalia Phenomenon* (Cleveland, TN: Pathway Press, 1966), p. 83; Stuart D. Currie, "Speaking in Tongues: Early Evidence Outside the New Testament Bearing on 'Glossais Lalein'," *Interpretation* 19 (1965):

292-293; George B. Cutten, *Speaking with Tongues: Historically and Psychologically Considered* (New Haven: Yale University Press, 1927), p. 36; George W. Dollar, "Church History and the Tongues Movement," *Bibliotheca Sacra* 120 (1963): 317; Robert G. Gromacki, *The Modern Tongues Movement* (1967; Grand Rapids: Baker Book House, rev. 1972), p. 15; E. Glenn Hinson, "A Brief History of Glossolalia," in Frank Stagg, E. Glenn Hinson, Wayne E. Oates, *Glossolalia: Tongues Speaking in Biblical, Historical, and Psychological Perspectives* (Nashville: Abingdon Press, 1967), p. 50-51; Harold Hunter, "Tongues-Speech: A Patristic Analysis," *Journal of the Evangelical Theological Society* 23 (1980), p. 128; Cleon L. Rogers, Jr., "The Gift of Tongues in the Post-Apostolic Church (AD 100-400)," *Bibliotheca Sacra* 122 (1965): 141-142; Hugh Wamble, "Glossolalia in Christian History," in Luther B. Dyer, ed. *Tongues* (Jefferson City, MO: Le Roi Publishers, 1971), pp. 29-30; George H. Williams and Edith Waldwogel, "A History of Speaking in Tongues and Related Gifts," in Michael P. Hamilton, ed. *The Charismatic Movement* (Grand Rapids: William B. Eerdmans Publishing Company, 1975), p. 67. Jimmy Jividen, *Glossolalia: From God or Man?* (Fort Worth: Star Bible Publications, 1971), p. 64 understands this passage to refer to speaking in tongues which is found in "contemporary religions of his [Celsus'] day." Cf. Ted A. Campbell, "Charismata in the Christian Community of the Second Century," *Wesleyan Theological Journal* 17:2 (1982): p. 8.

[45]Origen's response in *Against Celsus* 7.10 that "I think [Celsus] did this out of deliberate wickedness because he wanted to do all in his power to prevent readers of the prophecies from examining and studying their meaning" seems to point to the fact that Origen himself was convinced that these charges were a mere diversion employed by Celsus.

[46]*Against Celsus* 7.11; Cf. Num. 12:6-8; Hos. 12; 10; Ezek. 20:49.

[47]So Morton Kelsey, *Tongue Speaking* (1964; Garden City: Doubleday, 1968) Waymark Edition, p. 39; Chadwick, *Origen: Contra Celsum*, p. 403, n. 6.

[48]Matt. 1:18-25; 25:31; Luke 4:18-21; 12:49; 17:29-30; Mark 15:37; 16:6; John 3:16-19; 10:27-28; 14:3; and Acts 2:32-36.

[49]*Homily on Exodus* 3.2, P Fortier, trad., *Origène: Homélies sur L'Exode* (SC 16; Paris: Éditions du Cerf, 1947), 105, Translation mine. Cf. *Homily on Luke* 1.1.

[50]*Commentary on Romans* 1.13; Migne, *PG* 14:860; "*Arbitror diversis quidem gentibus inde eum effectum esse debitorem, quod omnium gentium linguis eloqui accepit per gratiam Spiritus sancti, sicut et ipse dicit: Omnium vestrum magis linguis loquor. Quia ergo linguarum notitiam non pro se quis, sed pro bis quibus praedicandum est accipit, debitor omnibus illis efficitur quorum accepit a Deo linguae notitiam.*"

[51]Francis A. Sullivan, S.J. " 'Speaking in Tongues' in the New Testament and in the Modern Charismatic Renewal," in Edward Malatesta, S.J. ed., *The Spirit of God in Christian Life* (New York: Paulist Press, 1977), p. 24.

[52]On Babel as a possible background to Pentecost see J. G. Davies, "Pentecost and Glossolalia," *Journal of Theological Studies* 3 (1952): 228-231, and on the possible background of the Sinai tradition see Stephen G. Wilson, *The Gentiles and the Gentile Mission in Luke-Acts* (SNTSMS 23; Cambridge: Cambridge University Press, 1973), p. 126 and James D. G. Dunn, *Baptism in the Holy Spirit* (Philadelphia: The Westminster Press, 1970), pp. 48-49.

[53]A textual variant on Origen's *Commentary on Romans* 7.6 Migne, *PG* 11:1120, n. 42 reveals the thought of "human languages (*linguis hominum loquar*)."

[54]Jenkins, 35, Fragment 52; *"glōssai pausontai hote nō homilēsō hō boulomai dialechthēnai."*

[55]A. Ramsbothan, "Documents: The Commentary on the Epistle of the Romans, III," *Journal of Theological Studies* 14 (1912): p. ix, Fragment 48; Cf. also *On Prayer* 2.4.

[56]*On Prayer* 2.4; Eric George Jay, *Origen's Treatise On Prayer* (London: SPCK, 1954), p. 86.

[57]Jenkins, 37, Fragment 57.

[58]Jenkins, 37, Fragment 59.

[59]Jenkins, 38, Fragment 61.

8

THE CHRISTIAN CATHOLIC APOSTOLIC CHURCH AND THE APOSTOLIC FAITH: A STUDY IN THE 1906 PENTECOSTAL REVIVAL

Edith L. Blumhofer

With Apostolic Authority I declare that the Church must not only be Christian and Catholic, but Apostolic; for some power must exist that can represent God on this earth in such a form that you can say "that man speaks with Divine Authority. (John Alexander Dowie, 1904)

We stand for the restoration of the faith once delivered to the saints . . . Glory to God for this Apostolic day! (Charles Parham, 1906)

In the fall of 1906, two restorationist teachings converged briefly in Zion City, Illinois. The two subsequently fragmented but their brief union resulted in the emergence of a third creative force that would survive as one of the formative influences in American Pentecostalism. The first centered in the ministry of Zion City's founder, John Alexander Dowie; the other focused on the evangelism of Pentecostal leader Charles Fox Parham. Though their views and methods differed considerably, both professed the "apostolic" faith. From a context shaped by their emphases would come important leadership for a movement that borrowed from each while disassociating itself from both. The significance of Charles Parham's apostolic message for the Christian Catholic Apostolic Church can best be assessed in the context of an examination of the ministry and objectives of Zion City's founder.

In the first years of the twentieth century, Dowie was an acknowledged authority figure for thousands of Americans. A reporter's claim that "no man of our time has ever secured anything like the personal following he has'' seemed well substantiated. Some 6,500 acres of farms, homes and businesses that constituted Zion City were legally his. Community life in the city on Lake Michigan was regulated by laws incorporating the distinctive ideals of Dowie's own ecclesiastical creation, the Christian Catholic Apostolic Church. Land was leased for 1,100 years to some 6,000 city residents who were required to be "born again" Christians, and Zion was a place where "breweries or saloons, gambling halls, houses of ill fame, drug or tobacco shops, hospitals or doctor's offices, theaters or dance halls, and secret lodges or apostate churches" were conspicuous by their absence. Also forbidden inside city limits was "hog raising, selling or handling."[1] The city was conceived as the headquarters of an international ecclesiastical organization which embraced at least 25,000 adherents before Dowie's death in 1907. Many factors combined to determine the dimensions of Dowie's ministry. This paper will focus on elements in the religious message which contributed to a milieu in which significant numbers of his followers would respond affirmatively to Pentecostalism.

I

John Alexander Dowie was born in Edinburgh in 1847. He emigrated to Australia as an adolescent, returning to the University of Edinburgh for theological training. In 1872 he again migrated to Australia to serve as a Congregational minister.

When a devastating plague struck eastern Australia in 1876, the focus of Dowie's ministry shifted from evangelism to healing.[2] After conducting some forty funerals in two weeks, Dowie, dissatisfied with his inability to offer his suffering parishioners healing, reflected on New Testament healing accounts and came to focus on Acts 10:38: "Jesus went about doing good, healing all that were oppressed of the devil; for God was with him." This thought, combined with Hebrews 13:8—"Jesus Christ the same, yesterday and today, and forever"— launched Dowie's healing ministry. He claimed that the application of this doctrine in prayer for the sick in 1876 ended the plague in his congregation. Some six years later, he committed the remainder of his life to healing evangelism.

The years immediately following 1876 were years of personal and vocational crises. Dowie withdrew from the Australian Congregational Union in 1878, charging that it was "terribly overladen with worldliness and apathy," and in 1883, he established an independent tabernacle in Melbourne.[3] His outspoken opposition to the medical profession and his public prayer for the sick assured him of publicity, as did his sustained vitriolic attack on the city's liquor interests. Publicity swelled the ranks of his followers. An able speaker and a stubborn, controversial campaigner for many causes, he claimed to have preached to as many as twenty thousand at one meeting and credited his growing prominence to miracles of healing to which many publicly testified.[4]

With regard to healing, Dowie maintained quite simply: "SIN is a cause, of which DISEASE, DEATH and HELL are the inevitable effects and consequences . . . HOLINESS is a cause, of which HEALTH, ETERNAL LIFE and HEAVEN are the glorious effects and consequences."[5] Dowie enumerated four modes of healing: 1) the direct "prayer of faith"; 2) the intercessory prayer of several; 3) anointing with oil by elders, with the "prayer of faith"; and 4) the "laying on of hands of those who believe, and whom God has prepared and called to that ministry."[6]

Although Dowie made virtually no reference to other teachers of healing, he was not unaware of contemporary ministries of healing in both Europe and the United States. He stood squarely in the tradition of those of his contemporaries who insisted that disease was real and that healing could be effected only through an act of divine intervention in human need. By the mid-1880s Dowie had begun to make an association between holiness and healing similar to that which characterized the teaching of William E. Boardman, Albert B. Simpson and Adoniram J. Gordon in Britain and America.[7]

Outspoken, ambitious, and unpredictable, Dowie throughout his life demonstrated a propensity for "moving on." Accordingly, he left Australia to establish ministry in the United States, arriving with his family in San Francisco in 1888. Evidence suggests that he had a considerable following in California and extended his American reputation through an itinerant ministry in "healing missions."[9] The 1893 World's Fair in Chicago beckoned him to the Midwest and the fulfillment of a dream to establish his headquarters in middle America. Dowie selected as the site for his ministry a wooden tabernacle located near the entrance to the fair, across the street from the camp of Buffalo Bill Cody. A reporter described that summer's ministry:

> Hundreds of thousands must have crowded into the "Little Wooden Hut" during the months of the World's Fair. Sometimes more than a thousand persons came in a week to have his hands laid on them . . . Pilgrims came on crutches and went away whole. Paralytics were borne in on litters, and literally "took up their beds and walked."

Despite widespread response during the fair, the months following proved difficult as scarcely twenty followers comprised Dowie's regular audience. In the spring of 1894, however, the ministry began to flourish, and Dowie moved his operation to downtown Chicago. His simultaneous decision to convert his own residence into "Divine Healing Home Number One" precipitated a chain of events which catapulted Dowie into prominence in the divine healing movement in the United States.

The concept behind healing homes was shared by other teachers of healing.[10] It involved opening a residence in which those who came for healing could find both reasonably priced room and board and the Bible instruction which was considered requisite to faith for healing. The Chicago Commissioner of Health regarded the matter differently, however, and in 1895 the Board of Health passed a "Hospital Ordinance" requiring that any dwelling used for reception of the sick be attended by a licensed physician. Dowie refused to comply: on principle he rejected all association with doctors and all use of medical remedies. In 1895, he had several healing homes which, he insisted were not hospitals: "No medicine is used. No 'treatment' is given . . . Divine healing has no association with doctors and drugs, or surgeons and their knives."[11] The controversy became so intense that Dowie claimed to have been arrested nearly 100 times in 1895 and to have expended twenty thousand dollars of his own money in his defense.[12] In the end, charges were dropped and the "Hospital Ordinance" was declared invalid. The publicity surrounding the events had generated widespread interest in Dowie, and converts flocked to the movement. The short, stocky, bearded Australian had become a public figure.[13]

In the midst of this controversy, Dowie began to institutionalize his growing restorationist vision: he created the Christian Catholic Church, housed in a tabernacle in Chicago, and organized an extensive network of related institutions including a publishing house, a college and an orphanage. Affiliated churches grew, especially in Illinois, Indiana, and Ohio: the proliferation of the movement was described by the *Outlook* as an "epidemic of credulity."[14]

The Christian Catholic Church was the logical result of Dowie's teaching and temperament. Personally unsuited to work under established authority or in fraternal fellowship with those who differed from him, Dowie also became increasingly critical of others who shared his interest in healing. As he contemplated the American religious setting—challeneged as it was in the late nineteenth century by new intellectual currents and unprecedented social change— Dowie opted for the restorationist approach of uniting believers in a movement he conceived as simply Christian, patterned on his understanding of the primitive church. Affirming the "historylessness" characteristic of restorationists, Dowie declared: "There can never be a new church unless it be a false church . . . We need the old-time Christianity of the first century."[15] By 1895, Dowie's conception of New Testament Christianity had come to incorporate not only distinctive conceptions of polity but also strong affirmations of the centrality of the charismatic component in the apostolic church. At the founding of his church, he stated his purpose to make provision in church order for all the offices and gifts listed in 1 Corinthians 12 and 14.[16] The use of these spiritual gifts he considered dependent on the divine calling of an apostle within the group. When one of his followers suggested that Dowie might, in fact, have an apostolic calling, Dowie demurred:

> I do not think that I have reached a deep enough depth of true humility . . . for the high office of an apostle. . . . The Apostolic Office means a high position truly, but the power of one that can take the lowest place.[17]

It was only a matter of time before Dowie's self-deprecation would yield to a sense of destiny.

Dowie's successes stimulated his immediate pursuit of a broader vision: the creation of a theocratic community. The essential components of his world view would be incorporated into life in a Christian city: restored apostolic polity, theocracy, political progressivism (shorn of its emphasis on direct democracy), millenarianism. Dowie's city, Zion, would be the first of many Zions actively preparing the world for Christ's return. The envisioned whole was undergirded by the central commitment to the practice of divine healing. This in turn, would become increasingly tied to the theme of restoration of spiritual gifts in the last days. Dowie anonymously purchased 6,500 acres of rolling farm land forty miles north of Chicago and, with a flair for the dramatic, unveiled his specific plans drawn on a twenty-five square foot canvas at the stroke of midnight to an audience that filled his Chicago Tabernacle for the watch night service, 31 December 1899. Dowie envisioned the city as a closed community in which all industries, schools, stores, hotels and the bank would be under church control. From 1900, realizing this goal claimed an ever increasing share of Dowie's attention.[18]

II

The essential message around which Dowie organized his community and broader ministries identify him closely with those American evangelicals in his day whose millenarian faith molded their religious perspective. His focus on the person and work of the Holy Spirit and on the restoration of a fuller ministry of the Spirit in the last days was widely shared by many from whom he ultimately disassociated himself.

In the late nineteenth century as part of a quest for the "fullness" of salvation, various evangelicals of different denominations, informed by their biblical literalism accepted baptism by immersion, experimented in "faith" living and taught divine healing as "in the atonement." In addition their millenarian persuasion determined their focus on the Holy Spirit and their urgency in evangelism. Among the evangelical leaders identified with such emphases were Reuben A. Torrey, Arthur T. Pierson and Adoniram J. Gordon all of whom had ministries with interdenominational appeal conducted through the Bible conferences and institutes that provided millenarians of the period with their social structure.[19]

In Dowie's Zion these themes remained central but were incorporated into an increasingly radical restorationist framework rather than developed through a millenarian perspective. Earlier in the century, Alexander Campbell's efforts to restore New Testament patterns had resulted in decentralization: Dowie's movement was in sharp contrast as his restorationism became increasingly exclusivist and authoritarian.

"Zion stands for salvation, holiness and healing" would be the oft-repeated claim of the faithful. (After 1900, the term "Zion" would be used to designate both specific communities and all members of Dowie's general organization.) Dowie stressed the basic sinfulness of humanity and the need for repentance and justification by faith. He further insisted that the initial conversion experience be followed by active pursuit of holiness. Obedience to the Bible was taught as requisite to healing: this included repentance, restitution, baptism—the "reordering" of the life. Dowie refused to pray for the healing of the unregenerate or unholy.[20]

As an essential expression of faith in God for healing, Dowie demanded that those who requested prayer relinquish all reliance on medicines and physicians. The depth of commitment he elicited was mirrored in the practice of Zion City which allowed no doctors, nurses, veterinarians or medicines in the city limits. It brought Dowie himself in May 1902 to the deathbed of his only daughter, the victim of severe burns, to offer fervent prayers but allow no medical aid. Evidence suggests that people in Zion "put their lives squarely behind their beliefs."[21] Across the front of his large tabernacles in Chicago and Zion City, Dowie had the words "Christ is All and in All" framed by "crutches, canes, trusses, bandages and braces" left by those who had been healed.[22]

Disagreements over the relationship between faith and medical "means" separated Dowie from some other advocates of divine healing, most of whom refused to condemn arbitrarily the use of remedies by those who lacked sufficient faith for healing, although they did affirm that medicines were "limited" and "uncertain," working naturally what God would rather perform supernaturally. Dowie seemed to thrive on controversy, and publicly denounced all those who differed with him, condemning all use of medicine and all teachers of healing who "compromised" on the issue of "means." "God has but one way of Healing," he insisted. "The Devil has a hundred so-called ways. Zion cannot go to medicine for healing. There is no fellowship between the blood of Christ and medicine."[23] In the Chicago area his railings against D. L. Moody and Moody's associates elicited from the popular revivalist the private observation:

"If Dowie is a man of God, then I am a fraud and do not know God."[24]

The demands of separation and commitment which he made on his followers were rooted in Dowie's conviction of his responsibility to reconstitute the apostolic church. He unquestionably influenced thousands of his followers (or reaffirmed their predilections) toward a literal biblical faith; related to this was his teaching that spiritual gifts were to be expected in the context of the true restored New Testament church of the last days. These themes, both of which were prominent throughout the most promising decade of his ministry from 1895 to 1905, attracted those of many denominational backgrounds to Zion where they frequently responded positively to the challenge to faith and the opportunity to live in "the strong moral environment" of a Christian city—a place, Dowie asserted, that was in covenant with God, for "Salvation, Healing and Holy Living."[25]

As his movement grew and his millenarian vision seemed to materialize in Zion City, Dowie began to stress the fact that the actual restoration of spiritual gifts and apostolic offices would immediately precede the imminent Second Advent. On 2 June 1901 in Chicago, he declared before his church his assumption of the role of Elijah. According to Dowie, Elijah had come in Old Testament times as a destroyer; in his second manifestation in John the Baptist he had been a preparer; in the third and final appearance he would be as restorer, and this Dowie claimed to be. "I take my commission from God," he asserted. "I stand here and tell you that you must obey God or perish."[26]

Religious leaders denounced this declaration, and Dowie's most sympathetic biographer dates from it a sustained decline in the church growth rate, but most members of Zion apparently accepted it and continued to respond enthusiastically to their leader's plans in Zion City.[27] His concern in his Elijah Declaration was initially for the contemporary realization of the prophetic office. It became, however, a step toward the announcement in 1904 that he was a God-ordained apostle.

The claim was publicly articulated on a cloudy, cool September Sunday afternoon before an audience of 7,200 at Shiloh Tabernacle, Zion City. Wearing the robes of the Old Testament high priestly office, Dowie addressed the "church throughout the world," proclaiming God's restoration through him of the apostolic office.[28]

In the New Testament church, he asserted, disharmony among the apostles had precluded the development of the full potential of apostolic authority. He declared it his purpose to pursue biblical "foundation principles" for the apostolic church, his goal being a church "restored and established in a manner which was beyond the power of the early Christians."[29]

The sign of an apostle, Dowie maintained, would be "his being possessed of the Holy Ghost to such a degree'' that the Corinthian Gifts characterized his ministry.[30] (Dowie in 1904 claimed to possess four of the gifts.) The gifts were primarily ''gifts for service,'' and Dowie considered that once one had been divinely chosen an apostle—having, as requisite, demonstrated at least one gift—all the gifts could be expected eventually to mark his ministry. His understanding of the granting of gifts to individuals within the church was less clearly formulated. He suggests that one and another (those in the church who were ''humble enough, and pure enough, and wise enough, and unselfish enough'') might possess one or more gifts without expectation of receiving them all.[31] That they were gifts, over the distribution of which one had absolutely no prerogative, he stressed: on the other hand, he suggested that an apostle could emerge only over time because ''that which is divine requires time to grow.''[32] He affirmed an orderliness and progression in the bestowal of the gifts both to an apostle and in the church.[33]

As Dowie formulated his outline for apostolic gifts and ministries for the contemporary church, his approach became increasingly less systematic until he concluded his public teaching on the subject without direct reference to the last three gifts (discerning of spirits, tongues, interpretation of tongues). His specific interpretations of passages relating to the functioning of the gifts in church life are less important, however, than the fact that he both repeatedly urged his followers to anticipate the restoration of the gifts and explained his own ministry of healing in terms of the operation of the gifts of healing. This central assertion helped set him apart from contemporary teachers of divine healing, and the context in which he presented it—a community of some six thousand and a broad following of some twenty thousand more, many of whom believed that they ''owed either their lives or their health'' to Dowie's use of the gifts—seemed to lend the message special validity. He focused attention on the subject, assumed a relationship (to which many of his contemporaries also alluded) between spiritual gifts and the last days, and challenged others to a response of specific faith.

This teaching, formulated with an apostolic claim, naturally elicited critical response and increased the gulf between Dowie and other Christian leaders. That Dowie's followers apparently accepted it probably indicates their perception of a relationship to themes that had dominated his teaching for at least a decade: literalist faith in an unchanging and soon-returning Christ Who demanded holiness as well as obedience and Who provided ''full'' salvation for spirit, soul and body. The gifts would exalt Christ—would demonstrate more fully through the Holy Spirit Christ's latter-day activity in and among His people. The three most prominent themes in Zion related closely to emphases characteristic in other groups that would soon provide leadership to the emerging Pentecostal movement:

restoration, millenarianism, biblical literalism. In Dowie's case, there was the additional claim of the manifestation of specific spiritual gifts in his restored apostolic context in Zion.

III

Although the emphasis on the "apostolic faith" became central to Dowie's religious conceptions, another level of his activities came to dominate public perception of his ministry. Confrontations with other religious figures became increasingly typical as his consistent concern for exposing "error" became an overwhelming drive by 1903. Affirming that he alone championed the biblical faith, Dowie vehemently denounced the denominations and their leaders. An illustration of the level of visibility to which he aspired was a huge nationally reported crusade in New York City's Madison Square Garden for which eight full trains were hired to transport three thousand of his members to New York. His "restoration host" systematically canvassed the city, leaving literature at each residence.[35] A world tour in 1904 brought further notoriety, as mob action and rioting in Australia and Dowie's outspoken criticism of King Edward VII seriously curtailed his public ministry in the British Empire.[36]

Such stimulating tours and controversies were costly, however, and it became increasingly apparent that something was seriously wrong with their supporting financial structure. In Zion City unemployment increased, payrolls could not be met, and additional credit was denied the city. At a critical time in 1905, Dowie determined to pursue his dream of creating another Zion community in Mexico. He planned to leave Zion City to negotiate a land purchase that his economic counselors considered ill-advised. As he concluded a five-hour farewell service on Sunday, September 24, Dowie suffered a stroke. Although initially he was only slightly incapacitated, Dowie would never again direct his people with the same authority and optimism.[37]

In spite of growing weaknesses, Dowie traveled that fall and winter to both Mexico and Jamaica, and those left in control in Zion City were forced to deal with economic dissatisfaction that was complicated by Dowie's continued demands for money on the one hand and by the persistent claims of creditors on the other. In Dowie's absence, cautious changes were made: the new leaders encouraged both limited private ownership and the seeking of employment outside of Zion City. Overseer Wilbur Voliva came at Dowie's invitation from Zion's Australian branch to direct the headquarters operations during Dowie's absence. Voliva inspired confidence in a context beset by major social and economic unrest and in April 1906 he led the move which suspended Dowie's leadership of the church. The reasons given Dowie for his removal from authority included financial mismanagement and questionable moral teachings. The latter referred to rumors that Dowie had quietly begun to advocate polygamy.[38]

Given the structure of Zion, removing Dowie from one office necessitated removing him from all. Though there is no proof that Dowie had wilfully attempted to defraud, the majority of Zion citizens had lost considerable money or endured hardships through the mishandling of funds. Most initially supported the new leadership in a reform program. A small minority of less than three hundred remained loyal to Dowie: his immediate family was among those who ultimately rejected him. The economic implications of loyalty to Dowie and the real fear of losing homes or jobs as a consequence further complicated the situation.[39]

In the church, the apostolic dimension was deemphasized, and Dowie was formally removed from his prophetic offices. However, even as Voliva gained firm control of administrative affairs, Dowie's former critics at the *Chicago Tribune* noted a subtle change that they considered boded ill for the future: the new General Overseer seemed to "lack an important ingredient essential to his position—a check upon bitterness, a saving element of mercy and kindness."[40] The former rapport between leader and people was notably absent.

By late spring 1906, the utopia was rapidly disintegrating. Dowie returned and became locked in a court battle with Voliva over ownership of the city. The Lake County Circuit Court sustained Voliva's contention that Dowie did not in fact own Zion but rather held it as a trust estate. The court then appointed a receiver for the city until its financial problems could be resolved and leadership for the church could be determined by democratic methods.[41] Every phase of city life, including the use of the public buildings, came under the control of the receiver. Schisms beset Zion. Elections in September 1906 officially confirmed Voliva's leadership. Although his followers included a majority of the Zion population, the degree of unanimity that had characterized Zion's earliest history would never again be achieved. Still, for most, the important element was Zion's teaching. Dowie might have been discredited but the practical effectiveness of his message remained visible for them in the crutches, tobacco pouches, casts and orthopedic shoes that covered the front wall of the tabernacle.

IV

One evidence that the resolution of legal problems had not restored harmony was the support that the disaffected gave several new "prophets"; Jehovah's Witnesses and Mormons reportedly made some converts as well. Into this situation, about the time of the court-mandated city election, a nucleus of residents who had heard of the Azusa Street revival invited Charles Parham.[42]

The Pentecostal message had, in fact, come to Zion earlier. One of those who had received the baptism with the Holy Spirit under Parham's ministry in Kansas in 1903 had moved to Zion City in 1904 and had opened her home for prayer meetings. When reports circulated in the city that a woman had spoken in tongues in one of these gatherings, Zion leadership had forbidden further meetings and had exerted economic pressure which had resulted in the family's moving away from the city.[43] Parham himself had visited Zion in Chicago just before founding his Bible school in Topeka in October 1900. Intrigued by the restorationist theme in Dowie's ministry and impressed by the emphasis on the Holy Spirit, holiness, and healing, Parham had nonetheless concluded that Dowie did not have the potential fulness of the Holy Spirit.[44]

Emphases in Dowie's ministry had clearly contributed much to the shaping of a context in which Parham's Pentecostal message could find support. Reports of the Welsh revival had also stimulated desire among some of Dowie's followers for similar renewal.[45] The economic and social as well as the spiritual unrest that had beset the city since 1905 resulted in the opportunity to extend a welcome to Parham; such an invitation could not have been issued a year earlier.

Local newspapers described Parham as one with "a pleasant and convincing manner that makes his discourse almost irresistible."[46] The rapid growth of his appeal seemed to attest this: the meetings, at first conducted in the city's large hotel, overflowed from two rooms into the hotel hallway and soon three daily meetings were scheduled to meet the increasing demand. By the end of the week, several hundred residents were sitting regularly under Parham's ministry, and Overseer Voliva had lamented that Parham was "winning some of our most faithful people."[47] Voliva succeeded in forcing Parham's ministry out of the hotel and in blocking Parham's efforts to rent schools and the tabernacle. Parham responded by holding meetings in five private homes, and audiences reportedly spilled out to the porches and lawns. Concurrent nightly meetings were conducted from 7 P.M. until midnight, with Parham traveling from one to the other, preaching and exhorting.[48]

Parham's message had much in common with Dowie's. Newspaper ads described his message as "Old-time Religion, Christ's Soon Coming, Repentance, Salvation, Healing, Sanctification, Baptism of the Holy Ghost."[49] He demanded two departures from Zion teaching: first, that the individual pursue a discrete experience of sanctification, which Parham considered a requisite for Spirit baptism; second, that reception of the Holy Spirit in Spirit baptism be evidenced by speaking in tongues. Parham taught that those "tongues" would be recognizable human languages of which the speakers had no previous knowledge. Dowie's emphasis on holiness and holy living made the first departure seem acceptable, especially when it was expressed in terms of entire consecration, (which Parham understood as integral to the experience) a theme which Dowie had addressed frequently.[50] The teaching about tongues, though new, was presented as both biblical and apostolic in a context where both of those characterizations were of primary concern. In addition, Parham maintained that he stressed the Holy Spirit rather than tongues. His claim that tongues simply demonstrated the *Spirit's* infilling made the glossolalic distinctive more acceptable in Zion. It is noteworthy that several of those who converted to Pentecostalism as a result of Parham's Zion City efforts would later reject the "uniform" aspect of the designation of tongues as "uniform initial evidence" of Spirit baptism while continuing to regard themselves and their ministries as pentecostal.[51] (These would affirm, rather, that all the gifts were manifestations of the Spirit and that any of them indicated the Spirit's endowment.)

After several weeks of meetings, individuals began to receive Spirit baptism, and observers sought to account for Parham's considerable following. A. F. Lee, general ecclesiastical secretary of the Christian Apostolic Catholic Church, resigned his position to identify with Parham. Hubert Grant, Dowie's personal secretary, joined the Pentecostals. F. F. Bosworth, prominent in the community as the conductor of the award-winning Zion City Band, welcomed Parham into his home. "The people in Zion are not in need of temporal power," the *Waukegan Gazette* theorized. "They are starving for want of a spiritual leader. All good church members, they deserted everything to come to Zion City." In Parham they apparently saw one to whom they could "entrust their interests," and thus "converts are flocking to his ranks daily, deserting the fold of the unspiritual Voliva."[52]

By 18 October, twenty-five had received Spirit baptism claiming, as evidence, to have spoken in German, French, Italian, Russian, Spanish, Norwegian and Chinese. One journalist recommended that high school students of foreign languages "get the Pentecostal Spirit and take advanced standing."[53]

Late in October, Parham traveled from Zion to Los Angeles, leaving behind several hundred followers, some fifty of whom had spoken in tongues.[54] Parham considered Pentecostalism "thoroughly established" in Zion. The response had been such that Parham had begun to consider the city his headquarters: he had moved the publication of his paper, the *Apostolic Faith*, to Zion, and he would soon move his family there. Parham's rejection at Azusa Street during this trip and his sharp criticism of the revival there undoubtedly contributed to the decision to resign as "Projector of the Apostolic Faith Movement" that he announced in Zion City in 1907.[55] Persistent press reports claimed that he aspired to replace Voliva and direct the affairs of Zion.

During Parham's absence, the revival continued to attract adherents.[56] Voliva instructed an audience at Zion College to "choose either me or this intruder who has stolen into our church" and deprived Parham's followers of membership in the Christian Catholic Church. Such deprivations had economic as well as social consequences: jobs were lost, families divided and Zion residents forbidden to socialize with those who accepted Pentecostalism. Anti-Pentecostal billboards posted throughout the city suggested that "these buzzards and buzzers" had no right "to come into our midst and try to supplant the principles of our community life."[57]

Parham reported that Dowie had criticized his "utterances and actions in Zion," but there is no direct indication of Dowie's attitude.[58] It may be inferred from his response to Pentecostalism in 1904. A later concensus among his supporters was that Dowie was most probably persuaded that, had the movement truly been "of God," it would have come through his church.[59]

Daily meetings continued for several months and the attendant disruptions of home life contributed to the decision to secure a lot near the center of the city and erect a tent. Since the city was in receivership, Voliva had no direct authority over the erection of the tent (which seated 2,000). He voiced complaints, but the civil authorities sided with the Pentecostals.[60] Parham returned to Zion with his family for the watch night service in the tent, 31 December 1906.[61]

By mid-January, when Parham left Zion for Toronto, the receiver had granted the Pentecostals' request for a building and had given them access to the city's one church, Shiloh Tabernacle, on week nights and alternate Sundays.[62]

Parham left in Zion a thriving Pentecostal work with capable leaders who had experience in ministry in Dowie's organization as well as in other denominations. The group had already begun to disperse as one and another accepted invitations to evangelize elsewhere.

Immediately after Parham's departure, press reports like those that dogged him elsewhere began to suggest that irregularities in his life had occasioned his departure from the city for the Toronto mission and that his ministry in Zion was finished.[63] Parham returned to Zion briefly in March, when Dowie's death earlier that month led some to speculate about Parham's intentions with regard to Voliva's permanent control, but Parham's public leadership in Zion was in fact ended. In 1907 he moved his family and his paper back to Kansas, and went on to minister in Texas. Increasingly separated by both personal inclination and adverse publicity from the leadership of Pentecostalism, Parham for years became "one figure modern pentecostals would just as soon forget."[64]

In June, William J. Seymour, leader of the Azusa Street Mission in Los Angeles, visited Zion and was reminded of "Old Azusa, ten months ago."[65] In remarks indicating the continuing of the Zion revival he reported that "people here receive the baptism in their pews while the service is going on, sometimes scores of them receive it. . . . There are little children from six years and on up who have the baptism with the Holy Ghost."[66]

As numbers of former Christian Catholic Church members received Spirit baptism, they endeavored naturally to spread Pentecostal teaching in the churches affiliated with that organization. By May 1907, an estimated thirty former Zion residents were engaged in itinerant ministries around the country. The contacts made through Dowie's Zion provided a network through which the Pentecostal emphasis could be effectively disseminated. The missions and churches affiliated with Zion, all of which were to some degree affected by the changes in Zion City, were systematically challenged with the Pentecostal message, either by Parham or by others from Zion.

Not all who had serious misgivings about Zion's structure and its theological innovations opted immediately for Pentecostalism. Some Zion ministers simply withdrew from the Christian Catholic Church and continued to proclaim Zion's essential message, shorn of Dowie's apostolic claims, in independent ministries. One of Dowie's prominent associates, William Hamner Piper, had founded the Stone Church in Chicago in December 1906 with about six hundred former Zion members. Piper had initially avoided addressing the issues raised by the Pentecostals, but by June 1907 he had become convinced of their message and invited his Pentecostal friends from Zion City to introduce it in his church.[67] The subsequent acceptance in the Stone Church of the Pentecostal message had far-reaching significance. In the years before the many independent Pentecostal groups in middle America began to organize, the Stone Church, through a schedule of special conferences as well as in its regular ministries and through its publication, *The Latter Rain Evangel*, functioned as a recognized center of American Pentecostalism. Reports in the *Evangel* helped maintain contact among itinerant evangelists; conferences attracted visiting ministers and missionaries from the Zion City group and elsewhere and provided both opportunities for extending fellowship and a sense of participation in a broader movement. Piper publicized announcements pertaining to Pentecostal conventions, Bible schools and ministries and generally made available to the movement the advantages of his own wide range of contacts. His *Evangel*, distributed free of charge, published primarily, but not exclusively, Pentecostal authors and became a source for Pentecostal teaching and devotional literature.

V

Dowie's literalist faith, his restorationist objectives and his millennial hope identified him with broad currents that converged, separated and reassembled unpredictably in the fluid late-nineteenth-century American religious culture. Through his ministry, thousands became convinced of the reality of divine healing in a context that also stressed holiness and the person and work of the Holy Spirit. His essential message inclined many of his followers toward Parham's ministry. Both Dowie and Parham were intent on restoring an apostolic component to the Christian faith, and thus both of their ministries were primarily organized around restorationist themes and sought to replace denominational organization with catholic apostolicity. Some undoubtedly saw in Pentecostalism the answer to Dowie's prayer:

> Give unto us, as we each are prepared, the Gifts that Thou has promised: the Word of Wisdom, the Word of Knowledge, Faith, the Gifts of Healings, Workings of Miracles, Prophecies, Discerning of Spirits, Tongues, Interpretation of Tongues . . . Let the Gifts be made manifest increasingly, in this Church.[68]

The discrediting of Dowie would create the climate in which Pentecostalism could flourish. Those who were indebted to Dowie functioned as an influential group in early Pentecostalism. Through their network of contacts, they continued to share fellowship and ministry, and to support one another's efforts. They frequently brought to their Pentecostal ministries both experience gained through years of pastoral and evangelistic activity and some perception of theological issues which many early Pentecostals—with their focus on the Spirit—lacked.[69] Many continued to acknowledge Dowie's influence, generally citing his example of faith. Marie Burgess Brown, who later ministered in the Assemblies of God, summarized succinctly her insistence that in Zion she had obtained her "foundation": "If it hadn't been for the truths of the Word of God as I learned them there," she maintained, "I would not be here today. I would never have been able to stand through all these years"[70]

Healing evangelist and author Lilian Yeomans who had been healed under Dowie's ministry would express a consensus when during a visit to the Zion Faith Homes (a Pentecostal ministry under the direction of former Dowieite Elder Eugene Brooks) in the 1930s she would state: "Some people say that Dr. Dowie's work is dead. No! It is more alive today than ever."[71] Those who came into Pentecostalism from Zion would consider that in Pentecostalism the real significance of Dowie's message was preserved and expanded. Shorn of the distractions of both secular concerns and externalization of the apostolic motif, Dowie's essential message of the full validity of New Testament Christianity for twentieth century believers found, they would claim, its logical and fullest development in Pentecostalism.

NOTES

[1]"The Passing of Dr. Dowie," *Word To-Day* 10 (April, 1906): 359; *Leaves of Healing* 8 (1901): 787. In a study of the communitarian aspect of Zion City, Grant Wacker cites an 1875 survey indicating a total of not more than 8,000 Americans living in seventy-two communitarian colonies. The Shakers, the largest single communitarian group, had between 1830 and 1850 some 6,000 members in numerous colonies. See Rosabeth Kanter, *Commitment and Community: Communes and Utopias in Sociological Perspective* (Cambridge, MA: n.p. 1972), p. 246; Grant Wacker, "Dowie's Zion: A Case of Charisma and Commitment," unpublished seminar paper, Harvard University.

[2]These events are discussed in Rolvix Harlan, *John Alexander Dowie* (Evansville, WI: n.p., 1906) and Gordon Lindsay, *The Life of John Alexander Dowie* (Dallas: n.p., 1951). There is some indication that an earlier concern over the apparent cessation of the church's apostolic ministry of healing reemerged during this 1876 crisis. Dowie later claimed that as an adolescent he had wrestled during his own illness with the church's silence on the subject of healing; later, while a student at Edinburgh, he had challenged the generally accepted premise that spiritual gifts had been given to the church on a temporary basis and had defended a thesis maintaining that they had never been withdrawn. John A. Dowie, "The Exercise of Apostolic Powers," *Leaves of Healing* 15 (1904): 173-177; John A. Dowie, "How God Gave Dowie the Ministry of Healing," in Gordon Lindsay, ed., *Champion of the Faith: The Sermons of John Alexander Dowie* (Dallas: n.p. 1979), pp. 22-28.

[3]Lindsay, *Dowie*, p. 45.

[4]Ibid., p. 76.

[5]John A. Dowie, "Wilt Thou Be Made Whole," *Bread of Life* 6 (March, 1957): 10.

[6]John A. Dowie, "God's Way of Healing," *Leaves of Healing* 15 (1904): 308.

[7]Lindsay, *Dowie*, p. 85. In a series on "The Exercise of Apostolic Powers," Dowie developed this thought. See *Leaves of Healing* 15 (1904): 275. In 1885 he received an invitation to an International Conference on Divine Healing and True Holiness sponsored by Boardman, proponent of the "Higher Christian Life" and organizer of a healing faith home in London. A report of this London conference indicated that London's "great agricultural hall was taxed to the utmost to accommodate the serious crowds that flocked to hear Boardman." See William E. Hull, "Divine Healing, or Faith Cure," *Lutheran Quarterly* 27 (April, 1897): 236-276.

[8]Lindsay, *Dowie*, pp. 190-194.

[9]John Swain, "John Alexander Dowie: The Prophet and His Profits: A Study, at First Hand, of 'A Modern Elijah,' " *Century Illustrated Magazine* 64 (October, 1902): 937.

[10]A. B. Simpson's associate, R. Kelso Carter, claimed that there were over thirty such "faith homes" in the United States in the 1890s. See Hull, "Healing," pp. 271, 275.

[11]John A. Dowie, "Divine Healing and the Chicago Doctors," *Leaves of Healing* 1 (1895): 518-520.

[12]John Julius Halsey, "The Genesis of a Modern Prophet," *American Journal of Sociology* 9 (November, 1903): 316-317.

[13]See John A. Dowie, "Victory," *Leaves of Healing*, II (1895): 177-179; Kenneth Mackenzie, *Our Physical Heritage in Christ* (New York: n.p., 1923), p. 20. Episcopalian MacKenzie would characterize Dowie as "the apostle of divine healing in his day." *Ibid.*

[14]"The Dowie Movement in Chicago," *Outlook* 68 (June, 1901): 429.

[15]Quoted in Lindsay, *Dowie*, p. 155.

[16]Ibid.

[17]Quoted in ibid., p. 186. See also John A. Dowie, "The Ministry of an Apostle—Is It For Today?" in Lindsay, ed., *Sermons*, pp. 113-125.

[18]The social and economic organization of the city are described fully in Philip L. Cook, "Zion City, Illinois: Twentieth Century Utopia" (Ph.D. diss. University of Colorado, 1965).

[19]See Edith L. Waldvogel, "The Overcoming Life: A Study in the Reformed Evangelical Origins of Pentecostalism" (Ph.D. diss. Harvard University, 1977).

[20]John A. Dowie, "God's Witnesses to Divine Healing," *Leaves of Healing* 8 (1900): 97; Gordon P. Gardiner, "The Apostle of Divine Healing," *Bread of Life* 6 (1957): 7.

[21]Wacker, "Zion," p. 17; Lindsay, *Dowie*, pp. 210-219.

[22]Kenneth Mackenzie, quoted in *Bread of Life* 6 (1957): 11.

[23]John A. Dowie, "The Everlasting Gospel of the Kingdom of God Declared and Defended," *Leaves of Healing*, V (1899): 713. For example, among his contemporaries in Chicago was R. A. Torrey, then Superintendent of Moody Bible Institute. Personally a believer in divine healing, Torrey neither taught the doctrine at the Institute nor publicly railed against physicians and medicines. Torrey once requested Dowie's prayers for his daughter. Dowie acquiesced, and then published in his *Leaves of Healing* a record of his correspondence and conversation with Torrey, claiming that Torrey and his colleagues at the Bible Institute lacked sufficient spiritual power to effect healings: they had been forced to humble themselves and to come to Zion. There is no evidence that the Institute took an

official stand against Dowie, although it is clear that Moody did not support the teaching that healing was "in the atonement." Dowie, on the other hand, publicly charged the Institute with lack of spirituality, claiming that the students of necessity came to his meetings in order to participate in meaningful Christian worship. Dowie's critical language and his focus on divisive issues gradually alienated him from contemporary clergy who did not join his movement. See *Leaves of Healing* 5 (1899): 457-464; Dwight L. Moody to A. F. Gaylord, Christian Catholic Church File, Moody Bible Institute.

24Dwight L. Moody to A. F. Gaylord, Christian Catholic Church File, Moody Bible Institute Archives.

25Among those who came to Zion City because of the environment it offered was F. F. Bosworth who, after a period of involvement with Pentecostalism, would join the Christian and Missionary Alliance and conduct a healing ministry that would merge with the resurgent healing revivalism of the late 1940s. See Eunice Perkins, *Joybringer Bosworth* (Dayton, OH: n.p. 1921), pp. 25-26; David Edwin Harrell, *All Things are Possible* (Bloomington, IN: Indiana University Press, 1975); F. F. Bosworth, "Bosworth's Life Story," (Toronto, n.d.).

26Dowie's "Elijah Declaration" was published in *Leaves of Healing* 9 (1901): 214.

27Lindsay, *Dowie*, pp. 184-192.

28John A. Dowie, "Declaration of John Alexander, First Apostle of the Lord Jesus, the Christ, in the Christian Catholic Apostolic Church in Zion," *Leaves of Healing* 15 (1904): 793-800. At this time, Dowie added the word "apostolic" to the church's title. It would be dropped in April 1906 when Dowie was removed from office.

29John A. Dowie, "Apostolic Powers," *Leaves of Healing* 15 (1904): 43.

30Ibid., p. 45.

31Ibid.

32Ibid., pp. 140, 208.

33Ibid., p. 139.

34For James Buckley's attitude see "Faith Healing and Kindred Phenomena," *Century Magazine* 32 (June, 1886): 222-236. The *Literary Digest* would comment about the New York crusade: "The spectacular descent of John Alexander Dowie and more than 3,000 followers upon New York City to wrest it from the grip of Satan has transfixed the attention of the entire country." *Literary Digest* 27 (October, 1903): 547-548.

35Cook, "Zion," pp. 276-288.

36Lindsay, *Dowie*, pp. 227-233.

[37]Arthur Newcomb, *Dowie: Anointed of the Lord* (New York: n.p., 1930), pp. 370-373.

[38]Cook, "Zion," pp. 373-379.

[39]This situation is described in detail in Cook, "Zion." Of the six who signed the document informing Dowie of his removal from office, three (Piper, Cantel, Speicher) would soon become Pentecostals.

[40]*Chicago Tribune*, 29 April 1906.

[41]Lindsay, *Dowie*, p. 247.

[42]Gordon P. Gardiner, "Out of Zion," *Bread of Life* 30 (October, 1981): 3; Sarah Parham, *The Life of Charles Parham* (Birmingham: n.p., 1930), pp. 155-156.

[43]Gardiner, "Zion," p. 3.

[44]Parham, *Parham*, p. 48.

[45]Bernice Lee, "When God Breathed on Zion," *Bread of Life* 30 (October, 1981): 7. J. R. Flower (whose parents were members of Dowie's work) later claimed that Dowie's ministry "awakened in many a desire for the supernatural and a longing for spiritual reality, which went a long ways toward preparing of the way for the rise of the Pentecostal Movement in the twentieth century." J. R. Flower, "History of the Assemblies of God," notes compiled for a course at Central Bible College, 1949, p. 9.

[46]*Waukegan Daily Gazette*, 15 October 1906.

[47]*North Chicago News*, 26 September 1906.

[48]Parham, *Parham*, pp. 156-157. The *Waukegan Daily Sun*, 15 November 1906, reported that as many as 300 attended a single house meeting.

[49]See, for example, the ad in the Toronto *Evening Telegram*, 19 January 1907.

[50]The relative ease with which some accepted Parham's teaching is reflected in Bernice C. Lee, "A Holy Jubilee," *Bread of Life* 5 (November, 1956): 3-4, 9-10. Parham stressed entire consecration, using that terminology rather than "Christian perfection," "second blessing," "entire sanctification," etc. He taught that one received "the assurance or witness of the Spirit" when one had consecrated entirely. This "witness" was the second work of grace. Interview with Pauline Parham, 28 November 1983.

[51]F. F. Bosworth would be the most prominent of those to reject tongues. His stance was applauded by the ministers of the Zion Ministerial Training Homes, all of whom were former Dowieites. The position remains characteristic of that group and its loosely affiliated churches today.

[52]*Waukegan Daily Gazette*, 20 October 1906.

[53]*Daily Sun*, 18 October 1906; *Waukegan Daily Gazette*, 19 October 1906. In a long article subtitled "How They Look and Act Under the Spell," the *Waukegan*

Daily Sun, 15 November 1906 analyzed the phenomenon.

[54]*Daily Sun*, 15 November 1906.

[55]Parham, *Parham*, pp. 161-177.

[56]Among those who received Spirit baptism during Parham's absence was an ordained minister of Dowie's church, Elder Cyrus B. Fockler. Another of those from Zion who would continue to emphasize healing in his Pentecostal ministry, Fockler attended the 1914 Hot Springs Convention and ministered in both the Assemblies of God and the Pentecostal Church of God in America, Gardiner, "Zion," *Bread of Life* 30 (November, 1981): 13-14.

[57]*North Chicago News*, 26 September 1906; *Bread of Life* 31 (February, 1982): 6.

[58]Parham, *Parham*, p. 159.

[59]Interview with Gordon P. Gardiner, 3 August 1982.

[60]Parham, *Parham*, pp. 171-172.

[61]Among those who accepted the Pentecostal teaching during the holiday meetings was Martha Robinson who, with her husband, was pastoring a branch of the Christian Catholic Church in Detroit. The Robinsons would return to Zion City to assist in the direction of the Zion Faith Homes and to organize Pentecostal ministries in the region. See Gordon P. Gardiner, *Radiant Glory* (New York: privately published, 1962).

[62]*Waukegan Gazette*, 21 January 1907; 22 January 1907.

[63]Gardiner, "Zion," *Bread of Life* 31 (January, 1982): 7-8; *Waukegan Gazette*, 21 January 1907, 23 January 1907; *Daily Sun*, 28 January 1907. Pursued by charges of sexual infraction, Parham was rejected by a large percentage of his followers in Texas and increasingly ministered on the peripheries of mainstream Pentecostalism. Parham, *Parham*, recounts his efforts.

[64]Grant Wacker, "A Profile of American Pentecostalism," unpublished article, p. 9.

[65]*The Apostolic Faith* 1 (June-Sept., 1907): 1.

[66]Ibid.

[67]William H. Piper, "Long Weary Months of Spiritual Drought," *Latter Rain Evangel* 1 (October, 1908), 3-6.

[68]*Leaves of Healing* 15 (1904), 209.

[69]The list of Pentecostal leaders who had been healed under Dowie's ministry and/or joined his movement and were committed to Zion would include F. F. Bosworth and his brother, B. B. Bosworth, Harry Bowley, Eugene and Sara Brooks, Marie Burgess Brown, Harry and Margaret Cantel, Cyrus Fockler, F. A. Graves, L. C. and Jean Campbell Hall, John Lake, D. C. O. Opperman, William Hamner and Lydia Piper, Anna Reiff, E. N. Richey, Charles E. and

Daisy Robinson, Henry and Martha Robinson, H. A. Ulrich, Fred Vogler, Helen
Innes Wannenmacher, E. M. Whittemore, Lilian Yeomans. Dowie encouraged
women to minister.

[70]Quoted in Gordon P. Gardiner, ''The Apostle of Divine Healing,'' *Bread
of Life* 6 (March, 1957): 15.

[71]Ibid.

9

DISCERNING THE WORK OF GOD

Paul G. Hiebert

The Charismatic Movement, defined in the broadest sense of that term, is one of the great movements in the history of the Christian church. It takes its place alongside the Reformation, the Anabaptist Movement, the rise of Pietism, the Evangelical Reawakening and other renewal movements in church history. Its impact can be seen in its rapid growth in less than a century to more than sixty-two million in the Protestant wing of the church and more than one hundred million in the church as a whole.[1]

THE GROWTH OF THE CHRISTIAN CHURCH BETWEEN 1900 and 1980

	1900			1980		
	Number in Millions	Percent of Protestant Church	Percent of Total Church	Number in Millions	Percent of Protestant Church	Percent of Total Church
Protestant Evangelicals	66.8	50		175.4	56.2	
Total Evangelicals	73.1		13.1	220.8		15.4
Protestant Charismatics	—			62.2	19.9	
Total Charismatics	—			100.0		7.0

Source: David Barrett, ed. *World Christian Encyclopaedia* Nairobi: Oxford University Press. 1982

REASONS FOR GROWTH

There are a number of reasons for this rapid growth of the movement. Certainly foremost among them is the continuing work of the Holy Spirit in the lives of God's people in fresh ways. God has in the past and continues in the present to work in ever new ways in the lives of his people to revive them, and to renew their witness in the world.

A second reason is the movement's emphasis on the affective dimension of human experience. Anthropologists refer to three such dimensions: the cognitive— thought and knowledge, the affective—emotions, and the evaluative—allegiances and responses. The Reformation stressed the first of these, namely the truth of the gospel. Certainly the early Reformers such as Calvin and Luther were deeply moved by feelings of worship in the presence of God, but their main battles were for orthodoxy. Their followers placed even less emphasis on emotional expressions of faith. In part this reflects the normal processes of institutionalization. Founders of new movements are often charismatic leaders (in the Weberian sense[2]) who give way in time to priestly leaders who are more cognitively oriented. However, in part, it reflects the fact that at that point in church history renewal required a return to truth.

The Anabaptist Movement that paralleled the Reformation emphasized the evaluative dimensions of the gospel. Truth and worship, Anabaptists argued, must lead to obedience, discipleship and holiness. The church is *in* the world but it must *not* be *of* the world. Intense persecution stifled the early exuberance of the Anabaptists and drove them into self-reliant communities that lived in uneasy accommodation with the world outside; institutionalization quenched the emotional intensity that characterized the movement at the outset. Nevertheless, they continue to remind us that renewal requires a return to discipleship.

Pietism introduced emotional expressions as central to the Christian experience. It stressed the feelings of inner peace, tranquility and a profound sense of awe in the presence of the majesty and greatness of God.[3] Hymns, the discipline of meditation and an orderly life, confession of sins, piety, and, in the extreme, transcendent experiences and a mystical sense of identification with God were the means used to generate and express these feelings. The result was a widespread renewal in the church and the birth of the modern Protestant mission movement. Here, too, institutionalization set in and these methods for affective expression lost their newness. One notable exception is the East African revival where an ongoing renewal of a pietistic nature has continued for more than forty years.[4]

The current Charismatic Movement reaffirms the importance of affective expression in Christian faith, this time in the feelings of joy and ecstasy[5] expressed by means of glossolalia, joyful music, raising of hands, dance, and, in extreme cases, spirit possession to the point of losing consciousness. To people whose hearts are too often empty, this renewed concern for the affective dimensions of worship comes as a breath of fresh air. They begin to feel the presence of God again in their lives. In many ways it is this restoration of the emotional expressions of Christian faith rather than a new call to cognitive insights or to discipleship that has been the main contribution of the Charismatic Movement to the broader church. To be sure, there are exceptions such as the stress on discipleship in some circles, especially among Roman Catholics and the Fort Lauderdale charismatics.

A third reason for the growth of the Charismatic Movement is its concern with making God's presence relevant to the problems of everyday life. Since the seventeenth century the Christian world view has increasingly been influenced by a neo-Platonic dualism that divides reality into two realms: the spiritual and the material. Any role God might have played in the world was increasingly confined to the former. The Hebrew concept of "creation" that stressed God's ongoing involvement in the maintenance of the world was replaced by the Greek concept of "nature" in which the world was seen as an autonomous system that operated in accordance with nature laws. God was no longer needed to describe and explain events in this world. These became the domain of science.

But science could not solve the spiritual problems of this world. It could not provide guidance for an uncertain future, prevent crises such as droughts, earthquakes and wars, give meaning to particular events such as unexpected deaths, or deal with the manifestations of human sin. It had demythologized the Western world by severing the link between the spiritual and material dimensions of reality, and by denying the existence of divine involvement in the order of this world. It appealed to "chance," "accident," and "luck" to account for events beyond scientific explanation.[6]

This secularization of the world eliminated witchcraft and fear of spirits that dominated the Middle Ages. It also left a deep spiritual void, for it left God largely out of the day-to-day experiences of human life. His actions were seen only in the miraculous, and for most people miracles were not everyday experiences. Science became the dominant mode for explaining human experience, which came to have little mystery or spiritual meaning.

In this context, the Charismatic Movement has made Christians aware again of God's work in this world and in the everyday events of human history. Medieval Catholics had appealed to the doctrine of saints, the Reformers to God's providence, and the Anabaptists and Pietists to the work of the Holy Spirit in sanctification with particular reference to the ongoing work of God in the world. But by the twentieth century even they were not free from the secularizing forces of modernity.[7]

The Charismatic Movement's emphasis on the ongoing work of the Holy Spirit in the lives of people was good news to many who had lost a sense of God's presence in their experiences. Unlike the literate religious leaders who tend to focus on problems of cognitive truth and ultimate reality, the common folk live much of their lives around the day-to-day crises and decisions they face. What they seek on this level is a demonstration of God's working in their lives. A message of divine power has great attraction.

This concern for power to solve the problems of life is not confined to modern humans. It is the central theme of folk religions around the world. While leaders of universal religions such as Hinduism, Buddhism and Islam are concerned primarily with questions of orthodoxy and orthopraxy, their followers appeal to magic, astrology, witchcraft, amulets, mantras and sacred medicines to deal with, *jinns, bhuts,* local spirits, and the evil eye. Many Western missionaries, influenced by the divided world view of their societies, responded by denying the reality of magic and earthly spirits. On the one hand they preached a gospel that dealt with questions of eternity, and on the other they espoused a secular science that handled problems of life on earth. It should not surprise us, then, that Pentecostal and Charismatic missionaries who reemphasize the manifestation of God's presence and power in the lives of unbelievers have found widespread responsiveness to their message.

THE NEED FOR DISCERNMENT

To open the door for the involvement of the spiritual dimension in human affairs is to allow the Holy Spirit to work more effectively in our lives. It also opens the door to the rulers and powers of darkness. What God does, Satan counterfeits. This is clear in Scripture for we are constantly warned about false prophets, false signs and wonders, and false teachings Col. 2:8; 1 Tim. 4:1-2; 2 Tim. 4:3). It should not surprise us, therefore, that the Charismatic Movement, like all movements before it, must face the possibilities of distortion.

In dealing with the spiritual manifestations in this life, the central question is one of discernment. Is it, in fact, the work of the Holy Spirit that we see in the lives of people or is it something else? We must test the spirits lest we be led astray (1 John 4:1; 2:26; 3:7; 2 Peter 2:1, 18; 3:17; 2 Thess. 3:2). But what test should we use?

Many Christians use particular phenomenological criteria to test the presence of the Holy Spirit, for these are easily applied. Some look for glossolalia, others for healings, miracles, ecstatic experiences and resurrections from the dead. But all of these are found in other major religions of the world and in tribal animism. The use of sacred languages and sounds is common in religious experience associated with trance or ecstasy, and is frequently linked with shamanism in tribal religions.[8] There are numerous testimonies of healings and other miracles performed by the Virgin of Guadalupe,[9] Tirupathi Venkateswara in South India, Voodoo spirits in Latin America, the Buddha, and many other gods, spirits and healers. Even the use of the name "Jesus Christ" is no test of the presence of the Holy Spirit. This name is widely used in South American spiritism, and in syncretistic Hindu-Christian movements in India such as that led by Subba Rao of Andhra Pradesh.[10] The fact is that spirit possession, feelings of ecstasy and joy, and resurrections are reported in all major religious systems. Even the Scriptures warn us that Satan's power will be demonstrated by powerful signs and miracles (2 Thess. 2:9). There are, in fact, no simple phenomenological criteria by which we can test the presence of the Holy Spirit.

The problem is not a new one. As Brown points out in his well-argued discussion of Christian beliefs regarding miracles, the early church was forced to defend itself against the charges that the miracles of Jesus were no different from those that could be witnessed in any marketplace of the day.[11] Origen did not appeal to some unique form to defend the divine nature of Christ's miracles. Rather he appealed to the changes that took place in the lives of people who had experienced these miracles. Origen wrote,

> They might have been comparable if he [Celsus] had first given sufficient proof of the similarity to those who employ trickery. But in fact no sorcerer uses his tricks to call spectators to moral reformation; nor does he educate by the fear of God people who were astounded by what they saw, nor does he attempt to persuade the onlookers to live as men who will be judged by God. Sorcerers do none of these things, since they have neither the ability nor even the will to do so. (*Against Celsus*, 1.68)[12]

If there are no simple phenomenological tests that we can use to examine whether or not spiritual experiences are manifestations of God's Spirit, what tests can we use? This question of discernment is one of the crucial issues facing the Charismatic Movement and the church in general in our day. Certainly in a short chapter no definitive answer can be given to the question. At best a few leads can be suggested that need further exploration.

The Glory of God

It is clear from the Scriptures and from the great church councils that the central purpose of Christianity is to seek the glory of God. Christ himself placed this at the center of his life and his death (John 7:18; 8:50; 12:27-28; 17:4). Consequently, as Calvin points out,

> Since Christ affirms this test of doctrine, miracles are wrongly valued that are applied to any other purpose than to glorify the name of the one God. (Deut. 13:2ff.)[13]

There is here a subtle but very real danger, particularly for leaders in the church, to take for oneself the glory and authority that belongs to God alone. This danger is particularly great in renewal movements for at the outset these are led by prophetic leaders who face two major temptations. On the one hand, they have a strong emotional component in their character. This accounts in part for their charism, but it also makes them particularly susceptible to the temptation of glory, power and sex. On the other hand, as Robeck points out, because they are prophets, they are tempted to claim for themselves absolute authority. He writes,

> Recently I asked a leader of charismatic renewal in Great Britain what he considered the greatest pastoral problem confronting the charismatic movement. Without hesitation he remarked that within the movement there had emerged a few leaders who were no longer willing to submit their prophetic words to any form of testing. In essence they argued that their personal authority as proven "prophets" was all that was necessary for others to accept what they spoke "in the Spirit."[14]

Leaders often see themselves as above the norms, spiritual exercises and disciplines they impose upon their followers. And they reserve for themselves the right to interpret the Scriptures. The result is movements in which glory is given to leaders. Mary Douglas points out,[15] that this is particularly true of highly individualistic societies such as modern cities where leadership tends to be in the hands of what anthropologists call "big men."

The Scriptures make it clear that while all Christians have gifts, Christ alone is the head. Human leaders are servants to the body. As Kraus points out in his excellent analysis, authority within the church is vested not in individuals, but in the church as a community. Without this check of the body as a whole, individual members, including leaders, go astray. This authority includes in particular the right to interpret Scriptures. Kraus writes,

> Thus the Scripture can find its proper meaning as witness only within a *community of interpretation*. Principles of interpretation are important, but secondary. There needs to be an authentic correspondence between gospel announcement and a "new order" embodied in community for Scripture to play its proper role as part of the original witness. The authentic community is the hermeneutical community. It determines the actual enculturated meaning of Scripture. . . .

And so it remains today. The Bible, as guide and exemplar for authentic witness, can find its rightful place and function only in a community of discernment of obedience. "First of all (we) must understand that no prophetic word of Scripture is a matter of one's own private interpretation (1 Peter 2:20)."[16]

Robeck adds,

> [T]he willingness to submit one's prophetic utterances to others within the community of faith to ascertain the appropriateness of timing, of method, of content, of lifestyle, or even of applicability to the congregation would seem to be indicative that one is truely submissive to the Lord of the Church (1 Cor. 14:29-33, 40).[17]

Paul himself tested his message with other church leaders to make certain that he was not running in vain (Gal. 2:11-12).

The Lordship of Christ

A second central test is that which forms the central theme of John's first epistle, namely the lordship of Christ. Lordship refers here not to an affirmation on the cognitive level of the deity of Christ. This is taken for granted. Even Satan knows this, but denies Christ's rule. Nor does lordship refer to a feeling of awe, adoration or ecstasy in his presence. It refers to obedience and discipleship (1 John 2:3-5 5:3; James 2:14-19). As Kraft points out, the question has to do with one's fundamental allegiances—the central commitments upon which one acts.[18] It concerns the center around which a person builds her or his life.[19] In Scripture even love is basically not a feeling but a commitment, for we are commanded to love, and emotions cannot be dictated.

There are two spiritual counterfeits offsetting the lordship of Christ. The first, and most obvious, is idolatry—to follow some other god. The second is Christian magic. This is clearly seen in the use of the name "Jesus Christ" in the curing rituals of Voodoo, South American spiritism such as Xango and Candomble, and Medieval European magic. This problem is not new. Already in Acts there were false prophets who used the name of Jesus to cast out demons (Acts 19:13-20).

A more subtle form of Christian magic, and one that constitutes an even greater threat to the church, is reflected by the attitude a person takes towards Christ. In worship the attitude is one of subordination and submission to the will of God in the person of Jesus. In magic it is an attempt to control Christ to achieve one's own purposes. In the former one's own will and desires are subordinated to those of God. In the latter one's will and desires become central. Religion becomes another means to gain one's own end.

The line between worship and magic is a fine one. The distinguishing mark is the attitude of the person and not the religious forms. Spoken words can be a prayer or a magical chant. Symbols can be reminders of God's presence, or means to control him. Even Scripture can be used as magic if we see it as ways of making God do our bidding. The question is one of submission versus control.

Christian magic promises believers a new and easy way to achieve their personal desires. This is illustrated in a recent flier I received in the mail. In it was a paper "prayer rug" that had been prayed over by a certain preacher. It promised that those who used it faithfully would be blessed with "salvation, joy, love, peace, extra money! new and better homes! new car! putting home together!—and the desires of their heart!" [*sic.* Exclamation points in the original]. It claims that one family used the rug and soon acquired "two restaurants, two motels, a Dairy Cream, a service station, thirty employees, four cars and three trucks."

This is obviously a blatant misuse of Scripture to manipulate God for personal ends. But we all face more subtle temptations to coerce God to do our bidding. We are exhorted to pray in the name of Christ, but when we see this as somehow empowering the prayer that is otherwise weak, it becomes magic. We are exhorted to pray for the sick, but when we feel that God *must* answer because we have used the right prayer and claimed the right verse, it becomes magic. This, in fact, lies at the heart of Satan's third temptation of Christ. He wanted Jesus to claim the promises of Scripture to satisfy his own desires, but Jesus responded by quoting the Scripture that deals with the misuse of itself, "Do not put the Lord your God to the test" (Luke 4:12, NIV). At its core, magic is an attitude of coercion. It is an attempt to use the right "formulas" to control power, including the power of God, to achieve our own goals, an attempt that we may mask even from ourselves by equating the goals with the Kingdom of God. The heart of Christianity is worship and submission to God, his goals and his methods.

The Scripture is particularly harsh in its condemnation of magic for it is a form of idolatry. It is to place one's self at the center rather than God. In the Old Testament the command is given to kill any prophet or miracle worker who leads the people away from worship and towards subordination to himself (Deut. 13). In the New Testament it is seen in the responses of Peter and Paul to magic (Acts 8:18-24; 13:8-11).

Agreement with Scriptures

As Robeck points out, a third test of spiritual practices is that of Scripture.[20] The question must always be asked, are they consistent with the truths revealed in the Bible? Moreover, those utterances that seek to add to or delete from Scripture must be counted as heresy (2 Peter 2:1).

The Fruit of the Spirit

A fourth test of prophecies and miracles to determine their divine nature is given by Paul when he lists the fruit of the Spirit (Gal. 5:22-25). As we have already seen, Origen appealed to these. Those who claim to have the Holy Spirit should be characterized by love, not a sense of spiritual superiority; joy, not a cloud of judgment and despair; peace, not an intense drivenness; longsuffering, not latent hostility; gentleness, not disregard for others; goodness, not legalism; faith, not cynicism; meekness, not a dictatorial spirit; and self-control, not uncontrolled emotionalism. Certainly these fruit have their phenomenological manifestations, but they are essentially qualities of the Spirit.

Maturity

The nature of our Christian experience is closely related to our spiritual maturity. Clearly Christ and the disciples used healings and exorcisms as signs that the Kingdom of God had come. They were evidence to unbelievers and believers alike of the presence and power of God.

The use of these demonstrations of power seems primarily to lead seekers to faith (Acts 2:22; 4:30; 14:3). Speaking to skeptical Jews, Justin wrote:

> [Jesus] was manifest to your race and healed those who were from birth physically maimed and deaf and lame, causing one to leap and another to hear and a third to see at his word. And he raised the dead and gave them life and by his actions challenged the men of his time to recognize him.[21]

These signs also manifested to the world the nature of the Kingdom of God, namely God's concern for the poor, the lame, the blind and the lost (Luke 4:18-19).

Scripture teaches plainly that miracles were never given as an end in themselves. When the disciples returned amazed after receiving power to heal and cast out evil spirits, Christ said to them, "Rejoice not that the spirits submit to you, but that your names are written in heaven" (Luke 10:20). Similarly when Herod and others demanded miracles, Christ refused to perform for them.

Little evidence exists that miracles played an important part in the ongoing lives of mature believers in the early church. In fact, Paul cautioned the Corinthian church against focusing upon them as the normative experience for the Christian congregation (1 Cor. 12-14). As faith grows, it depends less upon external signs and more upon a deep personal walk with God. The history of human faith is often a progression from belief rooted in God's work to belief rooted in God himself. This does not mean that God no longer heals Christians when they become mature, but for them this is no longer the center of their spiritual concern. Their focus has shifted from what happens to themselves to concern for a lost world and for the glory of God. And God is often more glorified through a life of faith and hope in the face of illness, suffering and death than in deliverance from them.

The way of mature Christian faith leads to submission to God's purposes, even though these call for suffering; to servanthood not self-advancement; and to the Cross, not from it. To pray in the name of Jesus is to pray as he prayed in Gethesemane when he placed himself in complete submission to the Father. This spirit is captured by Luther in his paraphrase of that prayer,

> Let it come to pass since the Father wants the devil to be defeated and weakened, not by might and power and magnificent miracles, as has happened heretofore through Me, but by obedience and humility in the utmost weakness by cross and death, by My submission to Him, and by surrendering My right and might. But in this very way I will take and wrest from the devil his right and might over you, since he is attacking and killing Me even though I am guiltless. Then he judged and condemned by his own guilt will have to give way, and flee from Me to the ends of the world.[22]

Brown adds,

> These (physical) miracles pale into virtual insignificance compared with the works of conversion and faith which overcome the power of evil and transform lives. In the last analysis, as the cross itself demonstrates, the ultimate victory is won through the self-surrender of Christ in weakness and not through a display of force. Paradoxically, the way of weakness is the way of strength.[23]

The fact that wonders play a greater role in winning unbelievers than in developing spiritual maturity explains largely why demonstrations of God's power are visible on the edges of the church where it ministers to unbelievers, particularly those who look for miracles to establish their faith.

Balance

One of the tests of Christian maturity is a balance in presenting the whole of the gospel (Acts 20:27; Eph. 6:11). As humans we are tempted to emphasize one aspect of God's message at the expense of the others, but partial truth presented as the whole truth is one of the more subtle forms of error. This lay at the heart of Satan's temptations of Eve in the garden and of Jesus in the wilderness.

The Lordship of Christ means that Christ is the center. From this center emerges the church as the manifestation of the Kingdom of God to the world, calling people to join that Kingdom through repentance and faith, and revealing the characteristics of that Kingdom through its concern for provision for the starving, healing for the sick, justice for the offended, liberation for the oppressed and peace for those caught in violence. All of these express the very nature of the church itself, and so long as Christ is the center, they are kept more or less in their proper balance.

Unfortunately, as humans we are tempted, often without realizing it, to make one of these the center of our Christian life. For some the gospel has been reduced to the message of peace. For others it is liberation of the oppressed, provision for the poor, or justice for the wronged. Within the Charismatic Movement there is a danger of focusing on healing and prophetic guidance and of ignoring the biblical concern for provision, liberation, justice and peace. But to shift the center from Christ himself is itself another form of idolatry.

The Unity of the Body of Christ

One test of the work of the Holy Spirit is the desire to maintain the unity of the body of Christ (John 17:11, 23; 1 John 2:9-11; 5:1-2). This does not mean that divisions will not occur. Again the question is one of attitude. Those led by the Spirit seek the fellowship of other believers. When divisions do occur, they have a deep sense of sorrow and a humility rooted in the awareness of their own spiritual inadequacies. And they retain a love and openness to those from whom they are separated.[24]

Unfortunately, divisions frequently occur when renewal takes place. This is true also in the Charismatic Movement, which, particularly in third world countries, has been characterized by divisions and sectarianism. This is due, in part, to the fact that those who have not experienced renewal may reject those who have. However, the onus of responsibility is on those who are more spiritual to seek to win the weaker brothers and sisters by not being an offense, and by showing a redemptive love that attracts (1 Cor. 8:9-13). The Scripture makes it clear that it is the strong that should not offend the weak. Too often the church has misused this principle to force young converts to conform to the dictates of the strong so as not to offend the strong.

There is little support in Scripture for the spiritually strong to withdraw from those who are weak in order to establish a more holy community. The spiritual life of a community of believers is partially reflected in its concern for those who are marginal. These include not only the widows and orphans, the poor and sick, the oppressed and forgotten, but above all those who are spiritually young and weak.

It is in the church's ministry to the marginals that those who have no place for death, poverty, suffering and illness within the will of God on this earth face a serious problem. God does deliver people from these as a sign of his power, and they at times respond in faith. But God does not deliver all for whom Christians pray, or who call upon him. As Augustine points out in his reflections on the lame man at the pool of Bethsaida (John 5:1-18),

> (Jesus) entered a place where lay a great multitude of sick folk—of blind, lame, withered; and being the physician of both souls and bodies, and having come to heal all the souls of them that should believe, of those sick folk He chose one for healing, thereby to signify unity. If in doing this we regard Him with a commonplace mind, with a mere human understanding and wit, as regards power it was not a great matter that He performed; and also as regards goodness He performed too little. There lay so many there, and yet only one was healed, whilst He could by a word have raised them all up. What, then, must we understand but that the power and the goodness was doing what souls might, by His deeds, understand for their everlasting salvation, than what bodies might gain for temporal health.[25]

Why then did he not deliver them all? Augustine points out that God delivers some as a sign to all of the nature and coming of His Kingdom. Moreover, even for those who are healed it is only a sign for they fall ill again and finally die.

> What, then, must we understand but that the power and the goodness was doing what souls might, by His deeds, understand for their everlasting salvation, than what bodies might gain for temporal health? For that which is the real health of bodies, and which is looked for from the Lord, will be at the end, in the resurrection from the dead.[26]

To suggest that all believers should be delivered from these earthly sufferings is to condemn those who do not experience deliverance to feelings of spiritual guilt, despair, and ultimately to bitterness against God. But it is these who need most the spiritual support and encouragement of the community of faith.

To claim deliverance from suffering for all believers is also to overlook that God can and does use our afflictions, consequences of sin though they may be, to speak to the world, and to strengthen his children.

Wholism

Many meanings are currently assigned to "wholism." Here it refers to a rejection of the neo-Platonic world view that has led the West to compartmentalize reality into spirit and matter, and into supernatural and natural. The Hebraic world view makes no such divisions. All events in history are supernatural because they are dependent upon God's ongoing involvement in his creation. All events are also natural for they are part of the order of that creation. Cressey notes,

(S)criptures does not sharply distinguish between God's constant sovereign providence and His particular acts. Belief in miracles is set in the context of a world-view which regards the whole of creation as continually dependent upon the sustaining activity of God and subject to His sovereign will (cf. Col. 1:16, 17). All three aspects of divine activity—wonder, power, significance—are present not only in special acts but also in the whole created order (Rom. 1:20).[27]

God's self-revelation is seen as much through what appear to be ordinary events as through what appear to be extraordinary ones.

The loss of this sense of wholism through the adoption of the Platonic world view is one of the reasons for the growing secularism of Western thought. Nature came to be seen as an autonomous self-perpetuating system. God's activities were relegated primarily to miracles, and these by definition are not the everyday experiences of life.

As Frances Hiebert points out,[28] the Greek dichotomy must be rejected in our understanding of such terms as "signs" and "wonders." The danger is that we read into these terms our contemporary world view with its sharp separation of natural and miraculous. The Hebrew words translated "miracles," "wonders," and "signs" *(môpēth, pele', and 'ôt)* refer to events that were seen as signals or omens of the presence of God.[27] Sometimes these were normal events such as the sabbath which was a sign that God hallows his people (Ex. 31:13), and circumcision which was a sign of God's covenant with his people. Sometimes they were the timing of otherwise normal historical events such as the death of a king, success or defeat in battle (1 Sam. 17:23ff.), the death of two sons in one day (1 Sam. 2:34), the way people responded to a given situation (1 Sam. 14:10), and a good harvest (2 Kings 19:29) that took on particular meaning. Sometimes they were unusual events such as God's delivery of Israel from the land of Egypt (Ex. 13:9) or the sun reversing its movements in the heavens (2 Kings 20). Their significance lay not in that they were "miracles" or exceptions to some natural order, for the gods of the heathen could do the same. Their importance lay in the fact that they were indicators of the presence of God in the lives of his people. They were never ends in themselves. They were signs calling the people to faithfulness and obedience to Jehovah. But here again we are faced with the question of discernment for omens were both good and bad, true and false.

The New Testament also makes reference to miracles and signs *(sēmion, dynamis and teras).* While these are Greek words, and therefore carry the implicit world view of the Greeks, it is increasingly clear that Paul and the other writers of the New Testament thought in terms of a Hebraic world view, and used the Greek terms because they were the closest translations of their Hebrew counterparts. Here, too, the emphasis is not on the miraculous over against the natural order of things. Wars and famines are signs of the times (Matt. 24). Circumcision was a sign of the covenant (Rom. 4:11). Jesus and his disciples used acts of power when they worked among Jews and among the common people who sought such signs as evidences of truth, while Paul appealed to the Greeks through the logic they trusted. But Paul points out that in the end neither of these is the ultimate test on which Christianity lays its claims of truth. Rather, it is the unique set of historical events surrounding the person of Jesus Christ centering around his suffering and death. Paul writes:

> Jews demand miraculous signs and Greeks look for wisdom, but we preach Christ crucified: a stumbling block to Jews and foolishness to Gentiles, but to those whom God has called, both Jews and Greeks, Christ the power of God and the wisdom of God. (1 Cor. 1:22-23, NIV)

Miracles and reason must be understood from the perspective of faith.

The Greek dichotomy must also be rejected in our definitions of "health." In the Hebrew world view, illness is closely related to sin and evil, and health is primarily a restoration of right relationships rather than a state of physical well-being. Out of right relationships (shalôm) with God and with one's fellow humans spring psychological and physical health. Health begins in holiness and peace, which have the highest priority, and ends in bodily well-being.

Ironically, to the extent the Charismatic or any other movement stresses miracles in the Greek sense of the term, it is in danger of reinforcing modern secularism. True, it brings back a sense of the sacred into the lives of people by emphasizing God's intervention in everyday affairs, but by defining this intervention only in terms of "supernatural" experiences, it excludes God from the "natural" order. God is not seen in the ordinary events of life, as he was in the theology of divine providence. Moreover, when miracles fail, his presence is called into doubt. People need a steady diet of miracles to bolster their faith, and in the long run, even miracles lose their power to convince, for when they become common and predictable they no longer are miracles. Consequently, Christians are often forced to find every new manifestations of the miraculous to reinforce a faith that depends upon supernatural evidences with a secular context. The deep sense of God's superintending presence in all spheres of life, that has been the hallmark of most Christian saints, eludes such believers.

CONCLUSION

Peter, explaining the Day of Pentecost said, "This is what the prophet spoke of:

God says, 'This will happen in the last days. I will pour out upon everyone a portion of my spirit.' '' While the specific reference is to the events of that day, the general application is to the church as a whole. But with this great promise comes the warning of Jesus that like the wind, we cannot fully understand the work of the movement of the Spirit (John 3:8).

As we see the Spirit of God at work in the lives of his people in salvation and nurture, we need to keep a sense of divine mystery and subordination. The manifestations of the Spirit cannot be reduced to formulas, nor can we control him for our purposes. The Holy Spirit ever works in new and unexpected ways and we are called to worship and follow.

Moreover, as we see the Spirit of God at work, we need discernment so that we can distinguish between the work of God and spiritual counterfeits both without and within the church. Paul points out that discernment is one of the gifts given by the Spirit to the church (1 Cor. 12:10). Robeck points out that two terms are used in the New Testament with regard to it.[30] One refers to the weighting of prophetic content (1 Cor. 14:29), the other to the testing of prophetic words (1 Thess. 5:21) or spirits (1 John 4:1-6).

If anything, we need discernment now more than ever before because we live increasingly in individualized worlds in a sea of increasing religious pluralism. We must make sure like Paul that the race we run should not be run in vain.

NOTES

[1]David B. Barrett, ed. *World Christian Encyclopedia* (Nairobi: Oxford Univ. Press, 1982), p. 826.

[2]Max Weber produced a classical study on types of leadership. A basic introduction to his thought is found in his work *From Max Weber: Essays in Sociology*, H. G. Gerth and C. Wright trans. and ed. (New York: Oxford Univ. Press, 1958), pp. 196-252.

[3]For an extended discussion of the role of awe and mystery in religious experience see Rudolph Otto, *The Idea of the Holy* (Oxford: Oxford Univ. Press, 1968).

[4]J. W. Katarikawe and J. E. H. Wilson, "The East African Movement." M. A. Thesis, Fuller Theological Seminary. For an extended bibliography on the East African Revival see Jocelyn Murray, "Bibliography on the East African Revival Movement," *Journal of Religion in Africa* 8 (1976): 144-147.

[5]For a phenomenological discussion of the role of ecstasy in religious experience see M. Eliade's *Shamanism: Archaic Techniques of Ecstasy*. W. R. Trask, trans. (New York: Pantheon Books, 1964).

[6]Paul Hiebert, "The Flaw of the Excluded Middle," *Missiology* 10 (1982): 35-47.

[7]Peter and Brigett Berger provide an excellent analysis of the nature of modernity in *The Homeless Mind: Modernization and Consciousness.* (New York: Vintage Books, 1974).

[8]Eliade, *Shamanism*, pp. 96-99.

[9]Ena Campbell, "The Virgin of Guadalupe and the Female Self-Image: A Mexican Case History," in James Preston, ed. *Mother Worship: Theme and Variations* (Chapel Hill: Univ. of North Carolina Press, 1981), pp. 5-24.

[10]Kaj Baago, *The Movement Around SubbaRao* (Bangalore: The Christian Literature Society and the Christian Institute for the Study of Religion and Society, 1968).

[11]Colin Brown, *Miracles and the Critical Mind* (Grand Rapids: Eerdmans Publishing Co., 1984), p. 5.

[12]Origen, *Against Celsus*, 1.68. Quoted from Brown, ibid., 5.

[13]John Calvin, *Institutes of the Christian Religion*, 2 vols. J. T. McNeill, ed., F. L. Battles, trans. (LCC 20; Philadelphia: Westminster Press, 1960), p. 17.

[14]Cecil M. Robeck, "Prophetic Authority in the Charismatic Setting: The Need to Test," *Theological Renewal* 24 (July, 1983): 4.

[15]Mary Douglas, *Natural Symbols* (New York: Random House, 1973), pp. 89-91.

[16]C. Norman Kraus, *The Authentic Witness* (Grand Rapids: Eerdmans, 1979), pp. 71-72.

[17]Robeck, "Prophetic Authority," p. 9.

[18]Charles Kraft, *Christianity and Culture* (Maryknoll, N.Y.: Orbis Books, 1979), pp. 239-245.

[19]Cf. Paul G. Hiebert, "The Category 'Christian' in the Mission Task," *International Review of Missions* 72 (1983): 421-427.

[20]Cecil M. Robeck, Jr., "How Do You Judge Prophetic Utterance?" *Paraclete* 11 (Spring, 1977): 12-16.

[21]Justin Martyr, *Selections from Justin Martyr's Dialogue with Trypho*, R. P. C. Hanson, trans. and ed., (London: Lutterworth Press, 1963), p. 43.

[22]Martin Luther, *Sermons on the Gospel of John: Chapters 14-16. Luther's Works.* J. Pelikan and D. E. Poellot, eds. (St. Louis: Concordia Publishing House, 1961), p. 191.

[23]Brown, *Miracles and The Critical Mind*, pp. 14-15.

[24]Paul G. Hiebert, "So Right They're Wrong," *Eternity* 34 (1983): 28-29.

[25]Augustine, *Tractates on the Gospel of John*, quoted by P. Schaff, *A Selected*

Library of the Nicene and Post-Nicene Fathers, vol. 7 (ANF 7; Grand Rapids: Eerdmans, 1956), p. 11.

[26]Brown, *Miracles and the Critical Mind*, p. xxx.

[27]M. H. Cressey, "Miracles," *The New Bible Dictionary*, J. D. Douglas, ed. (London: The Inter-Varsity Fellowship, 1962), p. 829.

[28]I owe much, particularly in this section, to insights provided by my wife, Frances F. Hiebert, in our discussions on the matter of discernment.

[29]Here and in the following paragraphs I have drawn heavily upon James Strong's *Strong's Exhaustive Concordance of the Bible* (Nashville: Thomas Nelson, 1890).

[30]Cecil M. Robeck, Jr., Notes for the class NT576 Spiritual Gifts, Fuller Theological Seminary.

INDEX OF PASSAGES

SCRIPTURE INDEX

Old Testament

INDEX OF
EARLY CHRISTIAN WRITINGS

SUBJECT INDEX